KANT'S AESTHETIC

Kant's Aesthetic

Mary A. McCloskey

**MACMILLAN
PRESS**

First published 1987

Published by
THE MACMILLAN PRESS LTD
Houndmills, Basingstoke, Hampshire RG21 2XS
and London
Companies and representatives
throughout the world

Printed in Hong Kong

British Library Cataloguing in Publication Data
McCloskey, Mary A.
Kant's aesthetic.
1. Kant, Immanuel—Contributions in
aesthetics   2. Aesthetics
I. Title
111'.85'0924   B2799.A4
ISBN 0-333-41907-3

Contents

Acknowledgements

I would like to express my gratitude to the University of Melbourne for the study leave which made the writing of this book possible and for financial assistance for typing and footnoting. I extend warmest thanks to Valina Rainer for footnoting the work to the German text of the *Critique of Aesthetic Judgement*. Valina Rainer and Dr Jan Srzednicki were patient in explaining to me nuances lost in translation. Dr A. Lloyd Thomas and Professor H. J. McCloskey read drafts of the work and criticised sympathetically. Ingrid Barker took pains with the typing of the manuscript. May the work be indicative of my profiting from the efforts of these who have helped me.

I would also like to thank Oxford University Press for permission to quote from Immanuel Kant's *The Critique of Judgement*, translated by James Creed Meredith (1952).

MARY A. McCLOSKEY

> We are right, he said, and the others are wrong. To speak of these things and to try to understand their nature, and having understood it, to try slowly and humbly and constantly to express, to press out again, from the gross earth or what it brings forth, from sound and shape and colour which are the prison gates of our soul, an image of the beauty we have come to understand – that is art.
>
> James Joyce, *A portrait of the Artist as a Young Man*

1
Introduction

The aim of this book is to show that the *Critique of Aesthetic Judgement* is not a set of disconnected remarks about aesthetic matters more interesting because of the distinction of their author and their place in the history of the subject than in their own right. That work can be seen to present an integrated theory whose scope, depth and suggestive power mark it as deserving of study by all who work in the field of philosophical aesthetics.

Kant's handling of his material presents impediments to the acquisition of an integrated view of the *Critique of Aesthetic Judgement*. He fails to give explicit directions to the reader about the bearings of his discussions of his central topics on one another. Kant presents a sustained and detailed analysis of such judgements as, 'This tulip is beautiful', which he refers to as judgements concerning the beautiful. His examples are mainly but not exclusively examples where what is judged beautiful is a natural object. Kant also presents a less sustained yet reasonably well worked out analysis of such judgements as, 'This stormy seascape is sublime', which he refers to as judgements concerning the sublime. His examples of these too are drawn mainly but not exclusively from nature. After his analysis of the sublime Kant proceeds to what may well appear to be a set of discontinuous and not very well worked out remarks about aesthetic judgements made about works of art or, to use Kant's way of describing them, works of 'fine art'. Many of these remarks are forbiddingly obscure and some are evidently perspicacious. Confronting these main sections of discussion in Kant's book, the reader cannot but wonder what Kant's intentions were in juxtaposing his topics as he did and whether any integrated theory can be won taking them all together.

The presuppositions which twentieth-century readers bring to the work also afford impediments to the acquisition of an integrated understanding of it. Twentieth century readers frequently expect philosophical aesthetics to deal simply and solely with the philosophy of art. Judgements about works of art form only part of what Kant treats under the heading of aesthetic judgement. Twentieth century readers have a tendency to believe that 'beauty' and 'pleasure' are terms which are hopelessly inadequate to the task of even partially elucidating the problems about the nature and value of works of art. Kant believes those terms to be indispensable to that task.

Kant sometimes argues for the superiority of the value of appreciation of the beauty of natural objects over the appreciation of worthwhile works of arts. Even the best of commentators take him to imply that beautiful and sublime natural objects are of greater aesthetic value than worthwhile works of art. Given such a reading, it could be thought that such a misunderstanding of the subject matter of aesthetics must prevent its author from producing serious philosophical work in the area. Now while it is true that Kant does believe that appreciation of the beautiful and the sublime in nature shows excellence of moral character whereas appreciation of worthwhile works of art need not, he does not maintain that beautiful and sublime natural objects are aesthetically superior to worthwhile works of art. Another impediment to obtaining an integrated view of his work emerges therefore as being an insensitivity to Kant's carefully drawn distinctions. Understanding his work often requires abandoning familiar perspectives and common presuppositions.

Such are some of the impediments to the acquisition of an integrated appreciation of Kant's mature aesthetic theory. The early chapters of this book aim to dispel some of them. The later chapters provide an interpretation of the way in which the various aspects of Kant's investigation should be seen to be interrelated.

It is the aim of Chapter 2 to remove some major objections to Kant's methodology and presuppositions. Criticisms from recent writings in philosophical aesthetics are brought to bear upon Kant's manner of approaching aesthetic inquiry and upon the key terms of his analyses. Richard Wollheim's criticisms of the approach to aesthetic inquiry through aesthetic judgements made about natural objects rather than with judgements about works of art are examined.[1] Nelson Goodman's objections to beauty and pleasure as key terms in which to elucidate aesthetic merit are considered[2] as are Collingwood's strictures against works of art which aim to please ('amusement art').[3] It is argued that the difference in outlook between writers such as Collingwood and Goodman on the one hand and Kant on the other is based upon a difference about the nature and value of pleasure rather than a basic disagreement about the role of beauty and pleasure in art and aesthetics generally.

The argument of Chapter 3 aims to show that Kant does not share the conception of the nature and value of pleasure which underpins criticism of writers such as Collingwood and Goodman of pleasure and beauty as key concepts in the analysis of aesthetic judgement.

Chapters 4 to 8 constitute a detailed and critical analysis of the *Analytic of the Beautiful*. Kant's analysis is given in four Moments, each of which unpacks an aspect of such judgements. Three of these aspects are qualifications of pleasure taken in what is judged. The first qualification is that such pleasure must be disinterested, the second that it must be universal and the fourth, that it must be necessary. The third aspect specifies that in which or that because of which such pleasure is taken. This is maintained to be a special kind of formal quality which Kant calls *Form der Zweckmässigkeit*, translated by Meredith as the 'Form of Finality'.[4] Since this formal quality depends upon relationships between the sensible properties of the thing judged rather than the structural properties which satisfy the requirements for applying a determinate concept to it, Kant's Form of Finality may be glossed as perceptual as opposed to conceptual form. In Chapters 4 to 8 each of these four aspects of judgements concerning the beautiful is discussed separately and questions are raised concerning their relationships to each other.

Chapter 6 is devoted to a consideration of the question whether the aspect of the First Moment, disinterested pleasure, attributes to aesthetic judgement a unique aesthetic attitude. Criticisms launched by recent writers such as Marshall Cohen[5] and George Dickie[6] against the existence of such an aesthetic attitude are brought to bear upon Kant's contentions.

Chapter 9 is a discussion of what it is in Kant's estimate that gives us the entitlement to use such judgements as 'This tulip is beautiful' as we do. It is a discussion of what he calls the 'Deduction of Pure Aesthetic Judgements'.[7]

Chapter 10 treats of Kant's account of the sublime. This account throws into the picture of aesthetic judgement a feature additional to those involved in the analysis of the beautiful. As Kant develops it, the analysis of the beautiful makes reference to only those cognitive powers employed in perception. These are, for him, imagination as the ability to form images from diverse sensory data, and understanding as the ability to form and apply concepts. In his analysis of the sublime Kant adds reference to a third cognitive power, namely reason. In an initial summary of his position 'reason' can be glossed as the power of thought.

Kant's treatment of judgements concerning the sublime presents them as sufficiently like judgements concerning the beautiful to count as aesthetic judgements but as differing from them in having more than the mere powers of perception involved in them. It is not pleasure in perception alone which constitutes appreciation of something sublime but pleasure in a complex of perception and thought. It is the attribution of this additional feature of judgements concerning the sublime which links Kant's discussion of the sublime to his discussion of art, of 'fine art'. It is this, too, which explains his coupling of the sublime and fine art in the *Analytic of the Sublime*.

Chapters 11 to 13 are devoted to Kant's philosophy af art. It is argued that Kant singles out three major differences between aesthetic judgements about natural objects and works of fine art. Judgements of works of art unlike judgements of natural objects must take note of intent, thought content and communicative efficacy. First, works of art are put together as they are intentionally in order to please. Secondly, works of art are expressive of thought. Such thought, although not the same as the thought involved in the appreciation of the sublime in nature is both akin to it and can incorporate it. Kant calls being engaged in such thought having 'aesthetic ideas'.[8]

Both the ideas of Reason and aesthetic ideas lack the kind of congruence between concept and experience requisite for empirical knowledge. Ideas of reason have no adequate instantiation in sensory experience. Aesthetic ideas cannot be captured adequately by any determinate concept. Ideas of reason and aesthetic ideas are akin because they are both characterised by this lack of congruence. Aesthetic ideas can incorporate ideas of reason by serving them as substitute instantiations. Worthwhile works of art which Kant thinks of as exemplary models[9] of fine art are therefore to be estimated not merely by reference to their beauty but also by reference to the thought expressed by them. They are to be assessed too by reference to whether they render such thought communicable to those to whom they are addressed.

The communicability of pleasure in reflecting upon natural objects is essential to their being properly judged beautiful; the communicability of the thought expressed by works of art is essential to their being fit to count as exemplars of fine art. In works of art both whether they are perceptually beautiful and communicate thought are relevant to aesthetic judgement of them. It is argued in Chapter 13 that there is sufficient evidence to conclude that Kant believes that in works of art fit to function as exemplars the communicability of the pleasure in the perceptual aspect of them effects the communicability of the thought expressed by them. Kant calls the ability to express such thought, 'genius'[10] and the ability to discern the beautiful, 'taste'.[11] He maintains that both are necessary for the production of works of art but that where they are in conflict taste must prevail over genius. If the beauty of a work of art is that which effects the communicability of what the work expresses this decision of precedence is entirely comprehensible within Kant's terms of reference. A sophisticated and highly suggestive account of the interplay between the perceptual and the intellectual aspects of worthwhile works of art emerges.

In Chapter 14, it is argued that Kant's philosophy of art is preferable to that of Collingwood which it, in some ways, resembles.

In Chapter 15 two ways in which questions of value enter into aesthetics are considered. One can consider which amongst natural objects, useful man-made objects and works of art are of aesthetic value. One can also raise questions about the importance of things having aesthetic value. It is argued that it is a measure of Kant's stature as a writer in aesthetics that one is able to elicit from the *Critique of Aesthetic Judgement* not only a persuasive account of which things are of aesthetic value and which are not; but also a persuasive answer to the question why it is that appreciating things which are of aesthetic value is worthwhile.

2
Kant's Methodology and Presuppositions

It is obvious from a brief account of the central discussions of the *Critique of Judgement* that Kant's analysis of aesthetic judgement centres squarely upon his analysis of what it is for something, be it natural object, humble artefact or work of fine art, to be beautiful; and reference to pleasure is an essential part of that analysis.

It is obvious too that Kant's treatment of aesthetic judgement displays both a difference of assumption as to the scope of aesthetic judgements, and a difference of stress within that scope, from those explicitly adopted or implicit in the works of the majority of writers in contemporary aesthetics. The philosophy of art which is assumed to comprise the whole of aesthetics by most contemporary writers, is taken by Kant to comprise only a segment of the sphere of aesthetics. For him, judgements that something is beautiful and that something is sublime, count as aesthetic judgements, whilst the things so judged may include both natural objects and artefacts. 'Beautiful' is taken to apply equally well to flowers,[1] living creatures,[2] crystal formations,[3] summer-houses,[4] gardens,[5] pictures,[6] poems,[7] and pieces of music,[8] whilst 'sublime' is taken to apply equally well to the stars,[9] the cosmos,[10] raging torrents,[11] the Pyramids,[12] St Peter's in Rome[13] and 'the well known inscription on the Temple of Isis'.[14] Not only do the things about which aesthetic judgements are made include natural objects, humble artefacts and works of fine art, but Kant treats aesthetic judgements made about things other than works of fine art as if they were just as important in the context of the analysis of aesthetic judgement as works of fine art.

Again, not only does Kant take judgements about natural objects and humble artefacts as falling within aesthetics and as being full-blown examples of aesthetic judgements, he also sees such judgements as the most elementary and primitive aesthetic judgements there are. He believes that only by first coming to understand them can we come to understand judgements concerning works of fine

6

art; and that an analysis of the worth of a work of fine art will contain something identical with what is involved in judging something such as a tulip to be beautiful. This amounts to his taking simple judgements about natural objects and humble artefacts to be both epistemologically and constitutively primitive in aesthetics. Epistemologically, because he thinks that we cannot understand the one without coming to understand the other; constitutively, because he thinks that judging that a work of fine art has worth is identical in part with judging that a natural object such as a tulip is beautiful.

Kant, then, makes certain assumptions in investigating aesthetic judgement in the way he does. He assumes that understanding aesthetic judgements about natural objects and humble artefacts enables us better to understand aesthetic judgements about works of art; and he assumes that aesthetic judgements about both nature and art are, or include, judgements concerning their beauty. Furthermore, his analysis of what it is to be beautiful is partly in terms of the pleasure it gives. He therefore assumes that a discussion of pleasure is relevant to a discussion of aesthetic judgement.

These assumptions and points of reference cannot be left unquestioned if Kant's aesthetic theory is to be seen to be significant in the context of contemporary aesthetics and not merely to be an interesting part of the history of the subject or a part of his biography. It is therefore important to turn to the writings of those who in the contemporary scene have challenged and rejected Kant's method of approach to aesthetics and his central assumptions to see whether his theory can withstand the challenge.

It is often maintained that the kind of judgements which Kant chooses as his starting point and elects to analyse are borderline cases of aesthetic judgements or not aesthetic judgements at all. To use them as a point of reference for aesthetic judgement in general, is therefore thought to be bound to mislead, whilst to use them as models to be bound to falsify.

Wollheim for example argues that to start out on an investigation of aesthetic judgements from examples such as those used by Kant (and Bullough) is to start from peripheral cases rather than central ones, in a way which is bound to distort one's conception of the central cases should one think of them as modelled upon the peripheral ones.[15] Thus he contends, and does not in so far as I understand his later mitigating remarks[16] retract, that Kant's procedure is like the procedure of one who begins an investigation of

language with an investigation of what it is for a parrot to 'talk',[17] or
who begins an investigation of what it is to be a person, with an
investigation into the personhood of the personified animals, trees
and rocks of romantic poets or children's stories.[18]

Wollheim denies what Kant assumes to be true, that simple
judgements such as 'That tulip is beautiful' are impeccable and
central examples of aesthetic judgements, and takes them instead to
be 'secondary and peripheral'.[19] On the basis of this verdict
Wollheim suggests that the appropriate methodology for aesthetics
is to start with the central cases of aesthetic judgement identified by
him as judgements about what Kant would call works of 'fine art'.
Since he uses examples taken solely from works regarded as having
at least some merit, he takes it to be appropriate to start from central
cases of aesthetic judgements where the judgement is in favour, not
against, the work in question.[20]

Wollheim goes on to say that although Kant (and Bullough) make
a mistake it is not just a mistake but a way of making the point that
'art' is grounded in 'life'.[21] He takes that to mean that 'art' and 'life'
are asymmetrical, that:

> whereas we could feel concern for a real human being without
> ever having been affected by the depiction of misfortune in a play,
> the reverse is inconceivable. Equally, we could not have a feeling
> for the beauties of art unless we had been correspondingly moved
> in front of nature ...[22]

This with some qualification Wollheim accepts, and in accepting it
concedes what I have described as Kant's 'epistemological' contention about the status of judgements about natural objects and
humble artefacts.

What Wollheim does not accept is that there is something
identical between such judgements and judgements made about
works of art. Thus he argues, taking the example of 'the progression
of a cobbled street to a smooth building that grows upward from it',
that appreciating such progressions without and within (as constituent of) a work of art are radically different in kind from one
another.[23] So much so – if we are to take his earlier remarks seriously
– that to talk of them in the same way will be necessarily to
equivocate.

To sum up. Wollheim's contention that Kant's methodology
involves a mistake rests upon his contention that aesthetic judge-

ments about works of art are the central cases of aesthetic judgement. Wollheim's intuitions about what is central are plainly opposed to Kant's but that does not show Kant's methodology involves a mistake.

Again, Wollheim claims Kant's mistake commits him to draw misleading conclusions about aesthetic judgements about works of art. This would be conclusive against Kant's methodology if Kant thought that he could illuminate every aspect of judgements concerning works of art by analysing judgements about natural objects and humble artefacts. However Kant, like Wollheim, believes that unlike natural objects, works of art are intentionally made to be as they are;[24] and, that unlike natural objects and humble artefacts, they are works of genius and as such express aesthetic ideas.[25] He also believes that in estimating the worth of works of art we must take these differences into consideration.[26]

Kant none the less believes that something very important is common to our judgements about natural objects and humble artefacts and our judgements about works of art – they both concern perceptual form. The salient point to consider here can be brought out by considering whether appreciating a Sung porcelain bowl and appreciating a waterlily stand to each other in the way in which listening to a man talk and listening to a parrot 'talk' do.

If, however, we consider only what Wollheim calls 'the meaning properties' of a work of art Wollheim's point is well taken. Compare standing and considering what the meaning of a haystack in a flood might be, with considering what the phrase 'beside the haystack in the flood' means in a poem.[27] The difference is comparable with the difference between a parrot 'talking' and a man talking. It is Kant's intention to stress the importance of perceptual form but to rebuke him for that is not to find a mistake in his methodology.

As well as starting from judgements about nature and then moving to judgements about works of art, Kant's method of approaching aesthetics centres squarely on his analysis of the beautiful. Many writers have argued that this is unsatisfactory and have found it unsatisfactory in a variety of ways. It has been thought to be theoretically unhelpful and it has been thought to debase the value proper to works of art. Some argue that concentration upon 'the beautiful' obfuscates. Some argue that it trivialises.

Goodman argues that aesthetic theories which centre on the notion of the beautiful are either false or they obfuscate.[28] His argument is that such theories face a dilemma. If the notion of 'beauty' is clearly articulated then we can readily find counter-instances to the claim that beauty is constitutive of aesthetic excellence for we can find examples of things which are aesthetically excellent which are ugly. If, on the other hand, these apparent counter-instances are rejected as not being cases of things with aesthetic excellence which are not beautiful, then 'beauty' has become a synonym for 'aesthetic merit'.

To consider the first horn of this dilemma in relation to Kant's position. The 'problem of the ugly' is usually explained in connection with works of art rather than natural objects or humble artefacts. So Goodman explains it. Thus such works as Gruenewald's *Crucifixion*,[29] Sophocles' *Oedipus Rex* and Goya's *Witches' Sabbath* are thought of as works of aesthetic worth which are ugly or at least non-beautiful. Since Kant holds that being beautiful is a necessary condition[30] for a work's having aesthetic worth, such counter-instances count against his theory, given that they are accepted.

Much of the force of the appeal to such examples as counter-instances turns upon the tacit appeal made to our non-collusive agreement that such works are 'ugly'. However it is not at all clear that such agreement is forthcoming if what we are talking about is the work rather than what it expresses or depicts. Most of us find mutilations, incest and witches unpleasant topics for contemplation and we might well be prepared to count them as 'ugly' upon that count. It does not, however, follow that a work which depicts such topics and expresses something about them is itself necessarily 'ugly'. Kant is at pains to point out that there can be beautiful 'representations' (expressions, depictions) of ugly objects; and he carefully states that the beauty of art as opposed to the beauty of nature is the beauty of the representation not of what is represented. He is often rebuked for this, the suggestion being that he believed that ugly things should be depicted only as beautiful in art. However, that is only one way in which what he says can be taken. The more important philosophical way of taking it comes out more clearly if one emphasises as he himself does not, that just as there can be beautiful representations of ugly things, so too there can be ugly representations of beautiful things. Using the terms which I. A. Richards invented to analyse metaphor, one can express the philosophical point as being that 'beautiful' can be (and is) applied to the 'vehicle' not the 'tenor'[31] of the work; and if that point is taken, non-depictive works which perforce depict neither beautiful nor ugly things, simply point up the consideration in question. For Kant, what is depicted may be as ugly as you please and, if nothing is depicted at all, all that is at issue is the beauty of that non-depictive thing.

Once these considerations are taken into account, non-collusive agreement that the works cited as counter-instances are 'ugly' or even non-beautiful cannot be counted upon. The Goya, for example, is rich, glowing and evocative and therefore 'beautiful' in the simplest and most straightforward sense of that term. *Oedipus Rex*, for literary rather than visual reasons, seems hardly less so. The Gruenewald *Crucifixion* is another matter. Taken in its own right it is at least partly ugly, and partly ugly with a point. Much more importantly, however, the *Crucifixion* is only half of a work of art, since much of its force draws on the contrast between it and the picture of the risen Christ which is revealed when the folded leaves on which the *Crucifixion* is painted are opened up. Everyone knows, or ought to, that the parts of a beautiful object can be and often are non-beautiful, or even ugly.

So much for the exchange of intuitions. What anyone who advances criticism such as Goodman's against Kant has to show, is not so much that something can have aesthetic merit and yet may be judged intuitively to be ugly by us, but that something may have aesthetic merit and yet be ugly as Kant construes being ugly. The objection that there is a 'problem of the ugly' is purported to be pertinent so long as a specific meaning is given to 'beautiful'. The specific meaning Kant gives it, or finds it to have, is that it pleases and that it is proper to demand that it should please because it has a certain kind of perceptual form, the Form of Finality. It has the power to set the cognitive faculties of humans[32] into harmonious free play. A counter-instance then, would have to be something which has aesthetic merit, but which does not please, and where it is not proper to demand that it should please because it does not have the Form of Finality. Once again, it does not seem incontrovertible that examples usually appealed to as constituting incontrovertible counter-examples do constitute counter-examples of this sort. It is arguable that even the Gruenewald *Crucifixion* pleases; and that it is proper to demand that it should please, because it has the kind of perceptual form which has the power to set the cognitive powers of humans into harmonious free play.

Even if the criticism is re-put in relation to natural objects rather than works of art, an emendment which would make it more

immediately relevant to Kant's views than it is as it stands, one
needs to bear in mind that Kant continually issues warnings that we
are generally prone to mistake non-aesthetic responses for aesthetic
ones. For sharks, sting-rays, caterpillars, spiders, monkeys, dwarfs,
deserts and terrible storms to count as 'ugly' it is sufficient neither
for our unprompted intuitions nor for Kant's account that they
simply displease on some count or other. They must, to count as
'ugly', displease in respect of certain features rather than others, or
in a special way. It is certainly part of Kant's account that beautiful
things can displease, and that non-beautiful things can please.
Beautiful things can displease as being personally disagreeable,
scary, threatening, dangerous or as falling short of perfection after a
kind, and 'ugly' is often used to express just such displeasure. By
the same token, non-beautiful and ugly things can please for a
variety of different reasons and in a variety of different ways. The
appropriate counter-instances, for Kant, will have to be, as they
were in the case of works of art, cases where the natural objects or
humble artefacts have aesthetic merit and yet do not please, and
where it is not proper to demand that they shall please because their
perceptual form has the power to set the cognitive powers of people
into harmonious free play. It is not an incontrovertible fact that such
counter-instances are forthcoming and only if they are forthcoming
is there any 'problem of the ugly'.

Two things emerge. First, any difficulty for Kant's theory arising
out of the kind of criticism we have been considering is going to
turn, not so much on the rights or wrongs of his method and on his
stress upon the notion of beauty, but upon his views about pleasure
and different kinds of pleasure. Secondly, pressing him at the point
where it is claimed that a natural object can both have aesthetic merit
and yet be ugly tells, if it tells at all, as an illustration of a theory
forced back on to the other horn of Goodman's dilemma, the claim
that if 'beauty' is given a meaning which does not give rise to 'the
problem of the ugly' then it has come to mean the same as 'having
aesthetic merit' and is therefore useless in explicating it.

Discussion of pleasure will come later.[33] Here, all that needs to be
said is that Goodman's criticisms are coupled with a view of
pleasure which Kant would reject. The issue between them is no
longer who is right about methodology, or about the role of beauty
in aesthetics, but one as to the nature of pleasure. On Kant's analysis
he is able to give content to aesthetic pleasure as a special kind of
pleasure whereas on Goodman's assumptions that seems 'too
transparent a dodge to be taken seriously'.[34]

The second horn of Goodman's dilemma, that if the notion of beauty is extended to cope with the counter-instances which he believes we can produce to show that there is for the beauty-theorist a problem of the ugly, it becomes only an 'alternative and misleading word for aesthetic merit'. Since natural objects can also be judged 'sublime' it is not the only kind of aesthetic merit natural objects may have. Secondly, he can deny that 'beauty' as an alternative word for (one kind of) aesthetic merit misleads. In fact, one of Kant's aims in the *Critique of Aesthetic Judgement* is to use 'beauty' or what it is to be 'beautiful' to illuminate aesthetic judgements about works of art. 'Beautiful' is not just an alternative and misleading word for the sole aesthetic merit of works of art.

Kant's use of 'beautiful' as the key aesthetic term in his theory provides a focus for his claims as to the autonomy of aesthetic judgement, and its companion contention that the most important aesthetic values are not derivative values. The critical estimate of what he does therefore shifts to these. Before going on to examine them, however, it is important to consider a third kind of criticism which is often levied at Kant, the very familiar claim that to give an account of aesthetic judgement partly or wholly in terms of 'beauty' is to trivialise the notion of aesthetic worth.

One should notice just how totally opposed to Kant in outlook and presupposition this criticism is. To trivialise is to give a description or an account of something which makes it inexplicable why anyone should value such a thing. To say that judgements about the beauty of a tulip for instance, do not amount to much in the context of aesthetics, to say that such judgements concern 'mere beauty', will not do justice to what Kant believes us to be committed to even in connection with such a simple judgement as this.

It is Kant's thoroughgoing contention that such judgements are not to be brushed aside, that in aesthetics they rate and rate highly. For him they rate within aesthetics. No matter what the differences between natural objects and works of art are, these judgements still provide a paradigm. Secondly, the kind of value such judgements exemplify rates in comparison with the values of utility, morality and knowledge. Further, Kant believes that just because such judgements as 'That tulip is beautiful' rate taking note of them enables us to render the value we put on other grander and more complex aesthetic matters explicable. Hence once again what appears to be a criticism of Kant's method, collapses into a confrontation of value judgements, and should be treated as such.

The matter does not, however, rest here. Most claims or implications as to the triviality and superficiality of talking of 'beauty' in aesthetics, are grounded not so much in presuppositions about the nature and value of 'beauty', but in presuppositions about the nature and value of pleasure which are taken to be integral to it. Sometimes this issues in a confrontation of value judgements too – this time about the value of pleasure rather than beauty. A reminder here is in place. One does not have to be a hedonistic utilitarian to find it objectionable to have the consideration that something gives pleasure brushed aside by being described as 'mere pleasure'. Despite the fact that in ethics there are many situations where hedonistic considerations are completely irrelevant or are relevant but overridden by more important considerations, there are also very many situations where hedonistic considerations are the most important considerations there are. If there were not, traditional utilitarianism would not be the interesting and attractive theory it has always been. Pleasure has very good claims to be thought of as *an* ultimate good. Once stated it ought to be evident that to say of something that it is a source of pleasure (in a suffering world) cannot soberly be taken to trivialise it. Need one say that Kant is not a hedonist in ethics?

The criticism, of course, runs deeper than the above considerations would suggest. It is usually the nature of pleasure, not the value of it, which is basically at issue. If it is assumed, as it is more often than not assumed, that pleasure stands in an external relation to that which gives it (its object) then (a) what gives pleasure can on that count only have derivative value, and (b) there is no way which is not an arbitrary way of distinguishing one kind of pleasure from another. As an assumption the first of these lies behind Collingwood's account and dismissal of 'amusement' art[35] and the second behind Goodman's dismissal of aesthetic pleasure as 'too transparent a dodge to be taken seriously'. If the first were true in so far as the giving of pleasure entered into aesthetic consideration 'aesthetic' objects would become means to ends and their value consequently derivative.[36] If the second were true then difference in 'quality' of pleasure as opposed to duration and intensity[37] could not be defended. As a result 'aesthetic' pleasure would enter into free competition with such pleasures as for example, those of a comfortable bed or a spin in a fast car or plane, which whilst still being of value are indeed 'trivial' when contrasted with the graver considerations of life. Consider here choosing to sacrifice one's marriage or the future of one's children for the pleasures of speed or of a comfortable bed.

Criticisms such as Collingwood's or Goodman's are conclusive against Kant's procedure if and only if the conception of the nature of pleasure which underpins them is correct. It is one of the considerable virtues of Kant's account of aesthetics that he rejects that conception. Nor should we accept it since we, unlike Kant, have the advantage of Ryle's[38] criticism of such conceptions of the nature of pleasure.

When considering whether Kant's method stands up to the criticism connected with the second horn of Goodman's dilemma I claimed that, although it was plausible to argue that in some contexts Kant uses 'beautiful' as an alternative term for aesthetic merit, this is neither misleading nor useless since it enables him to drive home his claim that aesthetics is autonomous. Throughout the *Critique of Judgement*, both by the contrasts he draws and by explicit statement he insists that aesthetic judgements have a certain kind of autonomy. They are, he claims, distinct from simple expressions of likes and dislikes, from judgements about utility, from judgements as to whether something is good of its kind and from the judgements of morality, as well as from cognitive judgements aspiring to truth. He explicitly rejects empiricist and rationalist groundings of judgements of taste (aesthetic judgement) because to accept them is to deny such autonomy. We find him saying,

> In this way beauty would have its *locus standi* in the world completely denied, and nothing but the dignity of a separate name, betokening, maybe, a certain blend of both the above-named kinds of delight, would be left in its stead.[39]

This insistence that aesthetics is a separate field is simultaneously an insistence upon aesthetic values being non-derivative. Kant holds that aesthetic values are no more a sub-class of truth, personally idiosyncratic esteem, utility or morality, than is aesthetics a branch of knowledge, self-knowledge, biography, psychology or morality. Moreover, he defends the non-derivative character of aesthetic values at two levels, the one within aesthetics, in analysing what it is for something to be beautiful, and the other in comparing aesthetic values with other values, that is, in saying what is so important about something being beautiful, given the analysis he gives.

Empiricists and rationalists might well not be moved by Kant's

contention that their views threaten the autonomy of aesthetics.
Noting this, we might think that Kant was appealing disingenu-
ously to something which he held as a simple unfounded assumption. Such an interpretation does not do him justice. He does not
think that he or we have to assume autonomy as an act of simple
faith; he thinks both that our practice in making judgements about
beautiful natural objects and humble artefacts commits us to such
autonomy, and that our practice is as it is, bears witness to
something of considerable value. Further he thinks that our practice
is just as firmly anchored to our judgements about natural objects as
it is to our judgements about works of art.

Most contemporary critics of the autonomy of aesthetics[40] have
had as their targets a group of theories, such as those of Bell and Fry,
which can in a rough general way be thought of as theories which
defend 'art for art's sake'. They therefore challenge the autonomy of
aesthetic judgement as applied to works of art and argue for the
relevance and importance of subject matter and 'meaning' in art.
They see insistence on autonomy as opposing 'art' to 'life'. It is
therefore very difficult to bring their criticisms directly to bear upon
Kant's insistence upon autonomy. Kant does not deny that works of
art have 'meaning' nor that their subject matter is relevant to an
aesthetic understanding of them. Nor does he think that their
'meaning' or subject matter contributes nothing to their aesthetic
value. He thinks that works of art express aesthetic ideas and that
aesthetic ideas are what genius contributes to a work of art, and
hence that of which in addition to considering beauty we must take
note in making an estimate of them.[41]

Kant is, however, formalist in relation to *beauty* so one can think
of him as holding a view of 'beauty for beauty's sake' analogous to
'art for art's sake' and similarly opposing 'beauty' to 'life'. To do so
would not amount to a falsification. Kant does regard appreciation
of beauty as requiring perception not wholly geared to determinant
concepts and to action, and which is not precariously fraught with
the feelings of the perceiver. It would be, however, question-
begging to conclude that this amounts to opposing 'beauty' to 'life'.

One of Kant's strengths is the way in which he reminds us that
aesthetic judgements permeate day to day living. There is no
suggestion whatever that aesthetic perception and appreciation are
activated solely within galleries and concert halls and the like. Nor
does he imply that to have aesthetic merit something must be
particularly deep or solemn. Not only is this one of Kant's strengths

but coupled with his insistence upon the importance of such judgements and their role in 'life', it adds up to a consideration of major importance. Seeing a cabbage as the one best to cut to cook for dinner, or a fly as one that a trout might rise to, or seeing the fly as hateful or a creepy crawly are no more immediately part of 'life', and still less a more valuable part of it, than enjoying looking at a variety of crystalline formations, or the plumages of birds, or a rose, or a piece of landscape gardening or the ladies dressed for a party seen against the background of a well-furnished room. What commentators have been pleased to call Kant's philistinism makes it plain that he sees 'beauty' as part of 'life'.

Both Kant and Hogarth, whom he resembles, although formalist about beauty, have a far richer conception of 'form' than Bell[42] or Fry,[43] partly because both Kant and Hogarth do not require that the form in question be of necessity human-created form. Hogarth's little drawings which he uses to illustrate his points in the *Analysis of Beauty* include drawings of pieces of parsley, the various shapes of women's corsets, legs of chairs etc.[44] It is just as much of a mistake to think that Kant's examples show no more than the philistinism of his taste, than it would be to think that those Hogarth drawings do no more than show *his* philistinism.

This conception of aesthetic judgement as part of and not contrasted with 'life' needs to be seen alongside the fact that in the *Critique of Judgement* Kant has come to include capacity for aesthetic appreciation in men's capacity for rationality.[45] Since the ground on which Kant rests his claim that persons are of incomparable worth is their rationality[46] and he does not think of their rationality merely as a matter of what they know or how well they can argue, but of their capacity to see themselves and their world as totalities, to think of themselves as moral agents and to appreciate 'the beautiful', Kant's conception of 'beauty for beauty's sake', if we think of it as that, is, for him, a conception of aesthetic appreciation as one of the most important aspects of 'life'. None the less aesthetic appreciation for Kant is not an inflated notion. In order for someone to have aesthetically appreciated something he does not have to have done something as grand or as solemn as to have contemplated in awe Michelangelo's *God creating Adam*.

3
Pleasure

Kant, as we have seen, believes that taking pleasure in something is an indispensable aspect of making a judgement concerning that thing's aesthetic worth. It was argued in Chapter 2 that Kant's belief is only vulnerable to criticisms such as those of Collingwood and Goodman if Kant is assumed to share their philosophical conceptions about what is involved in taking pleasure in something. It was stated without argument or ramification that Kant does not share such a conception, but, on the contrary, makes use of a very different one. The time has come to examine the evidence for that claim and to extract Kant's account of pleasure.

Kant might plausibly be thought to share approximately the same conception of the nature of pleasure as Collingwood and Goodman if evidence were to be drawn from the works he produced before the *Critique of Judgement*. In *Observations on the Feeling of the Sublime and the Beautiful* he describes pleasure or enjoyment as a 'sensation' (*Empfindung*) and a 'feeling' but draws no distinction between the two descriptions.[1] He does draw a distinction between 'finer' feeling which includes pleasure in the sublime and in the beautiful and less 'delicate' pleasures but marks that distinction by reference to whether the pleasure can or cannot occur 'without any thought whatever'.

In the first and second *Critiques* and in the *Groundwork* Kant treats pleasure as a determination of 'sensibility'. As such it is the effect of objects upon percipients passively affected. He shows no interest in developing a philosophical analysis of what is involved in taking pleasure in or in enjoying something, being preoccupied with inclinations and appetites in connection with will and action. He describes pleasure as 'a sensation' and does not distinguish between different kinds of 'sensation'.

Alongside the change in Kant's understanding of aesthetic judgement, born witness to by his letter to Karl Leonhard Reinhold in the later part of the year 1787 where he announced, 'I have discovered a kind of **a priori** principle different from those heretofore observed', Kant's interest in and understanding of pleasure increased and developed. In the *Critique of Judgement* Kant is no more content to say that pleasure is 'a sensation' and leave it at that than he is to say, as he did in *Observations*, that 'The sublime **moves**, the beautiful **charms**'.[2]

To show that Kant has a conception of the nature of pleasure which differs from the kind of conception which is in the background of Collingwood's and Goodman's criticisms, it is therefore necessary to attend to the *Critique of Judgement* itself and to attend to both what he explicitly says about the nature of pleasure and to the way in which he distinguishes one kind of pleasure from another.

First, take the evidence of what Kant explicitly says. The key passage is to be found in the First Moment of the *Analytic of the Beautiful*. He is comparing pleasures of the three kinds which he believes to be the basic kinds of pleasure, namely, 'the agreeable', pleasure in 'the good' and pleasure in 'the beautiful'.[3] In that context he argues that there is a common misconception which frequently leads to the extension of the notion of 'the agreeable' to cover all of these three and which gives rise to disastrous consequences. Once this extension is made, he says, everything comes to be thought of as pursued solely as a means to pleasure, and as a consequence it is believed that men can only be blamed for folly or imprudence and not for baseness or wickedness. Given that pleasure in the good and beautiful are modelled on 'the agreeable',

then impressions of sense, which determine inclination, or principles of reason, which determine the will, or mere contemplated forms of intuition, which determine judgement, are all on a par in everything relevant to their effect upon the feeling of pleasure, for this would be agreeableness in the sensation of one's state . . . How this is attained is in the end immaterial . . .[4]

The misconception which Kant believes to licence this disastrous extension is that 'sensation' is univocal. When pleasure is said to be 'a sensation' and when the perceived green of a meadow is said to be 'a sensation', it is believed that 'a sensation' has exactly the same sense in both assertions. It is this that Kant is concerned to deny. He believes that the difference between the two is so great that it would be better not to call pleasure 'a sensation' but instead to mark its difference from green as 'a sensation' by calling it 'a feeling'. Whereas a sensation of green can and often does represent such states of affairs as the meadow's colour, pleasure cannot represent a state of affairs at all. At very least it should be called a 'subjective' rather than an 'objective' sensation. In his own words,

> The green colour of the meadow belongs to *objective* sensation, as the perception of an object of sense; but its agreeableness to *subjective* sensation, by which no object is represented: i.e. to feeling, through which the object is regarded as an Object of delight (which involves no cognition of the object).[5]

The point upon which Kant is insisting here, is that pleasure, far from being or being capable of being a representation itself, presupposes something which is or is capable of being a representation which is its object; and as its object functions without reference to whether it truly represents or not. The perceived green colour of the meadow pleases. The green colour as perceived can represent, but whether or not it does, the green colour is what is found pleasing. Pleasure in the perceived green colour cannot represent the meadow; and Kant adds, it cannot represent the perceiving subject either.

If we interpret 'represent' to mean it tells us something about the meadow or the person perceiving the meadow, it may be thought surprising that Kant maintains that the feeling of pleasure does not 'represent' the perceiving subject since we attribute the pleasure to our perceiving self in the same way as we attribute the perceived green of the meadow to the meadow. Kant repeats the contention in the Introduction to the *Metaphysic of Morals*,[6] so it is no mere casual aside. Pleasure construed as 'subjective sensation' cannot represent the perceiving subject.

It is the virtue of the interpretation of Kant's account which we have been considering that it enables us to make sense of this apparently counter-intuitive remark. Pleasure alone abstracted from what we would call its intentional object cannot function as a representation of the state of the perceiving subject. To function as representation of the perceiving subject's state, pleasure must be coupled with the intentional object of pleasure. To illustrate this consider the cases of one enjoying the champagne served at a wedding, or one who is delighted upon being complimented upon his clothes. In these examples, the perceiving agent's state is the state of enjoying the champagne or of being complimented upon his dress, whether or not it is champagne rather than carbonated white wine that he is drinking or whether or not someone is genuinely appreciating his dress rather than criticising it by being ironical.

To return to Kant's spelling out of the main difference between saying green is a 'sensation' and saying pleasure is a 'sensation'. He maintains that when we say that the meadow is green, 'green' functions as a representation of what the colour of the meadow is; and, what we are concerned with is whether, as representation, it is true or false. When on the other hand we say that the green of the meadow is agreeable, we say of the representation that we delight in it (the green colour); and are not concerned with whether green as a representation of the meadow's colour is true or false.

This reading of the passage shows the significance and importance of Kant's starting his book with his account of what it is for something to be beautiful in the way he does. He says:

> If we wish to discern whether anything is beautiful or not, we do not refer the representation of it to the Object by means of understanding with a view to cognition, but by means of the imagination (acting perhaps in conjunction with understanding) we refer the representation to the Subject and its feeling of pleasure or displeasure.[7]

Kant's two conclusions about pleasure in general are then that, (i) pleasure is incapable of being a representation but presupposes either a representation of sense, a principle of reason or a form of intuition as its object; and (ii) it is a response of a subject to something which is its object, not just another object amongst objects.

The particular conclusion in context is that it is quite wrong to try to distinguish 'the agreeable' by trying to distinguish sensory pleasures as such, but instead we should try to distinguish those pleasures which have sensations or 'objective' sensations as their objects.

It is a short step from these conclusions, if it is a step at all, to the view that pleasure is internal to its objects, that is that one cannot 'have' the particular pleasure that one does without 'having' its object. One cannot have the pleasure of eating a peach whilst not eating at all but whilst (enjoyably) squelching barefoot through mud. One cannot 'have' the pleasure of eating a peach whilst eating a banana – except in the case where one mistakenly thinks one is eating a peach. If pleasures are internal to their objects then one can have as many kinds of pleasure – qualitative kinds – as there are kinds of object.

Such a view as this jibes with Kant's intention in contrasting the false view of pleasure where everything comes to be seen as a means to pleasure, with his own view which has no such implication.

A. D. Lindsay notes the change in Kant's understanding of pleasure as it is expressed in the *Critique of Judgement* stressing the aspect of spontaneity. He says,

> Kant in his earlier writings represented pleasure as the passsive effect on the mind of its stimulation by objects. Our feelings of pleasure are then the mark of our animal or phenomenal nature, of our being part of the mechanically determined world. But our pleasure in the beautiful is the expression of our intelligible nature or the free spontaneous activity of the mind, and yet is caused in us by reflexion upon objects. Here at last is the mind in its freedom, affected by objects in a way which is not incompatible with its freedom. Here is something between the sharp alternations of actions from respect for the moral law and heteronomous actions determined by accidental pleasure.[8]

There are times where one wishes Kant had broken further from his earlier view. It impairs his capacity to accommodate aesthetic appreciation of sensations. One does not, however, regret his divergence from his earlier view.

Kant's explicit statements about pleasure in the *Critique of Judgement* are not by themselves conclusive evidence that he does not share the account of pleasure which underpins such criticisms of his kind of approach and beliefs about aesthetic judgements which are brought by Collingwood and Goodman. The second kind of evidence at our disposal is, however, much more conclusive. We have already looked at what he says; appeal must now be made to what he does, to the way in which he distinguishes one kind of pleasure from another in his overall handling of the whole programme of the *Critique of Judgement*.

Kant maintains that there are three basic (qualitative) kinds of pleasure which differ from each other in having three different basic kinds of object. The basic kinds of pleasure are pleasure in the matter of sensation ('the agreeable'), pleasure in the beautiful and pleasure in the good. Their objects are sensation, perceptual form and concepts. The telling point is that nowhere in his treatment of these kinds of pleasures does he speak as if the task of differentiating them could be accomplished by inspection relating to the pleasures abstracted from their objects. He neither says nor implies that we can distinguish one kind of pleasure from another in the way in which, for example, we can distinguish a black opal from a milky opal, or navy blue from powder blue.

Where Kant does not distinguish different kinds of pleasure by reference to different kinds of objects he distinguishes them by different relations in which the representations stand to the respective feeling. Thus we find him saying,

> The agreeable, the beautiful, and the good thus denote three different relations of representations to the feeling of pleasure and displeasure, as a feeling in respect of which we distinguish different objects or modes of representation.[9]

The differences between different kinds of pleasure turn for Kant entirely upon differences amongst and in relation to their objects. Since nobody is going to deny that there are differences between the things which give us pleasure, the claim that there is a distinctively aesthetic pleasure becomes dependent upon there being distinctively aesthetic objects of pleasure. One can argue against Kant's conception of what determines the distinctiveness of the objects of such pleasure, but one cannot dismiss the introduction of the notion of a distinctive kind of pleasure as a dodge 'too transparent to be taken seriously'.

If Kant had simply characterised the objects of aesthetic pleasure as differing from other objects of pleasure as producing or being capable of producing a peculiar aesthetic pleasure, we would be entitled to complain of circularity in his account, but Kant's account of what constitutes a peculiarly aesthetic object of pleasure is, as it should be, independent of reference to the kind of pleasure which it is or is capable of producing.

4
The Analytic of the Beautiful – Preliminaries

The main theme of the *Analytic of the Beautiful* is the development of an exposition or analysis of the kind of judgement which expressions such as 'This is beautiful' are used to make. Although Kant sometimes speaks as if he were analysing the judgement,[1] and sometimes appeals to our linguistic expressions and that to which our usage of them commits us,[2] there is no doubt that he thinks of himself as appealing to a practice in which people participate and which he expects them to recognise.[3] He accepts what Wittgenstein denies,[4] that 'This is beautiful' is in common use. His analysis of the judgements which we use expressions such as 'This is beautiful' to make, is, however, meant to proceed without prejudice to whether we really are entitled to use such expressions as we do.

Shorn of its many elaborations, Kant's analysis of our use of the expression 'This is beautiful' is that it expresses disinterested pleasure which we believe we are entitled to demand of any and everyone because the object judged is discerned to have a certain kind of perceptual form which is called by Kant the Form of Finality. The four points of this analysis are elaborated in four 'Moments', each with its own definition.

The definition of the First Moment is,

Taste is the faculty of estimating an object or a mode of representation by means of a delight or aversion *apart from any interest*. The object of such a delight is called *beautiful*.[5]

The definition of the Second Moment is,

The *beautiful* is that which, apart from a concept, pleases universally.[6]

The definition of the Third Moment is,

Beauty is the Form of *Finality* in an object, so far as perceived in it *apart from the representation of an end.*[7]

And the definition of the Fourth Moment is,

The beautiful is that which, apart from a concept, is cognized as object of a *necessary* delight.[8]

Because 'Moment' seems to be a rough synonym for 'element', and Kant calls his procedure 'analysis', one is inclined to think that each Moment extracts an independent constituent which is necessary for any judgement concerning the beautiful to have, and which taken together with those of the other Moments yields what is sufficient for such a judgement. On this reading, given that pleasure in a scientific specimen of, say a hook-worm, and pleasure in an isolated colour, say gentian blue, were disinterested, they would none the less not qualify as judgements concerning beauty, since they are not also pleasures which one can go on to demand of others, without making an appeal to a concept under which they are taken to fall.

The formulae of the definitions, on the other hand, suggest that Kant means us to believe that each definition lays down not what is necessary but what is sufficient for making a judgement concerning the beautiful. On this reading, granted that pleasure in a scientific specimen or an isolated colour is disinterested, it will qualify as a judgement concerning the beautiful, using the definition of the First but not the definitions of the other Moments. One would therefore be entitled to conclude that there can be discrepancies between the results obtained by making use of different definitions. Kant does not believe this to be a possibility. He thinks that any judgement which satisfies one of his definitions will automatically satisfy any of the others. So he cannot believe the criteria to be independent. In fact, he is inclined to maintain that one can derive one definition from another; but he is not always explicit about how the derivation is to be done.

Kant gives an argument for moving from the definition of the First Moment to that of the Second. It is that, if the judging subject can find no personal reason peculiar to him for the thing in question to give him pleasure, he must believe that the reason for his pleasure must be something which he can presuppose in every other person.[9] This argument is a bad argument. There is absolutely no reason to believe that what gives us disinterested pleasure is any less idiosyncratic than what gives us pleasure which is based upon our interest. The argument, even if good, would only entitle us to move from the definition of the First Moment to the definition of the Second.

Kant gives us no indication as to how he supposes we should derive the definition of the Third Moment from that of the First nor that of the First from the Third. Why, we might ask, *must* we feel disinterested pleasure in a certain kind of perceptual form (the Form of Finality) and in that alone? Why *must* we feel only disinterested and not interested pleasure in the Form of Finality?

Much more argument is directed towards showing that the definition of the Third Moment follows from that of the Second and Fourth. Here Kant argues that that which pleases universally and of necessity without reference to a concept must be a certain kind of perceptual form (the Form of Finality) since 'the matter' as opposed to 'the form' of sense, is of necessity private and contingent.[10]

The definition of the First Moment can be taken in either a negative or a positive way. We can construe 'pleasure apart from any interest' as pleasure in an object in which we have no 'interest' or as pleasure in an object considered in its own right or for what it is. Positively construed, the definition of the First Moment lends itself to application which is independent of the definitions of the other three Moments.

The definitions of the other three Moments complete each other. Both the definition of the Second Moment and that of the Fourth are negative. They only tell us that the universality and necessity of pleasure in the beautiful does not turn on the thing in question being subsumed under a concept; only the definition of the Third Moment tells us that upon which pleasure in the beautiful does depend. There are strong grounds for believing that Kant is working with two virtually distinct positive definitions which he claims, but does not demonstrate, to be logically interdependent.

The first definition differs from the other three in another way. Kant sees the task of giving an analysis of judging something to be beautiful and of formulating definitions of beauty in terms of distinguishing the beautiful from what he calls 'the agreeable' on the one hand and 'the good' on the other. In the definition of the First Moment by the single criterion of 'disinterested' pleasure, pleasure in 'the beautiful' is distinguished from both 'the agreeable' and 'the good'. Each of the other definitions contains explicitly or implicitly two considerations, one to distinguish 'the beautiful' from 'the agreeable', one to distinguish it from 'the good'. In the definitions of the Second and Fourth Moments 'pleases universally' marks off 'the beautiful' from 'the agreeable', whilst 'apart from a concept' marks it off from 'the good'. In the definition of the Third Moment the Form of Finality is implicitly contrasted with sensation which Kant takes to be the matter as opposed to the form of perception[11] and the object of 'the agreeable'; and 'apart from the representation of an end' explicitly distinguishes 'the beautiful' from 'the good'.

In this way a classification of pleasures into three basic kinds, 'the agreeable' and the pleasure of 'the beautiful' and 'the good', forms the background of Kant's attempts to define the beautiful. He sees analysing the judgements we are wont to make and express by such sentences as 'This is beautiful' as involving marking off one basic kind of pleasure from the other two. Since this background concerning basic kinds of pleasure is imported by Kant, not implicit in our practice, it needs to be brought out into the open.

Kant's classification of pleasures into three basic kinds is, it seems, meant to be both exhaustive and mutually exclusive. It can only be thought of as exhaustive at great cost. The intellectual pleasures one must suppose to be included under pleasures of 'the good'. The 'agreeable' must end up as a description which covers any pleasure which is not one of 'the beautiful' or 'the good', and hence must amount simply to a miscellaneous category of pleasures. Even as pleasure in 'the matter of sensation', it blankets cases of too diverse a kind. Consider the differences between the pleasure of eating oysters when one is starving, the pleasure of the taste of oysters and the pleasure of feeling oysters slipping down.

The problems of treating 'the agreeable' and pleasures of 'the beautiful' and 'the good' as mutually exclusive are even greater. On seeing a branch of ripe cherries we might feel pleasure and judge the laden branch to be beautiful and the fruit good, or the branch to be a good branch of a cherry tree. We have too, intuitions enough for maintaining that to judge the branch laden with fruit to be beautiful, is to make a different judgement from the judgement that the fruit or the branch is good. When, however, we consider our simple personal pleasure in the cherry branch laden with fruit, we cannot easily answer the question whether it is or can be, partly or wholly, different from our pleasure in its beauty and admiration of it as a good branch of a cherry tree. Kant's notion of 'the agreeable' is an invented category which is roughly equivalent with our notions about what is merely pleasant or pleasing. Our notion of what is pleasant or pleasing overlaps the pleasures of the beautiful and the good, and does not exclude them. To ensure the exclusion of 'the agreeable' from the pleasures of 'the good' and 'the beautiful' Kant has to insist on the difference between and the exclusiveness of their objects.

To apply this to the case in hand. Kant believes that only our pleasure in the Form of Finality is disinterested, and that we can only take disinterested pleasure in the Form of Finality because taking pleasure in anything else will be by definition pleasure in 'the agreeable' or 'the good' both of which are interested. He believes that we can take no other than disinterested pleasure in the Form of Finality because interested pleasure in such form is not pleasure in the Form of Finality but pleasure in what something with the Form of Finality produces or brings about.

Such manipulations conceal, but do not dispel, the tensions between the definition of the First Moment and that which emerges when one combines those of the other three.

The pattern of Kant's comparisons and contrasts between 'the agreeable', 'the beautiful' and 'the good', are notwithstanding interesting in their own right. We can map this pattern as follows. 'The agreeable' and pleasure in 'the good', in contrast with pleasure in 'the beautiful', are interested pleasures – pleasure in the beautiful' alone of the three being disinterested. Pleasure in 'the beautiful' and 'the good', in contrast with 'the agreeable', which is merely private, are universal and necessary pleasures. Pleasures which are universal and necessary count as 'communicable' pleasures, so pleasure in 'the beautiful' and 'the good' are 'communicable'. However, the communicability of pleasure in 'the good' differs from pleasure in 'the beautiful', by being communicable by means of a concept, whereas the communicability of the pleasure in 'the beautiful' is communicable by means of the Form of Finality.[12] Further, 'the agreeable' and pleasure in 'the beautiful', unlike pleasure in 'the good', are always immediate pleasures, whereas pleasure in 'the good' may be either mediated or unmediated.

5
The First Moment –
Disinterested Pleasure

In the First Moment Kant is primarily concerned to maintain that whereas pleasure in the agreeable and the good are 'interested' pleasures, pleasure in the beautiful is 'disinterested'. The fact that pleasure in the good counts as 'interested' for Kant should be noted, since noting it forestalls a too facile reading of what he means by 'disinterested'. The definition which concludes the First Moment includes along with the characterisation of beauty in terms of disinterested pleasure, specific reference to the aesthetic as distinct from aesthetic *value*. The way in which we must consider something when we are aiming to judge whether it is beautiful or not is disinterestedly, and what we judge when we judge that it is beautiful, is that it pleases when it is considered in that way.

What then does Kant mean by considering something in a 'disinterested' way? What does he mean by 'disinterested pleasure'?

He starts his explanation of what he means by 'disinterested' with a definition of 'interest' and an elucidatory example where he imagines contrasting attitudes and evaluations of people confronted with the question, 'Is this palace before you beautiful?'.

The definition of 'interest' is,

> The delight which we connect with the representation of the real existence of an object is called interest. Such a delight, therefore, always involves a reference to the faculty of desire. . . .[1]

He later goes on to say,

> All interest presupposes a want, or calls one forth. . . .[2]

The example he offers in elucidation of the above definition of interest and which by contrast is meant to elucidate 'disinterested' is as follows,

If any one asks me whether I consider that the palace I see before me is beautiful, I may, perhaps, reply that I do not care for things of that sort that are merely made to be gaped at. Or I may reply in the same strain as that Iroquois *sachem* who said that nothing in Paris pleased him better than the eating-houses. I may even go a step further and inveigh with the vigour of a *Rousseau* against the vanity of the great who spend the sweat of the people on such superfluous things. Or, in fine, I may quite easily persuade myself that if I found myself on an uninhabited island, without hope of ever again coming among men, and could conjure such a palace into existence by a mere wish, I should still not trouble to do so, so long as I had a hut there that was comfortable enough for me. All this may be admitted and approved; only it is not the point now at issue. All one wants to know is whether the mere representation of the object is to my liking . . .³

The first two of Kant's imagined reactions to the question, 'Is the palace before me beautiful?' illustrate ways of finding it 'disagreeable', the second two ways illustrate ways of judging it not to be good and finding it displeasing on that account, that is ways of disapproving of it. We are told quite bluntly that neither finding it disagreeable nor disapproving of it is to the point. Since all four ways of considering the palace are not indifferent to the real existence of the object being considered, the subjects are said not to be judging the palace aesthetically, and hence only appear to answer the original question in the negative.

It can be seen that Kant is making use of two criteria for 'disinterested', indifference to the real existence of the object of 'the representation' and not presupposing or calling forth a want. Later he maintains that these two criteria are identical.⁴ They certainly do not seem to be so.

To consider the first of these criteria, indifference to the real existence of the object of the representation. The way in which Kant presents the desert island consideration in his example quoted above makes it appear that he is, temporarily at least, using 'disinterested' construed according to this first criterion as sufficient for concluding that a judgement is aesthetic, and for concluding that any pleasure which is disinterested in that sense, and only pleasure which is disinterested in that sense, is aesthetic.

Both seem intuitively wrong. We do not seem to be indifferent to the real existence of all the objects we judge to be beautiful or not beautiful; and, where we are indifferent to the real existence of something, for example a certain kind of tiny frog becoming or having become extinct, considering it from that point of view does not seem to be a particularly aesthetic one. Moreover, if we were pleased by it, it seems we might be pleased for all manner of reasons. It might suggest a theory about other (really existent) frogs, it might be a perfect symbol or emblem for some society, it might suggest better than any existent frog a frog which might turn into a prince, to cite a few.

There is, I think, tension within the way Kant treats this criterion, tension which, not surprisingly, arises out of his very liberal and highly misleading use of the term 'representation'. The opening sentence of the *Analytic of the Beautiful* says that, 'we refer the representation by way of the imagination to the judging subject not by way of understanding to the object' thereby treating 'the representation' as really given. That there is something which we take to represent how things are before us is taken for granted and permits us, without using the expression in a Pickwickian sense, to say '*This* is beautiful'. It stresses the aspect of Kant's account of the beautiful which is taken up by Croce,[5] that aesthetic judgement is of particulars. The 'representation' (of imagination) of the palace considered by the man on Kant's desert island, is an entirely different matter. It is not a representation of any particular at all. Willing or not willing its existence would be willing *into existence*, a particular.

What these considerations bring out is that some reference to real existence is already contained in the notion of being 'a representation' as Kant standardly employs it; and that reference is essential to his contentions about aesthetic judgements being singular.[6] It is also essential to his insistence upon the object judged beautiful being sensed. When he cuts the notion of representation loose from its representative role altogether, or takes 'a representation' to mean something which can represent but is not necessarily representing anything, he defeats his own conclusions since both the particularly of aesthetic judgement and the sensory aspect of what is judged, disappear with the representative role, and what remains is something generic not *sensed* but at best imagined to be sensed.

What then of the second of his proposed criteria for 'disinterested', 'Not presupposing a want or calling one forth'? This criterion brings us much nearer to the colloquial meaning of 'disinterested' given that we construe the want in question to be the want of the person judging. We can in the colloquial sense of 'disinterested' take 'disinterested' pleasure in something not wanted by us personally. We can take disinterested pleasure in someone else's winning the lottery and in something which someone else would want, for example a fine axe displayed in a shop window can be admired by someone who does not have nor ever will have a use for axes. Kant does, I think, mean to construe the want to be the want of the person judging, and I think he would try to deal with the cases which the colloquial use of 'disinterested' deems disinterested but which he counts as 'interested', by maintaining that a want of the subject is not presupposed by the judgement but 'drawn forth'. He would interpret taking pleasure in someone else's winning the lottery, or in looking at a fine axe as judging those things to be good and since he believes that the good is what we *rationally* want,[7] the judgement 'draws forth' a want in the judger.

Kant's claim to be able to isolate the aesthetic by reference to 'disinterested' consideration, and aesthetic value by 'disinterested' pleasure, turn upon treating the ethical point of view and ethical values as 'interested' and not 'disinterested'. This is wholly in line with his conception of willing as rational wanting but it is, as the above considerations show, out of kilter with the colloquial usage of 'disinterested', and what the colloquial usage is, is not irrelevant to his purposes.

It is therefore hardly surprising to find him doing something suspiciously like a volte-face on whether or not pleasure in morality is disinterested, when he is maintaining that beauty is the symbol of morality in the *Dialectic*. One of the points upon which the analogy which he claims to hold between morality and beauty is that both please *'apart from all interest'*.[8] He hastily adds that morality although involving an interest is still, like beauty, not bound up with an *antecedent* interest.

If this, not being bound up with an antecedent interest, is the main thrust of his contention, one would have thought he could concede the point that pleasure in the beautiful, whilst not resting upon an antecedent want might, however, draw one forth. As things would then stand, being 'disinterested' would not peculiarly characterise the aesthetic, or aesthetic value, since they would characterise moral value as well. The distinction which Kant wished to preserve could still be made by pointing out that in the case of morality a want must be drawn forth but in the case of beauty it might or might not be. In a footnote,[9] he does seem to accept a conclusion somewhat like this one. It is coupled, however, with a curious conception of what the want drawn forth in the case of the beautiful might be.[10] He seems to think that we only want to have or get beautiful objects because we want to show them to others, or to show them off to others ('the empirical interest in the beautiful')[11] or, for moral reasons ('the intellectual interest in the beautiful').[12] He does not seem to think we could want to have or keep a thing of beauty simply to be able from time to time to admire it.

Kant's claim that his two criteria for being 'disinterested' are necessarily connected must be rejected on the grounds that some friendships, some loves of place, and some scientific prizings, involve pleasures taken in the real existence of something without necessarily presupposing a pre-existent want. That one is glad that some individual person or place exists, or that there is an Australian pelican as well as a European one, does not entail that one had a pre-existent want which these existents assuage. Nor does it entail that one wants 'to have' them or be with them. At most being glad that something such as these exist could be taken to entail that one ought to protect and preserve it should it be under threat. One can, however, say as much for the beautiful. It seems forced too, to press such examples into the pattern prescribed by Kant for 'the good'. Such affections need not be rational; our friends may be bad, our favourite places not peculiarly meritorious.

On the other hand, there are some grounds for thinking that there is a necessary connection between an antecedent or drawn forth want and interest in real existence. Wanting and willing are for realisations of what is wanted or willed. Even here we must not rush to conclusions. Consider the case of fantasy gratifications. A child may dream of getting a Bunyip for Christmas, St Anthony dwell on sensual gratifications in the desert and magazine readers gloat over glossy pictures of fine food. These pleasures are not solely, if at all, pleasures of anticipation. To accommodate them within the belief that there is a necessary connection between a want and an interest in the real existence of the object of the want, 'not indifferent to the real existence of the object of the want' must be taken as a more accurate description of the interest in real existence rather than 'delight in the real existence'. For fantasy gratification, what gratifies in fantasy, must be thought of as really existing, even though it does not really exist.

We must, I think, conclude that Kant's claim that his two criteria for being 'disinterested' are identical can no more be accepted than either of them alone. However, he has amongst his various loose descriptions of what he means, one which more accurately catches his meaning and provides a more defensible account of what it is to have a 'disinterested' as opposed to an 'interested' pleasure, and which does involve working his two criteria together. This description of an interested pleasure is as follows,

> Such delight is determined not merely by the representation of the object, but also by the represented bond of connection between the Subject and the real existence of the object.[13]

The mysterious character of what Kant's man on the desert island is doing when he asks himself whether he will bring a palace such as the one he is imagining into existence, and the contrasted case of aesthetically appreciating the palace, becomes much clearer if approached with this description of what it is to be 'interested' and what 'disinterested' in hand. To ask, 'Do I want one of these things here – on my island?' does bring in a represented bond of connection between the real existence of what is represented and the subject, in a way that to ask 'Is this beautiful?' or to say 'This is beautiful' does not.

This way of explicating the distinction between 'interested' and 'disinterested' also takes care of the case of fantasy gratifications. What pleases there is 'the represented bond of connexion' rather than 'the representation'.

It will also serve to show why such a powerful objection as that made by Marshall Cohen in the following quotation:

> Responding aesthetically to a woman may involve not raising questions about her morals; it does not require 'bracketing' her existence. Responding aesthetically to a pope might require the remission of papal politics; it would not entail meeting with equanimity the news that one had been gushing over a particularly startling creation from Madame Tussaud's,[14]

whilst devastating against the theory he advances it against (that of Vincent Tomas), is so much less effective against Kant's contentions. Responding aesthetically to a man or a pope does require that you attend to him rather than to the represented bond of connection between you and him.

On page 26 it was pointed out that both a positive and a negative interpretation of the definition of the First Moment are open to us. We may take 'disinterested pleasure' to mean solely a pleasure which does *not* presuppose a pre-existing want of the subject. On the other hand, we may take it to mean that it is a pleasure which is felt towards the object which itself pleases rather than towards the subject's getting, having or making use of the object. The positive interpretation is a matter of emphasis, since it proceeds against the background of the negative interpretation. Although it is a matter of emphasis it is not a mere matter of emphasis. The negative interpretation leaves room for the objection that 'disinterested pleasure' tells us only what aesthetic pleasure is not, not what it is. A whimsical pleasure and pleasure in anticipated causal consequences of something might be 'disinterested' on this showing. The positive interpretation purports to tell us what aesthetic pleasure is by telling us what it is taken in, that is by reference to its object.

The stress I have put upon disinterested pleasure as delight in 'the mere representation of the object' weights the positive against the negative interpretation. That such a weighting has been traced to Kant himself is shown by those writers who make the adoption of an aesthetic attitude central to aesthetic appreciation and judgement, is sufficient to bring home to us how important the interpretation of 'disinterested pleasure' as pleasure in the features of a thing in its own right, rather than in the relation in which it stands or is thought to stand to the judging agent, historically has been felt to be. One of the first of these writers, Schopenhauer, forcibly iterates the point. He says,

> Most men are almost always at this standpoint, because they lack objectivity, i.e. genius. Therefore they do not like to be alone with nature; they need company, or at any rate a book, for their knowledge remains subject to the will. Therefore in objects they seek only some relation to their will, and with everything that has not such a relation there sounds within them, as it were a ground bass, the constant, inconsolable lament, 'It is of no use to me.' Thus in solitude even the most beautiful surroundings have for them a desolate, dark, strange, and hostile appearance.[15]

This description of what it is to consider something in a disinterested way as opposed to considering it in an interested way, and of disinterested as opposed to interested pleasure in something, will not, however, serve to differentiate a certain kind of scientific interest from an aesthetic one. If one considers a mould which has grown in a cup of cold coffee, one must, in order to consider it either aesthetically or scientifically, avoid representing 'a bond of connexion between the Subject and the real existence of the object', that is one must avoid thinking of oneself as drinking it. A scientific and an aesthetic interest in the mould, and scientific pleasure in it, if it proves a significant mould for the study of moulds, and aesthetic pleasure, if it proves beautiful, are equally 'disinterested' on this showing.

What this shows is that, so far as the outcome of the First Moment goes, Kant has not produced what he has claimed to produce, a criterion of being 'disinterested' which *isolates* the case of pleasure in the beautiful. His theory will have to rely upon the outcome of the other Moments to differentiate the two cases above. When the scientist and the aesthetic connoisseur of moulds not only take pleasure themselves but go on to claim that others should take pleasure as well, the procedures connected with the two cases will differ. The one will, in defending his claim, need to adduce conceptual considerations connected with the classification of moulds and the role of this one, the other will need to appeal to other people's direct experience of the perceptual form of the mould. Kant's theory of the First Moment is incomplete where he thinks it is complete; but he can in the foregoing way call into play the conclusions of the other Moments to complete it.

Not only does Kant's use of being 'disinterested' as a criterion of aesthetic pleasure rule into the class of aesthetic pleasures cases such as the scientific case above which we would not, intuitively, count as such, Kant takes it to rule out of the class of aesthetic pleasures cases which we would be inclined to count as aesthetic. The striking examples of these are a class of pleasures of sense, or 'sensation' as he would call them, for example pleasure in the colour of gentians. It seems that here Kant simply misapplies his own criterion. We have noticed already that 'the agreeable' as a category of the basic kinds of pleasure tends to be a catch bag of very diverse kinds of case.[16] Not only do the cases in that category differ radically from each other, the characterisations of them with which Kant works vary. Sometimes he talks of the agreeable as what is found 'pleasing in sensation'[17] and sometimes he talks of it as what 'gratifies'.[18] Now among the various cases which count as cases of the agreeable, there are some which it is quite misleading to describe as 'what gratifies'. For some, that description is plainly false. If the description 'what gratifies' is to cover all of the cases of pleasure in eating oysters mentioned in Chapter 4,[19] 'what gratifies' will have to vary from case to case.

These differences are blanketed by the cover term 'the agreeable' in such a way that the case which comes closest to what is involved in something being beautiful is not distinguished by Kant. Take the oyster examples. There are good grounds for treating pleasure in eating oysters when hungry and pleasure in feeling them slip down as pleasures in eating, but none for taking pleasure in the taste of oysters, which is pleasure taken in *what* is eaten. It is just this which lends point to Kant's own remark,

> Only when men have got all they want can we tell who among the crowd has taste or not.[20]

Kant mentions as examples of pleasures in 'the agreeable', pleasure in the colour violet, in the tone of stringed and wind instruments, and in drinking a glass of Canary wine.[21] Now pleasure in the colour violet, or in the sound of the violin, are not at all like the pleasures of a man recovering lost capacities, or even of a man being released from imprisonment. A man recovering from impaired vision, or someone who leaves a room in which a deafening noise is being produced, or who gets out of gaol, may take intense pleasure in seeing and hearing. However, that is not the same thing at all as taking pleasure in what is seen and what is heard. In the case of sight and sound, since they do not work as taste does, by contact, there is no literal counterpart of taking pleasure in the oysters slipping down. There is no literal interpretation of the eye or ear being 'caressed'.

Some cases of drinking a glass of Canary wine will be cases where pleasure is taken *in drinking* not simply pleasure in what is drunk. Of them it will be in order to say that they are pleasure 'in the (truly) represented bond between the subject and the real existence of the object'. The case seems other and different with pleasure in the colour violet or pleasure in the tone of a violin. There, it is not pleasure in the (truly) represented bond of connection between the subject and the real existence of the object but pleasure in the 'representation', that is in what is seen and what is heard. Pleasure in the colour violet or in the tone of the violin does not seem to presuppose a want nor draw one forth. Nor does it seem obviously to provoke 'a desire for similar objects'.²² It is only by a sleight of hand, by equating 'what is pleasing in sensation' with 'what gratifies' that Kant deceives himself into thinking that he has shown that according to his own criteria of 'interested' and 'disinterested' *all* of the cases of pleasure in 'the agreeable' are 'interested' rather than 'disinterested'.

Curiously enough, in one of his tantalising turnabouts he seems to become to some extent aware of this. After he has spent most of the First Moment arguing that all of the agreeable (the taste of sense) is interested he says, in the Second Moment,

> The first of these I may call the taste of sense, the second, the taste of reflection: the first laying down judgements merely private, the second, on the other hand, judgements ostensibly of general validity (public), but *both alike being aesthetic (not practical) judgements about an object merely in respect of the bearings of its representation on the feeling of pleasure or displeasure.*²³

Characteristically Kant is not prepared to say of the pleasures of the agreeable that some are and some are not 'disinterested' pleasures. If some are 'disinterested' it means that his contention that 'sensations' alone (e.g. the colour of gentians) cannot be beautiful will have to turn upon our not being entitled to make a claim that others shall take pleasure in them as well, not upon the strictures of the First Moment.

When Kant claims that pleasure in the good is 'interested' not 'disinterested', it is not because he thinks that the pleasure presupposes a want but that it 'draws one forth'. If something we do not like doing or do not feel inclined to do is believed to be a means to what we think intrinsically good (i.e. what is 'useful') or is believed to be intrinsically good, Kant thinks that the thought that it is good draws forth a want to do it and that want when acted on, or thought of as acted on, pleases. The pleasure then, is not in the 'representation' but in the represented bond between the subject and the real existence of the object represented. Attributive uses of 'good' which do not necessarily involve a represented bond between the subject (taken to be the particular human making the judgement) and the object represented seem none the less to presuppose a want or draw one forth and turn on the represented bond of connection between a subject (some subject but not necessarily the subject making the judgement) and the real existence of the object. Admiring a good apple or a good axe does seem to presuppose that someone wants them and/or someone would want them if they, like you, who are making the judgement, judged them good. I have in mind here the case of a townsman admiring a good axe in a shop window, a townsman who never has, nor will have, a use for an axe. Kant would, I am sure, treat these cases as either examples of the useful or of the intrinsically good, thus reflecting errors incipient in that traditional treatment but errors which are not peculiarly his, nor errors which particularly affect the issue at hand.

6

The Aesthetic Attitude?

Theories which incorporate as their central feature the notion of an 'aesthetic attitude' have come under spirited attack by contemporary writers on aesthetics. The general description of such theories is that they maintain that a peculiar state of mind is a necessary, if not a sufficient, condition for anything's being 'aesthetic'. Thus George Dickie says,

> present day aesthetic attitude theories . . . maintain that anything can be aesthetic if and only if it is experienced while in the aesthetic attitude.[1]

Marshall Cohen characterises such theories in much the same way. He says.

> It is habitually assumed that there is an element common to our experiences of works of art (or to experiences called 'aesthetic'). Or if not, it is at least supposed that there are certain mental states necessary for the having of these experiences. I shall call the first assumption the doctrine of aesthetic experience and the second (in view of its most frequent form) the doctrine of an aesthetic attitude.[2]

As most of the contemporary writers who come under fire as holding 'aesthetic attitude theories' have been influenced by Kant's aesthetic theories it is, I believe, important to raise the question whether Kant himself puts forward such an aesthetic attitude theory and if so whether the criticisms which tell against the theories derived from his tell also against his own.

This is a good point at which to consider these issues since it is in the First Moment where Kant concentrates upon being disinterested which is, apparently, a state of mind, as a necessary condition of a judgement's being aesthetic. After the First Moment Kant, as the definitions themselves show, allows his account of 'the aesthetic', to retreat into the background of his discussion of what it is to judge that something is beautiful (of 'aesthetic merit'). It is left to us to draw conclusions about judging something not to be beautiful.

Since Kant's analysis of (a correct) judgement concerning the beautiful, after the discussion of all Four Moments, can be summarised as a judgement which expresses disinterested communicable pleasure which is not grounded on a concept but upon the Form of Finality, one is inclined to believe that a judgement that something is not beautiful will need to express communicable (that is universal and necessary) displeasure not grounded on a concept, but in the absence of the Form of Finality. He certainly does not say so, and I doubt that he was prepared to accept specifically that account of being not beautiful. Whether he was or not the suggestion is sufficient to bring home the fact that the role of disinterested reflection upon something, is not thought of by Kant as peculiarly characterising aesthetic merit. Kant certainly does not hold the view, as Fry and Bullough perhaps do, that confronting anything in a particular state of mind is sufficient for establishing that the thing confronted is 'aesthetic' when 'aesthetic' is taken to mean 'has aesthetic merit'. In Cohen's terminology Kant's is not an 'aesthetic experience' theory but at most a candidate for being an 'aesthetic attitude' theory.

Is Kant's an aesthetic attitude theory? Does he believe, to use Cohen's characterisation, that there are certain mental states necessary for the having of our experiences of works of art?

Kant's first definition can be read with the emphasis upon the negative or positive conception of 'disinterested' as pleasure and displeasure *not* dependent upon personal and private interest, or pleasure and displeasure dependent upon the directly perceived properties of the thing up for judgement. The emphasis upon the negative reading does almost certainly imply that being in a specific mental state is a defining characteristic of *aesthetic* judgement. Emphasis on the positive reading implies no such matter although it suggests a theory about how best to consider the directly perceived properties of a thing in their own right. It is helpful here to think of the recommendation that to fully register the tonal qualities of say, a sunset, one ought to look at the skyline upside down through one's legs.

In so far as Kant believes that there is a certain state, that of being disinterested, which is at least a necessary condition for considering whether anything is beautiful or not, he does believe that there is a certain mental state necessary for the experience of things judged beautiful, be they natural objects, humble artefacts, or works of art.

However, appreciation of the beauty of works of art is, for Kant, only a necessary condition and not a sufficient condition for appreciating a work of art. In order to appreciate a work of art one must not only appreciate its beauty but also take note[3] of the aesthetic ideas which the work expresses. Whether Kant means us to be committed to considering the aesthetic ideas expressed by a work disinterestedly is arguable. If we think of a work of art as comprised of a tenor and a vehicle, and think of the sensory bearer which expresses the aesthetic ideas as the vehicle, and the aesthetic ideas as the tenor, we can say that Kant thinks of 'beauty' or 'beautiful' as applicable to the vehicle. Whether or not we think that Kant believes his theory to be committed to considering the aesthetic ideas disinterestedly will depend on what we take him to believe about the relation between the vehicle and the tenor of a work. As what he says about that relationship is opaque, the issue is an arguable one.

An aspect of Kant's characterisation of wondering whether something is beautiful as it is presented in the First Moment which links Kant with typical contemporary attitude theorists, is his insistence upon aesthetic judgement being reflective, or contemplative. The contrast of aesthetic judgements with those of 'the agreeable' and 'the good', and his insistence that aesthetic judgements are not 'cognitive',[4] is enough to substantiate this emphasis without his frequent explicit statements. Considering something 'disinterestedly' does in fact seem to be what he means by reflection on or contemplation of something.

In so far as there is a strand of Kant's theory, the one which emphasises being 'disinterested', which is an aesthetic attitude theory, is it offensively so?

It would be, I believe, if Kant thought that being disinterested was a necessary condition for 'experiencing' things correctly judged beautiful but not for 'experiencing' things correctly judged not beautiful. It would be offensive, that is, if he held that being disinterested were a necessary condition of aesthetic merit rather than a necessary condition for counting as aesthetic. Stressing that he does not think anything of the kind takes the sting out of the criticism of his being committed to thinking that aesthetic judgements are reflective or contemplative. One only needs to reiterate that for Kant, the judgement that something is not beautiful or that it is ugly, is every whit as contemplative or reflective as the judgement that something is beautiful. Reflection is not for Kant a special state in which and in which alone we can discern merit, comparable with the purity of heart with which and with which alone one can 'see' the Holy Grail.

Cohen is right to draw analogies between the emphasis placed on contemplation in such theories as Schopenhauer's and those of Bell and Fry and the role of contemplation in religious contexts; but their theories relate contemplation peculiarly to aesthetic merit. Kant's does not. If 'feeling' the Form of Finality requires reflection so too does 'feeling' its absence.

When Kant thinks in terms of states of mind implementing or obstructing 'vision' he has much more mundane considerations in mind than those purported to interfere with religious revelation. What he stresses, is that preoccupation with some features of things involves one in the neglect of others. For example, a person can go on indefinitely drinking their morning coffee hastily from the same ill-made cracked cup and not stop to consider whether it is ugly or not. More suitable analogies than the one with religious revelation can be drawn between aesthetic cases and scientific cases where the job of investigating causes could not get under way until some way of looking at a phenomenon such as epilepsy or venereal disease was displaced.

One needs to add to this consideration that reflection in Kant's theory, unlike contemplation in those of Schopenhauer and Bell, is non-cognitive in Kant's meaning of that term. Kant does not think that aesthetic judgements constitute fragments of knowledge. Contemplation in Schopenhauer's and Bell's theories, as in putative religious experiences, features as a very superior kind of knowledge by acquaintance. Not only does Kant not think of reflection as knowledge, on his epistemological theory, he cannot think of it as such. Knowledge for Kant requires concepts, reflection *by definition* is not governed by concepts. It is not an accident that he speaks of the Form of Finality being 'felt'.

If Kant's attitudinal theory is not offensive in the ways in which later attitudinal theories sometimes are, it might still be entirely wrongheaded. Dickie[5] is careful to distinguish between the case where it is claimed that a certain mental state is necessary for the making of a judgement of aesthetic merit and the case where it is claimed that a certain mental state is necessary for the making of an aesthetic judgement (whether or not it be pro or con). He none the less wishes to argue that the latter as well as the former is mistaken.

His arguments to that effect, if they were successful, would tell more directly against Kant's position than do those of Cohen.

Dickie criticises Bullough's conception of 'psychical distance', Aldrich's interpretation of aesthetic seeing as 'seeing as', and Stolnitz's theory of disinterested attention, taking each to be a variant of aesthetic attitude theories. The variant closest to Kant's is Stolnitz's, and Dickie's criticisms of Stolnitz can be cast quite readily in terms which relate to Kant, even though Kant does not speak, as Stolnitz does, in terms of attention.

Against the view that the mental state thought necessary for characterising anything as 'aesthetic' is disinterested attention, Dickie argues that for 'disinterested attention' to make sense, there must be contrasting cases where it is proper to speak of 'interested' attention. Since according to Dickie these are not forthcoming, 'disinterested attention' is a myth.

Now of course Dickie is not denying that there are putative cases of 'interested' attention; the works of those who defend aesthetic attitudes abound with them. What Dickie is claiming is that all these putative cases of 'interested attention' turn out to be either (a) cases of inattention, or (b) different from the so-called cases of disinterested attention only in motivation.

(a) Attending to a beast one is about to shoot and attending to its shape, its colouring and the lustre of its coat both seem to be paradigm cases of attention. Both are inattentive to what the other is attentive to, that is they attend selectively to different aspects of the beast. Both, however, attend to the beast, and that is why it is completely arbitrary to pick out one of them as being inattentive. Each is inattentive only in relation to each other. In the light of these considerations it does not seem as wrong as Dickie leads us to believe, to speak of the difference between the two in terms of different kinds of attention. If we adapt the case to Kant, we will contrast the man who is wondering where best to shoot the beast so that the pelt will be least spoiled by the bullet hole; and the man who is considering whether the beast is beautiful. It does not seem so wrong to describe the one as considering the beast in a different way from the other, disinterestedly, as opposed to interestedly.

(b) However, such considerations do force the issue with regard to whether disinterested attention and interested attention are necessarily, rather than just as a matter of fact, different; and it is this issue which Dickie's second kind of dissolution of putative cases of 'interested' attention raises.

Dickie considers the case of two people listening to the same piece of music, the one listening to it with a view to being able to analyse it and describe it in an examination on the following day and the other listening to it for no ulterior purpose. Dickie's contention is that there may be, in such a case, no difference whatever in what is attended to and so, he argues, the difference is not a difference of attention but a difference of motivation.

What this case does not show is that the object of attention in practical activity or theoretical investigation is not by and large and on the whole different from the object of attention when considering something aesthetically. In shooting ducks and in drinking tea out of cups we do not normally attend to the same features of them as we would if we were forming an aesthetic estimate of them. Nor would we normally note the same features of the duck in trying to analyse and describe it for scientific purposes as we would when considering it aesthetically. Discovering the beauty of the duck or the ugliness of the cup can come as a complete surprise to one who pauses in the course of the practical activity of shooting or drinking, or to one who changes over from scientific investigation to aesthetic assessment.

Dickie's example is important in that it purports to show that although the objects of attention in practical and theoretical inquiries as opposed to aesthetic assessment are normally different, they are not of necessity so. Does Dickie's example show this?

It has been argued recently that it does not. Rader and Jessop state.

Without denying that there is a difference in motives, intentions and reasons, we think that this difference pre-supposes a distinctive mode of experience and cannot serve as a substitute for this original demarcation. The ultimate ground for the aesthetic motivation is to be found in the nature of the aesthetic experience itself. If Smith is really having an aesthetic experience and is not simply being bored, he finds listening to the music rewarding in itself. If he should cease to find it intrinsically rewarding, he would cease to listen to it aesthetically. Hence he focuses upon those aspects of the music that have intrinsic perceptual worth. Jones is not necessarily concerned with the music as fascinating for its own sake. With an ulterior purpose in mind, he focuses on the analytically describable features that he can later write about on the examination. Even if he should be bored, he will continue to listen and analyse the music in order to pass his examination. There is an intrinsic difference between his experience and that of Smith, and not simply an extrinsic difference in intention and motivation.[6]

This objection misses Dickie's point. By saying in the first sentence that difference in motive brings with it a difference other than difference in motive the authors reassert that the object of disinterested attention *must* be different from the object of interested attention and that is what Dickie's example is meant to challenge. Further, Dickie specifies that the people who are listening to his piece of music may both be enjoying the music or both be finding it boring. By doing this he insists that he is examining 'disinterested attention' as a candidate for being what it is that characterises listening to the music aesthetically and not as a candidate for aesthetic merit. Rader and Jessop reintroduce the notion of disinterested attention as characterising aesthetic merit and on the basis of that (*contra* Dickie's hypothesis) argue that there *must* be a difference in the intrinsic experience and hence in the kind of attention involved in it.

Dickie is simply arguing that one can assess something aesthetically without having a disinterested attitude to it and advancing an example to show that this is so. One can think of other examples such as the practice of professional buyers and sellers of opals and paintings. Now there is no contradiction in saying that in these cases the persons concerned must be disinterested in order to be interested, must take their project in stages so to speak. So as it stands Dickie's case is not completely conclusive. However, it does put the defender of the aesthetic attitude on a spot. Why should we say that it is necessary to consider what is to be judged aesthetically in a disinterested way rather than what Dickie says, namely that being disinterested is neither necessary nor sufficient for considering something aesthetically?

If we accept Dickie's conclusion, how does it affect our assessment of Kant's position? If the definition of Kant's First Moment is read with a negative stress and taken to lay down a sufficient condition for the aesthetic and for being beautiful; or if being disinterested is taken as one of the four necessary and jointly sufficient conditions for being beautiful, Kant is an 'aesthetic attitude theorist'. If we accept Dickie's argument we will therefore conclude that Kant in the First Moment is mistaken in putting

forward the criterion of being disinterested as defining or characterising what it is to consider something aesthetically – even though
he is not open to the objections which are conclusive against those
aesthetic attitude theorists (such as Schopenhauer) which make
being disinterested a defining characteristic of aesthetic value or
merit, and even though he is not committed to the view that our
attitude to the tenor as well as the vehicle of works of art must be
disinterested in order to be aesthetic (as is Bullough).

How important is being 'disinterested' to aesthetics generally and
to the negative reading of Kant's first definition in particular? One
must insist against Dickie who speaks of the 'myth' of the aesthetic
attitude, that something very like what Kant means by being
'disinterested' is of very great importance in the context of aesthetic
judgement. It is as useful in the context of aesthetic dispute as is the
Golden Rule in moral dispute. If it is possible for the object of
disinterested attention to be the same as the object of interested
attention it is still not very often the case that it is.

Dickie's example provides the test case he aims for only if of the
two persons listening to the piece of music the one who is listening
in order to do an examination about it the next day is a *good* student
preparing for a *good* examination. A student who is looking merely
for shortcuts toward passing an examination where the questions
are likely to be irrelevant or wrongheaded would certainly listen to
the piece in a different way from his friend who has no ulterior goal
for his listening.

One just cannot bring someone who responds, for example, to
one's judgement that a certain jellyfish is beautiful by replying that it
is a creepy, slimy thing, to consider whether it might be beautiful,
until one induces him to stop thinking of finding it in his bath. And
there are those who will not even contemplate the possibility of an
aerial bombardment[7] or a sick child[8] being beautiful since it is
evidently wicked to stand about staring when something can be
done to alleviate disaster and distress.

'Consider it disinterestedly' is often the right thing to say to get
someone to direct his attention to aesthetic considerations. As one
of the most interesting features of Kant's aesthetic is its heavy
emphasis upon aesthetic pleasures as communicable, it is not
surprising that he should also stress being 'disinterested'. However,
to treat being considered disinterestedly as on a par with the Golden
Rule in morality or to direct a person's attention amounts to treating
it as a test and not as a defining condition of aesthetic judgement.

Against a theory which posits such a condition as the sole criterion of aesthetic judgement Dickie's counter-example would be conclusive.

Dickie's example is pertinent to Kant's contentions in the First Moment because it separates what Kant assumes to be the same, the positive and the negative aspects of his definition, that is pleasure or displeasure *in the representation* and pleasure or displeasure which is *not* taken in an envisaged relation between the judging subject and the representation. Dickie's example brings Kant's negative aspect under attack. What Kant would have done in the face of such an attack is a matter of conjecture, but on the other hand, it is indisputable that should the negative aspect of being 'disinterested' fail, he still has the positive aspect to fall back upon. He could concede the claim that in order to determine whether the representation rather than the relation in which the representation is conjectured to stand to the judging subject pleases or displeases, the judging subject need not be *without* an interest in the representation and still insist that both the interested and the disinterested subject (Dickie's two persons listening to a piece of music) must attend to the representation and not to the represented bond of connection between it and them.

To so insist might still be thought to be incomplete. There might be much about the representation as opposed to how we stand to it, there might be many ways in which a subject might consider it. In dealing with a charge of incompleteness it is necessary to call to mind the definition of the First Moment is not Kant's only definition. What it is about the representation which pleases or displeases aesthetically, what about it which must please universally and necessarily without a concept is the presence or the absence of the Form of Finality. The demand that a subject consider the representation and not the envisaged relation in which he thinks he stands to it as an account of aesthetic as against unaesthetic pleasure or displeasure, is completed by the demand that the representation should be entertained with a view to seeing whether it is of such a form to be felt to set the cognitive powers involved in perception into harmonious free play.

To sum up. Kant's definition of the First Moment of *The Analytic of the Beautiful* is open to a negative and a positive interpretation of 'disinterested'. Only under the first interpretation is it vulnerable to the objections which are brought by such writers as Cohen and Dickie against contemporary theorists which they describe as 'aesthetic attitude' theorists. Cohen's attack confuses 'aesthetic' used to classify a kind of value be it pro or con with 'aesthetic' when it is used to mean being of aesthetic merit and *not* of aesthetic demerit. Kant's account of being 'disinterested' is meant to cover the first and not the second of these and is not therefore vulnerable to the main thrust of Cohen's attack. Dickie is much more careful to distinguish between using 'disinterested' to assist in the characterisation of the aesthetic where it covers both pro and con aesthetic judgements and where it covers only pro judgements. The example which he regards as decisive – the example of the two people listening to the same piece of music, the one in order to cope with a coming examination, the other simply aesthetically considering the music – is meant to challenge considering something disinterestedly as a complete or partial characterisation of aesthetic *pro or con* judgement. It connects as Cohen's criticisms do not directly with Kant's claims. We do not know what Kant would have done in the face of Dickie's criticism in so far as it, if accepted, forces the positive and the negative interpretations of 'disinterested' which Kant seems to assume to be the same apart. We do know, however, Kant has the positive aspect of his definition to fall back upon and we know that Kant does not intend the definition of the First Moment of the *Analytic of the Beautiful* to stand alone. That definition is completed by the definitions of the other three Moments the completion of greatest importance being that of the Third Moment. Where the definitions of the Second and Fourth Moments tell us only that aesthetic pleasure or displeasure must *not* be pleasure or displeasure based upon concepts, the definition of the Third Moment tells us that they must be based on the felt presence or absence of the Form of Finality. There is no trouble at all in explaining Dickie's example in terms of both listeners examining the music for the felt presence or absence of the Form of Finality. The challenge of the example can then be interpreted as bringing pressure upon Kant's insistence upon the inter-derivability of his four definitions.

7

The Second and Fourth Moments – Communicable Pleasures

The definition of the Second Moment is,

> The *beautiful* is that which, apart from a concept, pleases universally.[1]

and the definition of the Fourth Moment is,

> The beautiful is that which, apart from a concept, is cognized as object of a necessary delight.[2]

As these two definitions show, these two Moments contain discussion of those interpersonal claims which Kant is to maintain to constitute part and parcel of any judgement that something is beautiful. He holds that any judgement that something is beautiful lays claim to universal agreement; and given that it is correct and the thing in question is beautiful and not simply thought to be so, anyone who does not assent to it is constrained to assent to it. Since a necessary part of agreeing with or assenting to a judgement concerning beauty is taking pleasure in the thing judged beautiful, being constrained to agree is, in part, being constrained to take pleasure in the thing in question. A correct judgement that something is beautiful makes a demand to the agreement of everyone and anyone ought to assent to that demand. That is what Kant means when he speaks of pleasure in the beautiful being universal and necessary; and being universal and necessary in these senses is what he means by 'communicable'.

The framework of discussion in these Moments is still the framework of the threefold division of pleasure since the points of comparison and contrast between pleasure in the good and pleasure

50

in the beautiful is central to the development of Kant's analysis of judgements concerning the beautiful.

Kant contrasts the pleasures of the agreeable which are personal and contingent, with those of the beautiful and the good which he believes to be universal and necessary. As a result, he believes that whereas pleasures in the agreeable may be in purely private objects, pleasure taken in things judged beautiful or good must be in objects which are public.

Kant rests his contention that judgements concerning the beautiful lay claim to universal agreement upon the way in which we use the expression, 'This is beautiful'. He takes himself simply to be unpacking the implications of judgements we are prone to make. It is therefore useful to compare his contention with a similar one made by Stevenson when analysing 'good' according to his first pattern of analysis, namely that 'This is good', analyses into 'I approve of this, do so as well.'³ The 'do so as well' part of Stevenson's analysis is the counterpart of Kant's universal claim to the agreement of others. Both writers intend to elicit what we mean when we use 'This is beautiful' and 'This is good'. Both implicitly or explicitly contrast expressions which make a demand on others with those which do not. Like Stevenson, Kant believes that our use of 'This is good' commits us to making claim to the agreement of others and he believes this is true of 'This is beautiful' as well.

However, that is where the similarity between Stevenson's and Kant's views ceases. Whereas Stevenson sees the interpersonal claim simply as a personally issued imperative to be backed when queried by any sort of persuasive device which might be thought to be effective, Kant sees the interpersonal claim as one we think of ourselves being entitled to make, and one which is open to rational assessment, even though he believes that the kind of rational assessment appropriate to judgements containing 'good' differs radically from that appropriate to judgements containing 'beautiful'. Whereas taking note of the First Moment we conclude 'This is beautiful' expresses disinterested pleasure, taking note of the Second and Fourth Moments we conclude that it implies that anyone ought to take pleasure in the thing in question as well. Kant makes the point as follows,

It would . . . be ridiculous if anyone who plumed himself on his taste were to think of justifying himself by saying: This object (the building we see, the dress that person has on, the concert we hear, the poem submitted to our criticism) is beautiful *for me*. For if it merely pleases *him*, he must not call it *beautiful*. Many things for him may possess charm and agreeableness – no one cares about that; but when he puts a thing on a pedestal and calls it beautiful, he demands the same delight from others. He judges not merely for himself, but for all men, and then speaks of beauty as if it were a property of things. Thus he says the *thing* is beautiful; and it is not as if he counted on others agreeing in his judgement of liking owing to his having found them in such agreement on a number of occasions, but he *demands* this agreement of them. He blames them if they judge differently, and denies them taste, which he still requires of them as something they ought to have; and to this extent it is not open to men to say: Every one has his own taste. This would be equivalent to saying that there is no such thing at all as taste, i.e. no aesthetic judgement capable of making a rightful claim upon the assent of all men.[4]

It is clear from this passage that Kant is not maintaining that pleasure in the beautiful is universal in the way in which pleasure in eating ripe strawberries is wellnigh universal. In the case of the odd-man-out who does not enjoy eating ripe strawberries, even though some may demand that he takes pleasure in eating them as well, and may blame him for not doing so, they are not entitled to do so. Kant believes that, in the case of a judgement that something is beautiful, we not only make a claim to the agreement of others, we are also entitled to make it.

In criticising Burke's approach to aesthetics as too 'physiological' Kant says,

– if we attribute the delight in the object wholly and entirely to the gratification which it affords through charm or emotion, then we must not exact from *any one else* agreement with the aesthetic judgement passed by *us*. For in such matters each person rightly consults his own personal feeling alone. But in that case, there is an end of all censorship of taste – unless the example afforded by others as the result of a contingent coincidence of their judgements is to be held over us as *commanding* our assent. But this principle we would presumably resent . . .[5]

The demand to universal assent is not to predict what people will do, nor to pronounce what they must do according to the laws of the mind,[6] but to signify what they ought to do. The same kind of considerations hold in connection with necessity in the Fourth Moment.

It is, of course, important to realise that Kant is not putting it about that wherever he (Kant) says that something is beautiful everyone else ought to agree with him. He is saying that whoever says that anything is beautiful is making such a claim to agreement on the part of others, but that such claims ought to be acceded to only where the initial judgement is correct. Everyone using the expression 'This is beautiful' makes a claim but not every claim made is a rightful claim. Thus he goes on to say that when people disagree that they are 'not quarrelling over the possibility of such a claim, but only failing in particular cases to come to terms as to the correct application of this faculty'.[7] Later in the book he points out that people are indeed more prone to error in making aesthetic judgements than elsewhere.[8]

In connection with the claim made on others which Kant thinks to be implicit in judgements concerning the beautiful it is clarifying to draw on the comparison which he draws between 'singular empirical' judgements such as 'There is a bubble of water in this rock crystal' and aesthetic judgements. He uses this comparison to make a point about the kind of universality involved in judgements about beauty but it is just as appropriate as illustrative of what it is to lay a claim to the assent of others. On the basis of what someone personally sees when examining a piece of rock crystal he may say, 'There's a bubble of water in this piece of rock crystal'.[9] He thereby makes a claim to the assent of others. This claim is only a rightful claim if he has made a correct observation in the first place. However, even if he did not make a correct observation in the first place, he has still laid claim to the agreement of others but it is then not a claim that others ought to accede to.

PLEASURE IN THE GOOD

As we have seen Kant does not believe that it is a peculiarity of judgements concerning the beautiful that they express pleasure which is 'communicable'. Indeed, not only does he believe that pleasure in the good is to be communicable too but he believes pleasure in the good to be typically and comprehensibly communicable. He says,

In respect of the good it is true that judgements also rightly assert a claim to validity for every one; but the good is only represented as an Object of universal delight *by means of a concept* . . .[10]

Communication by means of a concept is the standard form of communicating anything, for example our thoughts and our knowledge, in Kantian epistemology. The universality and necessity of pleasure in the good is standard universality (he calls it 'objective') and the necessity is standard necessity governed by a formulable rule.[11]

There are three variants of 'the good' which Kant mentions, 'good for' which he identifies with what is useful, 'good in itself' which includes the moral good,[12] and good as the perfection of anything after its kind.[13] Kant claims that for each of these three the universality and necessity of pleasure in the objects judged depends upon their having a determinant concept applied to them. He probably has in mind something of the following kind. We take pleasure in wood as useful when we see it as 'fuel' or 'building material', we take pleasure in a certain action because we take it to be 'honest' or 'benevolent', and we take pleasure in a good horse because we place this beast as 'a horse' and so on. That we can demand universal assent and say that anyone ought to assent to our judgements turns upon their applying the same concepts to the objects in question and upon their bringing the same rules to bear upon the objects as we do. It is by way of the concept and the rules that we 'extort approval'.[14]

Pleasure in the good is for Kant the paradigm of communicable pleasure. In the case of pleasure in the beautiful, however, the position is different. He believes that pleasure in the beautiful is not based upon a determinant concept. He is usually interpreted to be saying that as pleasure in the beautiful is non-conceptual pleasure we cannot base our claims upon others to take pleasure as well on a concept. The correct interpretation is, I believe, that he holds that with pleasure in the beautiful we cannot base our claim to others taking pleasure as well upon a concept, so pleasure in the beautiful is non-conceptual. On this interpretation it is very important to ask why Kant believes that our claim that others should take pleasure as well cannot be mediated by a concept.

Approval which is characteristic of our attitude to the good is to be strictly contrasted with delight in an object we judge to be beautiful. Kant wants to stress that in order to get another person to approve what we do, we must first get him to judge as we do. Argument about the good is directed at agreement of judgement with an ensuing agreement in approval. Kant wants to stress that in the case of the beautiful, interpersonal agreement includes communicated delight and a delight which is not based on intellectual beliefs. Hence a concept cannot effect it.

Since the agreement when effected is not, however, fortuitous, Kant believes that something which is like a concept in that it is both public and regulative must mediate it, and that that something mediates agreement in delight not by being thought but being 'felt'.

The peculiarity of the case of judging something to be beautiful is, for Kant, that it involves the sort of universality which is not based on a concept and, ostensibly, an 'ought' which is not governed by a rule.

UNIVERSALITY

The peculiarity about the kind of universality involved in judgements about the beautiful is marked in Kant's terminology by calling them 'subjectively' rather than 'objectively' universal. 'Subjectively' universal judgements are valid (i.e. hold good) for all judging subjects, but not for all objects of the same kind. I take it that he is contrasting 'This swan is beautiful' with 'All swans have webbed feet' and 'Telling lies is always wrong'. 'This swan is beautiful' is subjectively universal since it holds (if it does) for all judging subjects, but not of all swans, whereas 'All swans have webbed feet' and 'Telling lies is always wrong' hold, if they do, not only for all judging subjects but of all swans and all lies. Judgements about beauty are about individuals and are singular. He compares them, as we have already noted, with singular empirical judgements. About that comparison he says,

It must always be only through reflective perception that it [the taking of pleasure] is cognized as conjoined with this representation. As with all empirical judgements, it is, consequently, unable to announce objective necessity or lay claim to *a priori* validity. But, then, the judgement of taste in fact only lays claim, like every other empirical judgement, to be valid for every one, and, despite its inner contingency this is always possible. The only point that is strange or out of the way about it, is that it is not an empirical concept, but a feeling of pleasure (and so not a concept at all), that is yet exacted from every one by the judgement of taste, just as if it were a predicate united to the cognition of the Object, and that it is meant to be conjoined with its representation.

A singular empirical judgement, as, for example, the judgement of one who perceives a movable drop of water in a rock-crystal, rightly looks to every one finding the fact as stated, since the judgement has been formed according to the universal conditions of the determinant judgement under the laws of a possible experience generally. In the same way one feels pleasure in simple reflection on the form of the object, without having any concept in mind, rightly lays claim to the agreement of every one, although this judgement is empirical and a singular judgement. For the ground of this pleasure is found in the universal, though subjective, condition of reflective judgements, namely the final harmony of an object (be it a product of nature or of art) with the mutual relation of the faculties of cognition, (imagination and understanding,) which are requisite for every empirical cognition. The pleasure in judgements of taste is, therefore, dependent doubtless on an empirical representation, and cannot be united *a priori* to any concept (one cannot determine *a priori* what object will be in accordance with taste or not – one must find out the object that is so); but then it is only made the determining ground of this judgement by virtue of our consciousness of its resting simply upon reflection and the universal, though only subjective, conditions of the harmony of that reflection with the knowledge of objects generally, for which the form of the Object is final.[15]

Kant, in this passage, is maintaining that 'This is beautiful' and 'There is a bubble of water in this rock crystal', that is a judgement of taste and a singular empirical judgement, are alike in that, on the ground of something intrinsically private, they make a demand upon the assent of everyone. In this context Korner's resumé of Kant's contention concerning a singular judgement is apposite.

First, an objective empirical judgement refers to an object and not merely to the subjective impression. Second, an objective empirical judgement is, if true, true for everybody. It is not qualified by some such clause as 'in my consciousness' or 'as it seems to me' but is generally valid, i.e. for everybody in every consciousness or, in Kantian terms 'in consciousness in general'.[16]

The species of universal validity are for Kant: Objective universal validity which is unconditionally valid for all members of a class of objects and for all judging subjects, and subjective universality which is of two sorts, that which rests on concepts, for example 'There's a bubble of water in this rock crystal' and that which does not, for example 'This rose is beautiful', neither of which are valid for a class of objects but are valid for all judging subjects.

If a judgement has objective validity it also has subjective validity, but from its having subjective validity nothing follows as to its having objective validity. The basic aesthetic judgement is always singular.[17] Given the summation of singular judgements we could reach a conclusion about all of a sort of thing, for example 'All roses are beautiful', but we could never acquire such a generalisation without a summation of singular judgements, nor could we conclude that a rose we had not seen must be beautiful. Contrast, 'All swans have webbed feet' and 'Telling lies is always wrong'.

Liking something is therefore said to stand to judging something to be beautiful, in the way that having 'a sensation' stands to an empirical judgement. Consider Kant's saying in the *Prolegomena*,

All our judgements are at first merely judgements of perception; they hold good only for us (that is, for our subject), and we do not till afterward give them a new reference (to an object) and desire that they shall always hold good for us and in the same way for everybody else;[18]

'NECESSITATION'

The peculiarity Kant sees in the 'necessity' about taking pleasure in something correctly judged beautiful is that it appears to be an exception to what he believes to be a general truth that 'necessitation', that is 'oughtings to' are governed by rule. Objective universality is based on concepts, necessitation depends on a rule, and rules are usually and typically formulable in the way that 'One ought not to tell lies' is a formula for a moral rule.

It is noticeable that in dealing with the peculiarities of a judgement concerning the beautiful involving necessitation, Kant does not, as he does with the peculiarities of its being universal, begin to speak of 'subjective' as opposed to 'objective' necessitation. What emerges, is that he thinks that the necessitation involved in judgements concerning the beautiful is, after all, only an apparent exception to the general truth that all 'oughts' are governed by a rule.

The apparent contradiction between, 'There can, therefore, be no rule according to which any one is to be compelled to recognise anything as beautiful',[19] and, 'being such a necessity as is thought in an aesthetic judgement, it can only be termed *exemplary*. In other words it is a necessity of the assent of *all* to a judgement regarded as exemplifying a universal rule incapable of formulation',[20] is dispelled by reading the first as meaning that 'there can be no formulable rule according to which . . .' since the 'ought' connected with judgements of taste is governed by a rule incapable of formulation, a rule based essentially upon reference to examples (exemplars). The rule which governs the 'ought' connected with judgements concerning the beautiful can, unlike the moral rule, 'It is always wrong to tell lies', only be taught by the use of examples – by, we might add, 'example, test and correction'.

With pleasure in the good, universality is thought to be based upon a concept and necessitation upon a formulable rule; with pleasure in the beautiful, despite the fact that there is a comparable universality and necessitation there is no concept and no formulable rule. Thus,

> In respect of the good it is true that judgements also rightly assert a claim to validity for every one; but the good is only represented as an Object of a universal delight *by means of a concept*, which is the case neither with the agreeable nor the beautiful.[21]

and,

> Nor yet is it [i.e. delight in the beautiful] a practical necessity, in which case, thanks to concepts of a pure rational will in which free agents are supplied with a rule, this delight is the necessary consequence of an objective law, and simply means that one ought absolutely (without ulterior object) to act in a certain way.[22]

Again,

> First, one must get firmly into one's mind that by the judgement of taste (upon the beautiful) the delight in an object is imputed to *every one*, yet without being founded on a concept (for then it would be the good), and that this claim to universality is such an

essential factor of a judgement by which we describe anything as *beautiful*, that were it not for its being present to the mind it would never enter into any one's head to use this expression, but everything that pleased without a concept would be ranked as agreeable;[23]

and,

Therefore they must have a subjective principle, and one which determines what pleases or displeases, by means of feeling only and not through concepts, but yet with universal validity.[24]

That which resembles a concept in mediating communicability in the case of judgements concerning the beautiful, which is public and regulative, is according to Kant – the Form of Finality.

8
The Third Moment – The Form of Finality

In the Third Moment Kant gradually develops the notion of that which, were there to be such a thing, would justify those claims to the agreement of others which he has argued to be implicit in the judgements we make concerning the beautiful. He calls it the Form of Finality. He does not, however, think of it as a single 'form'. The name is not to be taken as a proper name as in Plato's Form of the Good. It is a shorthand description of a kind of form.

Kant's discussion of this kind of form is at once part of his analysis or exposition of judgements concerning the beautiful, and part of the transcendental argument which constitutes the *Deduction*. It is part of the *Analytic* because, since Kant believes that if and only if there is a Form of Finality, we can justify our claims to the agreement of others implied by our judgements concerning the beautiful. He also believes that in making such judgements we presuppose that there is such form. By using the expression 'This is beautiful' we commit ourselves to making a claim to the agreement of others and also to all that is involved in the making of such a claim.

Kant's discussion of the Form of Finality is also part of the *Deduction* since if he is right about what would justify the claims to the agreement of others which are implicit in our judgements concerning the beautiful, then all that is left for the *Deduction* as opposed to the *Analytic* to do is to provide a proof that such form must exist. The Third Moment and the *Deduction* form in this way a continuity of theme.

The conditions which have to be satisfied by that which can justify the claims to the agreement of others implicit in our judgements concerning the beautiful, are that it has to be something (a) public or interpersonal, (b) regulative and (c) worthwhile in its own right. Kant's notion of the Form of Finality is of something which satisfies these conditions.

THE 'FORM' AND NOT THE 'MATTER' OF SENSATION

Kant maintains that any appeal to what he calls 'the matter' of sensation could not be used to justify our claims to the agreement of others because such appeal is, of necessity, appeal to something private. He means by 'the matter' of sensation, 'intuitions' which approximate in his epistemological theory to 'sense data'.[1]

He argues that we cannot defend our entitlement to claim the agreement of others to our judgements concerning the beautiful, by appealing to sense data, because we can never be sure that any two persons 'have' the same sense data. He says,

> a person who is without a sense of smell cannot have a sensation of this kind communicated to him, and, even if he does not suffer from this deficiency, we still cannot be certain that he gets precisely the same sensation from a flower that we get from it.[2]

Kant here needs to be taken to be making a general point about all of the senses. What applies to the taste, the palate, and the tongue applies also to that of the eye and the ear. 'A violet colour is to one soft and lovely: to another dull and faded.'[3]

Because he expresses this point in epistemological language, it could be thought that Kant believes sensation to be only contingently private. If that were so one could counter with the question, 'And what if one could be certain that another person had the same sensation as ourselves?' Kant does not believe that that question is pertinent. We cannot be certain about the sensations of others because they are of necessity private. If we were endowed only with 'sensibility' (the passive faculty for perceiving sensations or having 'intuitions') we could not escape from the egocentric predicament. In Kant's epistemology humans escape from the egocentric predicament because their active cognitive powers, imagination and understanding, impose an interpersonal and public pattern upon sensation, that is they bring the categories of a conceptual scheme to bear to order or regulate it.

Moreover, if one grants Kant his contention that 'that which is pleasing in sensation' is the same as 'what gratifies', then the object of each person's pleasure in such cases is not the sensation had by that person, but that person's having that sensation. Such objects of pleasure, or enjoyment, *are* necessarily private. If what I am enjoying in eating oysters is the oyster slipping down my throat, even if you are simultaneously eating your oysters and enjoying your oysters slipping down *your* throat, then the object of my enjoyment is of necessity not the same as yours. Thus, concede Kant's contention that 'the agreeable' is always 'what gratifies', and considerations drawn from philosophical psychology endorse the conclusion of his general epistemological position. The 'matter' of sensation cannot be simply contingently private, it is necessarily so.

The claim, implicit in a judgement concerning the beautiful, to the agreement of others, cannot therefore be justified by reference to sensation. Whatever it is that is to fulfil the justificatory role has to be, in contrast with sensation which is private, public and inter-personal. Kant believes that only the 'form' as distinct from the 'matter' of sensations can satisfy this condition.

Kant has already argued that the form and not the matter of sensation, if it is to be thought of as that by reference to which we can justify our claims to the agreement of others in judgements concerning the beautiful, cannot be conceptual form. The form and not the matter of sensation is not the structural organisation of a thing. How calyx, corolla, stem, etc., of a daisy are put together is distinct from how the gold colour of the circular centre, the radiating band of white petals and the green stem are configured. The mammalian structure of whales is an entirely different matter from the fishlike configuration of their sensory properties which misled early scientists.

Kant contrasts the form, and not the matter, of sensation not only with 'intuition' or sense data, but with the way in which the parts of things are structurally ordered. This difference I have been marking by contrasting 'perceptual' with 'conceptual' form. Although reference to a thing's conceptual form' would be sufficiently public or interpersonal to justify a claim to the agreement of others, Kant has already argued that such a 'form' falls foul of the conditions for a judgement concerning the beautiful laid down in the Second Moment. Such forms cannot ground the communicability of un-mediated pleasure.[4] His insistence upon publicity together with his contention that conceptual agreement cannot constrain taking pleasure as well, commits him to a quite distinctive kind of formalism about 'the beautiful'.

There has been much criticism of his theory on that count. He has often been taken to task for denying that isolated sensuous properties such as individual colours may be beautiful. He is uncharacteristically hesitant to affirm this apparent implication of his theory.

We have already seen that by lumping together too many diverse cases under the heading of 'the agreeable', he has introduced considerable confusion into the issue as to what counts as 'the matter' as opposed to 'the form' of sensation.[5] Drinking the next mouthful of Canary wine is a very different matter from admiring the colour of Parma violets. If both are claimed to 'gratify', 'gratifying' needs to be treated as vague and perhaps equivocal in meaning in a way in which Kant does not believe it to be.

In fact, Kant is inclined to argue that some isolated colours and tones can be beautiful. For this to be consistent with his theory he has to deny that such an isolated colour or tone *is* part of the matter and not the form of sensation. His argument to that effect is strained, obscure, and far from impressive. It amounts to his maintaining that, since we do find some isolated colours beautiful, we must, in perceiving them, tacitly detect formal elements of them without being consciously aware of doing so.[6]

The weakness of this argumentation should not blind us to the soundness of Kant's insight into the cases in point. I have been arguing that Kant's treatment of the Form of Finality is not so much as an implication of our use of 'This is beautiful', or as a datum of aesthetic experience, but as part of a transcendental argument aiming at the justification of the interpersonal claims made in making judgements concerning the beautiful. However, conclusions arrived at by such *a priori* processes are not necessarily false. There is nothing to stop them chiming with aesthetic experience. Although the Form of Finality is not introduced by Kant as something discovered by aesthetic experience there are absolutely no grounds for thinking that it cannot capture something in aesthetic experience.

The insight of which I spoke is a case in point. Isolated as opposed to isolatable colours and tones, are not very often the objects of our aesthetic judgements. Further, the pleasures we find in isolated colours and tones are comparatively irrelevant to judgements concerning the beautiful on two counts. First, nearly all of our experience is of complex wholes. When, for example, we cite the colour of claret as a counter-instance to Kant's contention that a certain kind of form and that alone can entitle us to demand that others take pleasure in what pleases us, we fail to note that in appreciating the colour of claret in a glass twisted in front of a light,

we are taking note of an interrelationship between shade, translucency and depth, and not in the 'colour' alone. Most of us would, I
believe, be very surprised to be presented with a matt colour sample
which was simply the same 'colour' as a good claret.

Secondly, that which is beautiful in comparative isolation, for
example the odd isolated patch of paint dabbed on a palette, the
hank of embroidery thread ready for use, bears little or no
relationship to that which is beautiful *in situ*. That red-gold hair
which is so beautiful in combination with a honey-coloured
complexion looks carrotty in another combination. The honey-
coloured complexion itself looks sallow and sickly when combined
with mouse-coloured hair.

Kant goes wrong, I believe, more because he is committed by his
epistemology to thinking that the distinction between 'the matter'
and 'the form' of sensation is an absolute one, than because of his
insistence upon the importance of perceptual form. It is much more
helpful to think of the distinction as being relative to cases, and to
realise that what counts as complex in the context of one case, may
be and is, taken as simple in another, and vice versa. To consider
whether the colour of the wine in one's glass is beautiful is to
consider the colour of the wine as a complex of its depth,
translucency and shade, but to consider the colour of the wine as
contributing to the beauty of the displayed feast is, or can be, to treat
it as simple component of a different complex. When looked at in
this way, what we would say of an absolutely simple sensation
becomes one of the wilder conjectures of metaphysics rather than a
common or garden counter-instance to maintaining that form is
essential to beauty.

Kant goes even further wrong in another way. He shows no
awareness of the fact that *perceptual* form can be determined by the
sensory components which it configures. He speaks sometimes of
colours being 'added' to pictures as if it were possible to have the
same picture and therefore the same 'form' with or without, added
colours. Some perceptual forms grow out of certian colours being
opposed and related – witness Matisse's practice in starting a
picture.[7] A person's dark hair by turning white can alter the whole
configuration of the face. A pattern of black dots is a different
pattern from a pattern of black and blue dots. Some things cannot
have the perceptual form which they do have, without having just
the sensory properties that they do have. Consider how 'the look'

on a pansy's 'face' changes with just one colour change in the markings. Kant's epistemology debars him from accepting this, for such forms would, on his showing, have to be necessarily private just as their component sensations are held to be.

Serious as this failure is, it is important not to overplay the point. Although the components which are conformed may be essential to a perceptual form's being what it is, they need not be. What the colours of a thing are, can be unrelated to the perceptual form of the thing, that is they can be altered without altering the perceptual form. In many cases the perceptual form can be maintained if the colour 'values' are maintained. For example, some violas, pelargoniums and pansies have two dark upper petals and three light lower petals. The perceptual form of these flowers can be preserved whilst changing their colours so long as the two dark upper petals are kept 'balanced' against the three light lower petals, although should you alter the dark colouring (say change maroon to blue-purple) of the upper petals you might have to alter the shade of the light lower petals to preserve the original form.

Colours in paintings are neither generally essential to, nor generally inessential to the perceptual form of the pictures. They can be just as inessential as Kant makes them out generally to be. In some pictures they are splashed on as gilt is on some elaborate picture frames. Even in the light of this objection Kant can therefore still argue that such colour is merely part of a thing's charm, not of its beauty. What the objection undermines is the strict line of demarcation which he is at pains to maintain between the privacy of sensation or sense data on the one hand and the publicity or interpersonal validity of form on the other.

A FORM WHICH IS FINAL PERCEPTION

The condition, that the object of a judgement concerning the beautiful has to be public or interpersonally valid, and hence pertain to 'the form' and not 'the matter' of sensation, amounts to no more in Kant's theory than a condition for the judgement's counting as aesthetic at all. It is a condition of a judgement's being either aesthetically favourable or unfavourable. Of what kind must a perceptual form be, for it to afford a justification for the claims to the agreement of others which are implicit in judgements concerning the beautiful which are not merely aesthetic but also aesthetically favourable?

The answer to this question is given by Kant in terms of two difficult notions, that of an 'end' and that of 'the harmonious free play of the cognitive faculties'. As I read him, Kant's answer put briefly, is that such forms must be final, that is 'ends' for perception; and that forms which are ends for perception are those which set the cognitive faculties of imagination and understanding in harmonious free play. He holds that whether a given form is or is not final for perception cannot be determined by applying a formula but can only be 'felt'.

First, what would a form which was 'final for perception' be? Kant has an extremely obtruse conception of 'an end' and an extremely complex way of classifying 'ends'. To make the task of interpretation worse, he seems also to have a developing notion of what an 'end' might be. However, when he talks of finality of form, he means, in some sense of that elusive word, that such a form is 'an end' for perception.

Like Aristotelian 'final causes' ends relate to goods and explain why the design of anything is what it is. Unlike Aristotelian final causes they are not that which a certain kind of thing 'seeks' or 'tends towards'. Kant's 'ends' do not necessarily relate to wills of creatures and they are not necessarily 'that for the sake of which' some creature acts. Persons both have and are 'ends'. They have subjective ends which they themselves pursue and they are ends in themselves.[8] Useful objects (e.g tools) and things which are of use to persons, for example rivers which carry silt and thus increase the area of fruitful soil, have ends.[9] Mathematical figures have ends[10] and so too do organisms.[11]

To compare such 'ends' with each other Kant classifies them along four different axes, subjective–objective, formal–real, internal–external and unconditional–conditional (i.e relative–absolute). The 'ends' which depend upon a person's will are subjective, real, external and relative. The 'end' which a person is, is objective, real, internal and absolute. Useful and adaptable things[12] (tools and things in nature which are of use to persons) have subjective, real, external and relative 'ends'. Mathematical figures have subjective formal, external and relative 'ends'. Using this manner of mapping 'ends' beautiful objects have 'ends' which are subjective, formal, internal and, surprisingly, absolute 'ends'.

Before looking at the changes which occur in Kant's conception of 'an end' from the *Groundwork* to the *Critique of Judgement*, it is worth noticing a further curious aspect of Kant's conception of the 'ends' of beautiful objects. It hovers between being thought of as an 'as if' end and a genuine end. He thinks of beautiful things 'as if' they were made just in order to be reflected upon by us with pleasure and as really being in their own right to be reflected upon by us with pleasure. Thus the Form of Finality or the Form of Purposiveness without a Purpose hovers between not being genuine finality at all (cf. a 'form of marriage') and being something approaching the quintessence of 'an end'.

Now, if we compare Kant's account of ends as it is developed in the *Critique of Judgement* with that presented in the *Groundwork*[13] one difference which is extremely important when considering 'end' as it applies in the context of judgements concerning the beautiful emerges. In the *Groundwork*, all subjective ends are said to be relative. In the *Critique of Judgement* subjective ends can be relative (the aims and goals of persons) and absolute (forms final for perception). However, the ground which Kant gives for judging the aims and goals of persons and the values based upon them to be 'relative' in the *Groundwork*, is that such 'ends' are conditional upon the wants and inclinations of the agent. Persons viewed as ends-in-themselves are 'absolute' ends because they have a value independently of what any agent may happen to incline towards or want.

In the *Critique of Judgement* the First Moment of the *Analytic of the Beautiful* defines judgements concerning the beautiful as 'disinterested' where being 'disinterested' involves not being based on, and hence not being relative to, the wants and inclinations of an agent. Unlike persons who are ends in themselves,[14] reflection upon the beautiful is an end of the subject (although not an end of the agent); but like persons who are ends in themselves, reflection on the beautiful is an internal end, that is, worthwhile in its own right, not worthwhile as a means to something else.[15]

One might be inclined to press the point that even if judgements concerning the beautiful are by definition disinterested (i.e. not relative to wants and inclinations) that does not warrant their being dubbed 'absolute' (or unconditioned). They are, on Kant's account, relative to the cognitive powers of subjects being what they are.

Kant, I believe, would be happy enough to accept this. What he is stressing is that such judgements must not be relative to anything as idiosyncratic as the inclinations or wants of an individual person. Secondly, he believes that one difference between the value of beautiful objects and the value of persons and moral actions is that whilst the second holds for all rational creatures, the first holds only for creatures who are rational *animals*.[16]

There is an additional reason for Kant not to be troubled by the point that in his account the end of beautiful objects or the finality of perceptual form is relative to the cognitive powers which a subject has. Rightly or wrongly he believes that 'it must be the universal wish of every rational being to be free from . . .' his idiosyncratic wants and inclinations.[17] Not only does he not think that every rational creature must wish to be rid of his cognitive powers, his epistemology commits him to viewing such a wish as suicidal on the part of the subject. As he seems to regard the very idea of common or garden suicide to be inconsistent[18] he would regard a subject's wishing to be rid of its cognitive powers as positively incoherent. On Kant's presuppositions what is final for perception, begins to take on something of the inescapable quality of moral imperatives and the worth of persons.

That is not all. In both the passage from the *Groundwork* and in the *Critique of Judgement* 'ends' which depend on our wills, and ends which (seem) to depend on nature's (or God's) will, are contrasted. Forms which are final for perception, that is perceptual forms as 'ends' can be considered from both the point of view of nature, and the point of view of judging subjects. From the point of view of nature, Kant thinks that the finality of perceptual forms like that of mathematical figures is merely formal. It is 'as if' nature had the end of presenting us with something pleasing in perception and had deliberately put together certain sensory configurations to that end.

However, looked at from the point of view of judging subjects, it is not merely 'as if' certain perceptual forms are final for perception. On the contrary they *are* final for perception. They are internal and absolute subjective ends, and ends which such subjects can only abrogate by ceasing to be subjects and therefore persons. To abrogate them, judging subjects would have to surrender not their wants and inclinations, which any rational creature would be glad to do, but their cognitive powers. Such abrogation is unthinkable.

Since an 'end' for Kant is not simply that which determines the design of a sort of thing, but is, or determines, that thing's value or worth, perceptual forms which are final for perception will also be in their own right worth perceiving or reflecting upon. Further, the value of such perception or reflection rates very high in Kant's scale of values. Being capable of appreciating the beautiful is second only to being capable of acting as a moral agent and both are rated well above the capacities of clever men of prudence.[19]

THE HARMONIOUS FREE PLAY OF THE
COGNITIVE POWERS

If we ask Kant which are the perceptual forms which are final for perception, he cannot give in reply such answers as 'Forms which exhibit closure' or 'Forms governed by the ratio of the golden section' or 'Forms which unify the maximum of variety' and so forth. Such answers involve subsuming the individual case under a concept, or concepts; and proceeding upon a formulable rule. Kant's contention is that,

> In forming an estimate of Objects merely from concepts, all representation of beauty goes by the board. There can, therefore, be no rule according to which any one is to be compelled to recognize anything as beautiful. Whether a dress, a house, or a flower is beautiful is a matter upon which one declines to allow one's judgement to be swayed by any reasons or principles. We want to get a look at the Object with our own eyes, just as if our delight depended on sensation.[20]

Kant's answer must be different in kind from those indicated above. It is that those perceptual forms are final for perception which are apt or suitable for setting the cognitive powers, imagination and understanding into harmonious free play. It is included in this answer that such suitability can only be 'felt' – in taking pleasure in the perceptual form of something we discern that which is apt for setting the cognitive powers into such play. His answer is therefore a rejection of further questions as to which perceptual forms are the ones which are suitable for setting the cognitive powers into harmonious free play. Answers to them would again commit Kant to the subsumption of the individual case under a concept and an application of a formulable rule. To know which perceptual forms are apt or suitable for setting the cognitive powers into harmonious free play one has to try reflecting upon them and 'see', or 'feel', that is one has to subject them to direct experience.[21] In feeling pleasure we feel the mutually invigorating engagement of our cognitive faculties, the pleasure being what the purring sound is to the smooth operations of an engine being tuned.[22]

Kant's answer needs to be seen against his view of the role of the cognitive faculties in ordinary perceptual knowledge where the faculties are seen as being engaged in harmony with each other, but not as free.

Kant believes three cognitive powers to be involved in ordinary perceptual knowledge. One of them, 'sensibility', is passive. It is the capacity of a subject to undergo changes of subjective state in the presence of sensory stimuli. The other two powers, 'imagination' and 'understanding', are abilities of the subject to order and interpret what comes through sense.

Both the acquisition of perceptual knowledge, and the formation of a judgement of taste in Kant's epistemology require the synthesis of sensations or 'intuitions' by the imagination. In the case of perceptual knowledge concepts are then applied; and the synthesis of the imagination and the concept of the understanding chime together. We can think of this as perceptual coinciding with conceptual form, a case falling neatly under the rule.

Kant sees the cognitive faculties as being in harmony or accord with each other; but also as being constrained in perceptual knowledge. He thinks of the imagination as being constrained because it is 'at the service of'[23] understanding. He thinks of the understanding as constrained too. The subject cannot synthesise and apply concepts as it pleases since the aim of the procedure is to ascertain truth or to solve a problem. Understanding is constrained by the task in hand and 'we have merely the value set upon the solution that satisfies the problem, and not a free and indeterminately final entertainment of the mental powers . . .'[24]

In the case of perceptual error, I think we would have a case of lack of accord or disharmony between the cognitive powers; perceptual form failing to coincide with conceptual.

When the perceptual form is a form final for the perceptual powers Kant sees the two faculties as being in harmony as they are in perceptual knowledge, but also in free play as in perceptual knowledge they are not. The imagination is free because it is not 'at the service of' the understanding and understanding is free because not under the constraints of ascertaining truth or solving problems of practice. The imagination can, as it were, take the understanding for a walk. The understanding can come along because freed from its usual constraints its role is simply to keep the imagination's synthesisings thinkable. The interaction of both is described as a mutual 'quickening'. That the cognitive powers are free and harmoniously in play is and can only be discerned by our pleasure in such engagement of our powers, that is by 'feeling'.

Although there is much which is unclear, and much that one would want to reject in this account, enough emerges and survives translation into the terms of a different epistemology, to bring home the point that forms, which Kant believes to be final for our perception, and which would provide justification for the claims to the agreement of other implicit in our judgements concerning the beautiful, are radically different from 'forms' construed as regular figures or shapes. His conception of form stands in direct contrast with that of Plato of the *Philebus* and that of his more recent adherents.[25] Forms final for perception cannot complete the activity of perceiving; they must invite and sustain it.[26]

> All stiff regularity (such as borders on mathematical regularity) is inherently repugnant to taste, in that the contemplation of it affords us no lasting entertainment.[27]

To sustain the activity they must be at once graspable and suggestive.

> Now geometrically regular figures, a circle, a square, a cube, and the like, are commonly brought forward by critics of taste as the most simple and unquestionable examples of beauty. And yet the very reason why they are called regular, is because the only way of representing them is by looking on them as mere presentations of a determinate concept by which the figure has its rule (according to which alone it is possible) prescribed for it.[28]

The contrast Kant has in mind is with the 'free beauties of nature',[29] but the point holds just as well if one thinks of the forms of stones used in making some Japanese gardens.

FORMS WHICH ARE REGULATIVE

When Kant is criticised as being philistine in aesthetics he is probably being interpreted as defending a philosophical theory which supports the man in the street's 'I know what I like'. He is remembered to have said that there are neither empirical nor *a priori* proofs which can be adduced to compel a person to reverse an aesthetic judgement which he has once made.[30] He is quoted correctly, as saying, 'I stop my ears: I do not want to hear any reasons or any arguing about the matter.'[31]

However, Kant, unlike the man in the street, is not in these cases putting his authority behind disingenuous obstinacy but emphasising the role of judgement in estimating beauty. Only if appeal to the opinions of others or *a priori* rules exhausted the ways in which a judgement might be corrected, would it follow that Kant's theory endorsed philistinism in the above way. They do not. Kant, unlike the man in the street, believes that there is a proper procedure for correcting judgements and settling disputes which is not a matter of appealing to generalisations about how other people judge, nor of adducing *a priori* proofs, but a procedure which is based upon appeal to examples.

In the first place he does not reject conflict between one's own judgement and the opinions of others as downright irrelevant. He takes it to be relevant in that it may make a person question 'whether he has formed his taste upon an acquaintance with a sufficient number of objects of a particular kind'.[32] What he does reject is the view that appeal to the opinion of others *consitutes proof* that one's own judgement, which is at odds with theirs, is wrong.

Again, in the case of the youthful poet who,

> refuses to allow himself to be dissuaded from the conviction that his poem is beautiful, either by the judgement of the public or of his friends,[33]

but who later comes to agree with them, the correction of judgement occurs because, in the interim, his judgement has been 'sharpened by exercise'.[34] It is clear that Kant believes the young poet's judgement has to be sharpened upon particular examples which function as models or paradigm cases of beautiful things. Kant rounds off the discussion of this section with the remark that,

> Taste, just because its judgement cannot be determined by concepts or precepts, is among all faculties and talents the very one that stands most in need of examples of what has in the course of culture maintained itself longest in esteem.[35]

Again, in rejecting the relevance of the *a priori* rules of celebrated critics to judgement, he does not conclude that critics as such, are useless. He says,

> There is, however, a matter upon which it is competent for critics to exercise their subtlety, and upon which they ought to do so, so long as it tends to the rectification and extension of our judgements of taste. But that matter is not one of exhibiting the determining ground of aesthetic judgements of this kind in a universally applicable formula – which is impossible. Rather is it the investigation of the faculties of cognition and their function in these judgements, and the illustration, by the *analysis of examples*, of their mutual subjective finality, the form of which in a given representation has been shown above to constitute the beauty of their object.[36]

One of Kant's most illuminating comments about the correct manner of rectifying taste comes at a point where he is considering the attempt to produce, rather than the attempt to discern, a beautiful form. In drawing a contrast between invention or inspiration in the production of works of art and the near-to-drudgery labour of imparting a form which is final for perception upon the vehicle which is to express such inspiration, Kant describes the artist as one who controls his work after 'having practised and corrected his taste by *a variety of examples from nature or art*'.[37]

One wishes, of course, that Kant had developed his account of the rectification of taste in more detail. However, one cannot doubt that his theory includes a view of a procedure anchored firmly to examples. Discerning which things are beautiful on his account is not simply 'feeling' the harmonious free play of the cognitive powers; *but also* of proceeding upon a rule which is neither *a priori* precept, nor empirical generalisation about what most or all people find pleasing to reflect upon; but one won from particular examples functioning as models, or exemplars.

If the claims implicit in judgements about the beautiful are to be justified there must therefore be something which constitutes the form and not the matter of sensation, which also is final for perception, and which can function as an exemplar for the development of taste.

KANT, ST THOMAS AND DEPENDENT BEAUTY

The kind of form which Kant argues in the Third Moment to be decisive of whether a given thing is beautiful or not, the Form of Finality is totally distinct from the articulated structure of a thing, the way in which the thing as material object is put together. To understand articulated structure, the individual thing must be subsumed under a concept which determines what it is to be. Whether any given thing is perfect or good of its kind will be at least partially determined by its articulated structure but not by reference to its having the Form of Finality. Judgements concerning the beauty of an object and judgements concerning the perfection of the same object or whether it is good of its kind are therefore for Kant totally independent of each other. Whether a girl's pale skin goes with her red-gold hair is one thing, whether her lack of skin pigmentation is due to a genetic defect is another. Examining the same girl's alimentary and respiratory tracts is relevant to judging her perfection as a girl but entirely irrelevant to her beauty.

Kant goes on to admit that there are some cases of judgements concerning beauty to which reference to a concept and relation to an end are relevant and it emerges that the above account is an account of what he dubs 'free' as opposed to 'dependent' beauty. He says,

> There are two kinds of beauty: free beauty (*pulchritudo vaga*), or beauty which is merely dependent (*pulchritudo adhaerens*). The first presupposes no concept of what the object should be; the second does presuppose such a concept and, with it, an answering perfection of the object. Those of the first kind are said to be (self-subsisting) beauties of this thing or that thing; the other kind of beauty, being attached to a concept (conditioned beauty), is ascribed to Objects which come under the concept of a particular end.[38]

This admission, that some beautiful things do not universally and necessarily please without reference to a concept, or without reference to what they are to be, could be thought to undermine Kant's whole account of judgements concerning the beautiful. His acknowledgement of 'dependent' beauty seems to constitute acknowledgement of a not inconsiderable range of counter-instances to his contentions.

If, up to the point at which Kant introduces the distinction between 'free' and 'dependent' beauty, we take him to be arguing that every single judgement concerning the beauty of something is non-conceptual and does not involve reference to that thing's relation to some end, then there do seem to be a large number of possible counter-instances to that contention, the cases which he goes on to describe as cases of 'dependent' beauty. If, on the other hand, we take Kant to be maintaining that *typically* judgements as to the beauty of something are non-conceptual and do not involve reference to some end, then we can call into question his judgement of what is 'typical'. If Kant chooses 'free' beauty as setting the paradigm of the beautiful the fact that other writers have settled on other paradigms might be thought to call his choice into question.

If the examples of judgements concerning the beautiful which Kant describes as 'dependent' beauty were to be accepted as paradigm, then all those conclusions which he has been so concerned to reject re-enter the picture. The universality and necessity of judgements concerning the beautiful would be conceptually tied, would involve a presupposition of what the thing judged is to be, and so would be in some way the same as judgements concerning the perfection of the thing or of its being good of its kind, and aesthetic judgement would not be autonomous.

Contrast Kant's views with those of St Thomas Aquinas to sharpen one's conception of the central features of aesthetic theory which Kant aims to reject. Aquinas's views stand in sharp contrast with those of Kant. He appears to take cases of judgement of beauty which Kant would describe as 'dependent' as paradigm and endorses those conclusions which Kant is at pains to reject. St Thomas says,

Beauty and goodness in a thing are identical fundamentally; for they are based on the same thing, namely, the form; and consequently goodness is praised as beauty. But they differ logically, for goodness properly relates to the appetite (goodness being what all things desire); and therefore has the aspect of an end (the appetite being a kind of movement towards a thing). On the other hand, beauty relates to the cognitive faculty; for beautiful things are those which please when seen. Hence beauty consists in due proportion; for the senses delight in things duly proportioned, as in what is after their own kind – because even sense is a sort of reason, just as is every cognitive faculty. Now, since knowledge is by assimulation, and similarity relates to form, beauty properly belongs to the nature of a formal cause:[39]

and again:

The beautiful is the same as the good, and they differ in aspect only.[40]

St Thomas believes that the beautiful is the same as the good because he holds to Aristotle's division of 'causes' into four kinds, material, formal, efficient and final, and to the view that the formal and final cause of a given thing are, in a sense, one. His own account of Aristotle's 'formal cause' is,

In another sense cause means the form and pattern of a thing, i.e. its exemplar. This is the formal cause, which is related to the thing in two ways. In one way it stands as the intrinsic form of a thing, and in this prespect it is called the formal principle of a thing. In another way it stands as something extrinsic to a thing but is that in likeness to which it is made, and in this respect an exemplar is also called a thing's form. It is in this sense that Plato held the Ideas to be forms. Moreover, because it is from its form that each thing derives its nature, whether of its genus or of its species, and the nature of its genus or of its species is what is signified by the definition, which expresses its quiddity, the form of a thing is therefore the intelligible expression of its quiddity, i.e., the formula by which its quiddity is known. For even though certain material parts are given in the definition, still it is from a thing's form that the principal part of its definition, comes. The reason why the form is a cause, then, is that it completes the intelligible expression of a thing's quiddity . . . And not only is the whole definition related to the thing defined as its form, but so also are the parts of the definition, i.e., those which are given directly in the definition. For just as two-footed animal capable of walking is the form of man, so also are animal, capable of walking, and two-footed.[41]

Of Aristotle's 'final cause' he says,

In a fourth sense cause means a thing's end, i.e., that for the sake of which something is done, as health is the cause of walking.

And since it is less evident that the end is a cause in view of the fact that it comes into being last of all . . . he therefore gives a special proof that an end is a cause. For to ask why or for what reason is to ask about a cause, because when we are asked why or for what reason someone walks, we reply properly by answering that he does so in order to be healthy;[42]

and again:

There is a fourth formal aspect of casuality inasmuch as some things are said to be causes in the sense of the end or good of things. For that for the sake of which something else comes to be is the greatest good 'and the end' of other things, i.e., it is naturally disposed to be their end.[43]

A quotation from Ross's commentary on Aristotle may bring home how it is that Aristotelians see formal and final causes as related. Ross says,

'Form', for Aristotle embraces a variety of meanings. Sometimes it is used of sensible shape, as when a sculptor is said to impose a new form on his material. But more often, perhaps, it is thought of as something which is an object of thought rather than that of sense, as the inner nature of a thing which is expressed in its definition, the plan of its structure. And even sensible shapes can be thus expressed, the shape of a statue could be expressed by a mathematical formula, though necessarily a very complex one. . . . *The form is the plan of structure considered as informing a particular product of nature or of art. The final cause is the same plan considered as not yet embodied in the particular thing but as aimed at by nature or by art.* But to speak thus, as Aristotle often does, is to speak abstractly. Neither nature, nor art is for him a force existing by itself. Nature is a collective name for the respective natures of all natural objects, art is a name for actual knowledge resident in individual artists. The final cause in art is strictly, then, a certain structure which some artist is consciously striving to embody in a particular material. The final cause in nature is a structure common to a whole *infima species*, to which individual members of the species strive without conscious purpose to give a fresh individual embodiment.[44]

If formal and final causes are thought of as so related it is easy to see why Aquinas considers beauty and goodness as aspects of one thing and as identical fundamentally. Beauty relates to the formal cause, but the formal cause is the final cause when aimed at but not yet perfected; whereas the final cause is the formal cause when enmattered, when the aim is achieved and perfected. The sculptor chiselling out his Hermes from the stone is moved by the formal cause acting as final cause, for it is that for the sake of which he wields his tools; the sculptor who admires his Hermes is finding the formal cause of Hermes pleasant to apprehend. Thus goodness (that for the sake of which, the final cause) and beauty (the formal cause) can be said to be one for their relationship is not modelled on different views (from the east and from the west) of the same town; but on the town as destination to be achieved and as achieved. It is the same town that we see from afar and at which we arrive. The aspects are not the aspects from different points in place but different points in time.

To sum up. St Thomas believes that judgements concerning the beautiful are cognitive, conceptual, concerned with the real exist- ence of the thing judged, and are, in a sense, identical with judgements concerning the perfection of the kind of thing the object is. Thus he believes, with Wittgenstein of the *1914–16 Notebooks*, that aesthetics and ethics are one.[45]

If we put Kant's argument into this Aristotelian framework, we can think of him as arguing that since the Form of Finality is different from the formal cause of a thing, judgements concerning beauty are indifferent to concepts and ends, and beauty and perfection (or 'good of a kind') are distinct and aesthetic judgement is auton- omous.

It is clear that Kant does not and cannot defend the central tenets of his own account of judgements concerning the beautiful and entertain examples of 'dependent beauty' to be counter-instances of his theory. Neither can he accept them as paradigmatic of judge- ments concerning the beautiful. How then does he see them? He argues that they are secondary and compound aesthetic judgements dependent upon prior judgements concerning 'free' beauty and which involve judgements resembling judgements of congruence between free beauty and perfection of 'good of a kind'.

In a judgement of 'dependent' beauty as it is analysed by Kant, the notion of what the thing is to be does not delineate how that thing is to be if it is to be beautiful, instead it provides criteria for ruling out as inappropriate or unsuitable some amongst the possible freely beautiful forms. He expresses it thus,

> Much might be added to a building that would immediately please the eye, were it not intended for a church. A figure might be beautiful with all manner of flourishes and light but regular lines, as is done by the New Zealanders with their tattooing, were we dealing with anything but the figure of a human being. And here is one whose rugged features might be softened and given a more pleasing aspect, only he has got to be a man, or is, perhaps, a warrior that has to have a warlike appearance.[46]

The notion of what the thing is to be does not delineate how it must be if it is to be beautiful, instead it provides criteria for ruling out as inappropriate or unsuitable some amongst the possible freely beautiful forms.

If judgements concerning dependent beauty involve judgements of fit or congruence of this kind judgements of free beauty and judgements concerning perfection must be independent of each other. One has to know, for example, that for the sake of which a church is as it is, that is what the thing in question is to be, and to feel that a certain sensory complex has the Form of Finality, and to judge that complex suitable for a church, or a face or a warrior.

9

The Deduction

Whereas the *Analytic* shows that in using judgements concerning the beautiful we lay claim to 'universality' and 'necessity', the *Deduction* is directed towards giving a justification of such claims. The 'universality' in question is the demand to everyone's assent; the 'necessity' is the 'ought' which is governed by a rule which we take to apply to those who fail to assent. Although Kant often thinks of this rule in terms of something which connects one person's reaction to another's in a single case of judgement, if the *Deduction* is to be complete, it must also deal with such a rule in so far as it relates various judgements made at different times by the same person.

As we have seen, in the Third Moment of the *Analytic* Kant simultaneously develops an analysis of the kind of perceptual form by reference to which a justification of our use of 'This is beautiful' could be effected if it could be proved that there were such forms; he also produces a major step of the *Deduction*. Part of one's assessment of the success of the *Deduction* will therefore be an assessment of the view that the existence of such forms would provide us with the means to justify the claims to universality and necessity which the *Analytic* has shown to be implicit in our use. To play such a justificatory role, such forms must satisfy the conditions of being public or interpersonal without being conceptual, of being final for perception and of being capable of functioning as exemplars. These conditions reveal what Kant believes the process of justification to be.

Kant's emphasis throughout is heavily upon the first condition, that of the publicity or the interpersonal character of the object of pleasure. He is insistent that anything by reference to which we *could* justify our use would have to be public, open to interpersonal access, a view which commits him, his epistemology being what it is, to its concerning the form and not the matter of sensation of the thing judged. He is quite right to think this condition to be of the utmost importance. It is important in relation to both the case where two subjects simultaneously consider the same thing, and the case of one subject judging a variety of different things at different times.

In the first case the claim to universal assent would be beside the point if one could not secure the identity of the object of pleasure; in the second there could be no rectification of taste if we could not compare objects of pleasure with each other.

However, in both these cases, in justifying a claim to the agreement of others on a particular occasion and in justifying the bringing together of a variety of things as all being beautiful, that the object of pleasure must be public or interpersonal constitutes only a necessary and not a sufficient condition of justification. All that the publicity of form ensures in the first context is that different subjects *can* take pleasure in the same object, and that pleasure can be communicated one to the other rather than simply shared between them. It is not sufficient to provide backing for a claim that either person *ought* to concur with the other's judgement to show that they can so concur. 'Ought' implies 'can', but 'can' does not imply 'ought'. All that the publicity of form ensures in the second context is that the same subject *can* render his or her own judgements made at different times consistent with each other. It is a general condition for their being ordered at all, not for their being ordered in any specific way. Being able to find out a universal for a set of particulars[1] is one thing; which universal we find is another.

In order to justify these 'oughts', as distinct from the respective 'cans' implied by them, that by reference to which we achieve a justification must satisfy the second of Kant's conditions. The second condition is that the perceptual form (the public object of pleasure) shall be one which is 'final for perception'. So we have to ask whether given there were such perceptual forms, would they provide something by reference to which we could justify the universality and necessity of judgements concerning the beautiful?

The basic trouble with this condition lies in interpreting what it means. Frequently it has been taken to mean that such forms would have to be forms worth contemplating or reflecting upon 'for their own sakes'. On this interpretation we read Kant as saying that, if and only if there were perceptual as opposed to conceptual forms which were worth reflecting upon 'for their own sakes' would we be entitled to demand that others take pleasure as well in what we judged to be beautiful and to classify objects judged beautiful together.

Although such an interpretation of the way in which there being perceptual forms which were final for perception would justify our use of the expression 'This is beautiful' partly captures, it is bound to strike one more as a firm reiteration of the contention that one jolly well ought to take pleasure in a certain thing rather than a justification of maintaining that one ought. If the process of justification is presented simply as removing the puzzling feature of the 'ought' by introducing an equally puzzling reference to what is 'worth' reflecting upon, the enquiry does not seem to have been much advanced.

Kant would hardly have needed to place his discussion of aesthetic judgement so carefully within a general theory of 'ends' if that were all that he meant by there being forms which were final for perception. One line of connection between the two parts of the *Critique of Judgement* is that both aesthetic judgement and teleological judgement concern 'ends'. One major contrast between them is that the one concerns 'ends' which are subjective and the other 'ends' which are objective for judgement. Objective ends are organisms, subjective ends are perceptual forms of a certain kind.[2] It is also in the *Critique of Teleological Judgement* that the argument for the existence of God and immortality which is based on practical or moral considerations occurs.[3] Mysterious as this argument in some respects is it is none the less inspired by teleology – the notion of a final 'end' of the world. For Kant the 'end' is man under moral laws.[4] Thus, the *Critique of Judgement* is permeated by a teleology reminiscent of Aristotle's.

If we give full weight to this Aristotelian style of thinking and think of forms final for perception along those lines, we can think of justification effected by reference to them as being similar to the 'explanation' given in terms of final causes in Aristotelian theory.

A final cause is at one and the same time 'that for the sake of which, something acts or is as it is, and 'the good of' that act or that kind of thing. If Kant is interpreted to be saying that the existence of forms final for perception would justify our use of the expression 'This is beautiful' as he analyses it, in the way that final causes do in Aristotelian theory, then forms final for perception will be that 'for the sake of which' we exercise our perceptual powers, and forms whose existence constitute 'the good of' those powers. The 'good of' locution here is to be contrasted with the predicative 'is good' which is a rough synonym for 'worth doing for its own sake' in the previous interpretation.

Kant can then be taken to be saying that in perceiving beautiful objects and in perceiving them alone, do we perceive that for the sake of which we exercise our perceptual powers and realise their good. He can be taken to be saying that only in perceiving beautiful objects do we fully realise our perceptual powers.

This account of the way in which perceptual forms final for our perception would justify our use of the expression 'That is beautiful', unlike the previous one, despite the replacement of the puzzle about 'ought' by the puzzle about 'good of', is not merely a reiteration of the original contention that we ought to take pleasure in such forms. It provides a reason for thinking that contemplation or reflection upon such forms is an activity which is 'worthwhile for its own sake'.

Moreover, that reason is not contingent upon the private wants, purposes and inclinations of individual persons. Like the categorical imperative, it holds good whatever the goals of action the individual agent may or may not have adopted; but unlike the categorical imperative, it holds good because the perceiving subjects are what they are, not because there are objectively valid laws of the Kingdom of Ends.

Such an interpretation of what Kant means by 'forms final for perception' of course presupposes that our cognitive powers in general are such that they can and do have ends or purposes. If that seems an unlikely belief for Kant to have, it ought to be borne in mind that he does think in exactly that way about another of our faculties, namely Reason. In the *Groundwork* he argues that the exercise of prudence and the pursuit of happiness cannot be the end or purpose of Reason since we can realise that end or achieve that purpose as well or better than we would by using Reason, by a kind of instinct.[5] The end or purpose of Reason is, he maintains, to live the moral life, that is, to live in accordance with the moral law out of respect for it. To interpret Kant as thinking of the perceptual powers teleologically is not, therefore, to foist an alien Aristotelian presupposition upon Kant's thinking.

Furthermore, it seems in keeping for a man who argues that it is not prudence but morality which is 'the end' of Reason, to argue that it is not perceptual knowledge but awareness of beautiful objects which is 'the end' of human perceptual powers.[6]

It could be argued that such an interpretation of Kant's views presents him as simply positing a very eccentric 'end' or purpose for our perceptual powers. It could be said that, just as the first interpretation amounts to a mere reiteration of what is said in saying that someone 'ought' to comply with a demand to his agreement because doing so is worthwhile for its own sake, so does the second

interpretation simply reiterate that he ought by laying it down that a
certain kind of perception form is that 'for the sake of which' we
exercise our perceptual powers and that which constitutes their
'good'.

This criticism can be softened by pointing to Kant's account of
what the end of our perceptual powers is, and partly met by
demonstrating that the purported reiteration in the second interpretation is not so unhelpful as that of the first.

On the first point. One ought to remember that Aristotle says:

> Since every sense is active in relation to its object, and a sense
> which is in good condition acts perfectly in relation to the most
> beautiful of its objects . . . it follows that in the case of each sense
> the best activity is that of the best conditioned organ in relation to
> the finest of its objects. And this activity will be the most complete
> and most pleasant.[7]

Both Kant and Aristotle therefore believe that the end of
perception is only fully realised in perceiving beautiful objects.
Where their views diverge is in their respective analyses of the
beautiful. Where Aristotle takes the beautiful to be pleasure in a
thing's final cause (its perfection), Kant takes it to be pleasure in a
form which is not final for the thing perceived, but for perceiving
subjects.[8]

To show that Kant is not alone in his belief about what the end of
our perceptual powers is, is not, of course, to show that he is right in
his belief. That both Kant and Aristotle are inclined to that belief
should none the less show that it is worth considering and is not an
arbitrary posit.

Secondly, a justification in terms of what fully realises the
perceptual powers is a more helpful answer to the person who is
inclined to reject the claim to his assent, than to answer which
amounts to a direct appeal to an ultimate value described as what is
worthwhile for its own sake. There are more ways in which one can
assess whether one's perceptual powers are or are not being fully
realised, than there are for assessing whether something is or is not
worthwhile for its own sake.

To return to the issue as to whether the existence of perceptual
forms which were final for our perception would enable us to give a
justification of our use of the expression, 'This is beautiful'. Kant, as
we have seen, is inclined to make more of the importance of

producir.g a justification of the claims to the agreement of others which he finds to be implicit in that use. He tends to emphasise the need to back up the contention that everyone shall and anyone ought to take pleasure in things correctly judged beautiful. Thus, he often takes the basic problem of the *Deduction* to be how 'the delight of any one person may be pronounced as a rule for every other'.[9]

However, besides that problem, there is the additional one concerning how several objects, each of which has been individually judged beautiful, stand in relation to each other; and hence this problem concerns the rationale of adding a new member to their number. It is this problem which is heightened by the section where Kant considers correction or 'rectification' of judgements of taste.[10] When a person sharpens his taste by exercise upon a variety of examples, he is concerned with a rule which binds these cases together and which enables him to add new cases and by reference to which he can rectify any particular judgement which is out of line.

If I read Kant correctly, it is because of this second aspect of judgements concerning the beautiful that he thinks of 'understanding' as well as 'imagination' being involved in them and why they count as 'judgements' at all. If he is then to give a 'Deduction' of judgements concerning the beautiful which is complete, that which entitles one to make a claim to the agreement of others in a particular case must also provide a rationale for classifying a collection of judgements about a variety of cases together.

If it were true that certain perceptual forms were final for our perception, and that some things had such forms, then anyone who took pleasure in something's being of such a form would be entitled to demand that all perceiving subjects shall, and any perceiving subject ought, to take pleasure in that thing as well. Failure to comply with the demand would amount to refusal to exercise one's cognitive powers to the full and to be only partially alive[11] to the world. Such a perceiving subject would be lacking something that he or she ought to have and consequently it would be appropriate to blame him or her.[12] Such a person too would be missing out on something 'worthwhile for its own sake'.

If there were kinds of perceptual form which were final for our perception, and if there were things which exhibited those forms, it would also be possible to give a rationale for classifying particular cases of judging things to be beautiful together, for proceeding to new cases from old and for 'rectifying' taste. To treat a particular case as an exemplar is to treat it as playing a particularly important

role in explaining what a given rule might be. It is one of the basic
principles of Kant's aesthetic that the rationale for classing particular
objects together as beautiful, and for teaching what is rule-like in the
relation of one beautiful object to another, cannot be fully articulated
in a formula. In order to learn the rule one has to learn it in
connection with a set of cases treated as exemplars.

Perceptual form which is not conceptual is a presupposition of
any rule being teachable by reference to examples but not by a
formulable rule. Forms final for perception are a presupposition of
one specific rule being taught rather than another.

Kant believes that if there were things which had perceptual
forms which were final for our perception, we could justify our use
of the expression ' This is beautiful' by reference to them. We have
been examining plausible interpretations of the way in which such
forms would effect such a justification. It remains to be shown that
things which exhibit such forms exist.

What Kant aspires to do, however, is to show not merely that such
forms exist but that they must exist. The *Deduction* aspires to be a
transcendental argument. In the section entitled *Deduction of
Judgements of Taste*[13] he presents a brief and cryptic argument which
is in substance a repetition of an argument he has already presented
in the Fourth Moment of the *Analytic*. He repeats it in different
words in the next section.[14] Shortly we will see that these two
versions cannot be taken to be complete. An attempt to see how he
meant the argument to be completed will be drawn from his first
statement of it in the *Analytic*.

The argument seems to be that there must be perceptual forms as
well as conceptual and perceptual forms which are final for our
perception, because their being such is a presupposition of our
coming to know sensible objects, that is a presupposition of
perceptual knowledge, empirical knowledge. What he says is that
the subjective finality of an object is no more than the subjective
condition of the cognitive powers for coming to know sensible
objects. Obscure as this idea is, Kant's elaborations and repetitions
of it show that he believes that we can argue from our having
empirical knowledge and being able to impart empirical information
one to another, to the conclusion that judgements concerning the
beautiful are, and are not merely taken to be, communicable that is
'universal' and 'necessary'.[15] To put the argument in terms of three
of his customary contrasts between empirical judgements and
aesthetic ones, he thinks that if the objective conditions for

judgement are satisfied the subjective ones must be satisfied too; that if we do apply concepts to things there must be perceptual as well as conceptual forms; and that if there is a determinant use of judgement there must also be a reflective or indeterminant one.

What the argument achieves, if it succeeds, is to secure the condition the the object of pleasure in judgements concerning the beautiful must be interpersonal. If it does that then it provides grounds for maintaining that people *are able* to comply with the demand that they shall take pleasure in objects correctly judged to be beautiful; but not for maintaining that they *ought* to. Again, whilst the conclusion of the argument is sufficient to remove intellectual objections to the view that the rule which relates objects correctly judged to be beautiful to each other is a rule teachable only by ostention, it does nothing at all to underpin one ostensively teachable rule rather than another.

If Kant's argument in Section 38 is correct, and if proving the universality and necessity of judgements concerning the beautiful requires no more than ascertaining that the subjective conditions for making empirical judgements are satisfied, reference to any perceptual form at all, rather than to one which is suitable for setting the cognitive powers into harmonious free play, would be sufficient to underpin such a judgement. It is plain that Kant does not believe that to be so. Some perceptual forms are suitable for setting the cognitive powers into harmonious free play and some are not. Some, for example, impose 'an irksome constraint upon the imagination'. When he considers the comparative aesthetic merits of the pepper garden and its jungle surroundings[16] the fact that we can have empirical knowledge of both does not provide us with grounds for establishing the universality and necessity of pleasure taken in both. Kant there is arguing that it is wrong to judge the pepper garden to be beautiful; and right to judge the jungle to be so. We must therefore conclude that the argument put forward in Section 38 and labelled the *Deduction of Judgements of Taste* is incomplete.

It is necessary to look elsewhere to find the way in which Kant meant it to be completed. It has recently been argued[17] that one should look to the end of the *Critique of Aesthetic Judgement* where Kant argues that the beautiful is the symbol of the moral[18] to find its completion. That procedure yields an interpretation which I believe to be incompatible with the views Kant expresses in the whole of his book.[19] It seems more pertinent to look back to Kant's anticipatory discussion of the *Deduction* in the Fourth Moment of the *Analytic*.[20]

He presents us there with a piece of *a priori* psychologising about an inner mechanism which seems to have been modelled on a musical analogy. The cognitive powers of the perceiving subject have to be tuned for perception, and in each perception the accord of the different notes (i.e. sensations) played upon the instrument is governed by a different 'proportion' or 'ratio'. Interesting as this account is, the details do not concern us. The whole passage cannot be treated as a substitute for the argument given in Section 38. What does concern us is that, not only does Kant argue that the fact of empirical knowledge vouches for the subjective conditions of judgement, but also that those communicable subjective conditions *include* differences amongst these 'ratios' or 'proportions'. He puts it this way,

> But if cognitions are to admit of communication, then our mental state, i.e. the way the cognitive powers are attuned for cognition generally, and, in fact, the relative proportion suitable for a representation (by which an object is given to us) from which cognition is to result, must also admit of being universally communicated, as, without this, which is the subjective condition of the act of knowing, knowledge, as an effect, would not arise.[21]

The fact of empirical knowledge therefore is taken to guarantee the existence of differences in the internal ratios requisite for perception of different things. Kant then goes on to argue that there must be one amongst these internal ratios or proportions which is best suited for the mutual quickening of the cognitive powers, and best suited for cognition generally, one which is best suited for setting the cognitive powers on the alert for acquiring knowledge.

With this supplementation from Section 21 the *Deduction* does provide us with some sort of an argument that there must not only be perceptual as distinct from conceptual forms; but that there must be amongst them some best suited to our cognitive powers.

The argument is, however, a very weak one. It can be taken in one of two ways. It can be taken to mean that amongst the things which 'through the intervention of sense' we experience, some must be of such a form to produce the internal ratio best adapted to our cognitive powers. Or, it can be taken to mean that, since different things experienced by us produce different ratios, there must be some imaginable ratio which is best adapted to our cognitive powers. Thus one can interpret, 'There must be one in which this internal ratio suitable for quickening (one faculty by another) is best adapted for both mental powers in respect of cognition (of given objects) generally. . .' to mean either that there must be one amongst the existent ones or that we can extrapolate one.

On the first interpretation Kant's argument fails. There is nothing in the argument which establishes that of the things experienced by us some must have perceptual forms displaying those 'ratios' or 'proportions' which are best suited to our cognitive powers. It may follow that some will be better than others. On the second interpretation, it does follow that there must be a best, that is, we could extrapolate one. However, such a conclusion is not sufficient for Kant's purposes. We scarcely need such a roundabout argument to show that forms final for our perception are possible or thinkable.

Whichever way one looks at Kant's *Deduction*, the argument does not succeed in doing what he means it to do. His arguments for the necessity and universality of our judgements concerning the beautiful do not amount to a transcendental proof.

It could be argued, however, that in trying to produce such a proof Kant has needlessly set himself a task which cannot be accomplished. Where it is highly plausible to contend that we cannot do without such categorical concepts as those he lists in the *Metaphysical Deduction* in the *Critique of Pure Reason*, it is highly implausible that we cannot do without the notion of the beautiful. What is called for in giving a justification of our use of the expression, 'This is beautiful' does not seem to need to amount to a transcendental proof. If it just so happened that there were perceptual forms which were final for perception, it would seem that reference to them would serve just as well, if not better, than an argument which showed that there must be such.

Kant is always insistent that, being able to give a *Deduction* which is a transcendental argument, does not render our judgements about particular cases one whit more reliable. Even if we establish without a doubt that we cannot do without the notion of causation we still have before us the task of determining what causes what in any particular case. In that task the universal law of causation does not protect us from error.[22] Since the particular is even more important than any general consideration in the case of the beautiful than in the case of causes and substances, it seems more important to establish that we are indeed confronted with things which display forms final for our perception than to establish that there must be

such somewhere which can be confronted by us. Kant has to fall
back upon an appeal to aesthetic experience of a kind. Indeed, he
often writes as if he takes it as a starting point,[23] but his efforts to do
more than that are not useless. They serve to help crystallise our
conceptions of the particular role such experience must fulfil and to
remove intellectual difficulties in the way of accepting that as its
role.

The whole of the interpretation of Kant's justification for the
universality and necessity of judgements concerning the beautiful
which I have developed is consistent with treating the 'ought'
involved in them as a non-moral 'ought' and functioning independently of the moral 'ought'.

In a recent book Donald W. Crawford argues that Kant's
Deduction is only completed when he discloses the relationship of
the beautiful to the moral and when the 'ought' involved in
judgements concerning the beautiful is shown to be a variety of or
derivative from the moral 'ought'.[24]

There are two sections of the *Critique of Aesthetic Judgement* which
appear to support this interpretation. The first is the section
entitled, 'An intellectual interest in the beautiful',[25] and the second is
the section entitled, 'Beauty as the symbol of morality'.[26] To treat the
Deduction as an extended argument completed only by the latter one
must take these two discussions as parts of one argument.

That they are not parts of one argument can be shown by the
consideration that the first of them terminates in the conclusion that
we can exact the feeling in a judgement of *taste as a sort of duty*[27] only
in the special case where the judgement in question is about a
natural object. If this argument is taken to be part of the *Deduction* no
judgement we make concerning the beauty of works of art or of
humbler human artefacts can have their implicit claims to universality and necessity rendered legitimate by it.

In fact, Kant explains quite clearly that the discussion in Section 42
is about whether we are entitled to demand that other people take
an interest in the beautiful, and whether we are entitled to claim that
they ought to take such an interest. Judgements concerning the
beautiful have in the First Moment been maintained to be disinterested and being disinterested has been analysed to include being
uncommitted to preferences one way or another as to real existence.
In this section Kant explicitly states that one who has an interest in
the beautiful 'is not alone pleased with nature's product in respect of
its form, but is also pleased at its existence'.[28] Having an interest in

the beautiful therefore presupposes that pleasure in a thing's form is universal and necessary, that is, that everyone ought to take pleasure in it. That one ought to take an interest in beautiful things cannot be adduced as a justification of pronouncing them beautiful.

Kant does think, and there is nothing inconsistent in his thinking, that we are entitled to demand that others take *an interest* in the beautiful in nature and not entitled to demand that they take an interest in the beautiful in art. Interest in the beauty of nature alone is akin to interest in the morally good. Judgements about what is beautiful generally (both in nature and art) are by contrast disinterested. He is not in this section developing an analysis of the 'ought' involved in them; he is assuming it. He is concerned with a different 'ought', that which one would address to a person who never sought to put himself in the company of beautiful things in nature. That 'ought' is certainly akin to the moral 'ought' but it has no bearing upon which things we pronounce beautiful as opposed to which things we find agreeable.

The case is different with Kant's discussion of the beautiful as the symbol of morality. Here he is speaking not of interest in the beautiful in nature being akin to interest in morality; he is speaking of the beautiful as such, being a symbol of the moral. The remark,

> Now, I say, the beautiful is the symbol of the morally good, and only in this light (a point of view natural to every one, and one which every one exacts from others as a duty) does it give us pleasure with an attendant claim to the agreement of every one else . . .[29]

is about the 'ought' involved in judgements concerning the beautiful generally. There is no question of arguing that it is not.

Although Kant makes this remark I cannot see it as anything but a rash overstatement of the point he certainly is making in Section 59 that the beautiful as a symbol of the moral has claims to our attention which are additional to those it has by simply being beautiful. Kant is given to using the word 'only' very loosely.

One must consider Kant's remark as rash, because if one does not, one has to see him as asserting something which is incompatible with the context in which it occurs as well as with most of the main contentions of his book. I take the first of these – incompatibility with the context in which it is made, more seriously than the second. A man may, after all, near the end of a book, argue himself into

defending a position which is inconsistent with most of the
conclusions he has argued for earlier on. If, however, a remark is
indefensible in its immediate context one has no choice but to treat it
as an ill-considered and careless overstatement.

Kant's remark that, only by seeing the beautiful in the light of its
being the symbol of the morally good, does it give pleasure with an
attendant claim to the agreement of everyone else, in inconsistent
with its context. This is because the main discussion of the section in
which it is made is about what it is for something to be a symbol of
something else, and with showing that the beautiful is indeed the
symbol of the morally good.

Kant explains that a symbol is an indirect presentation of a
concept working by the aid of analogy. On the basis of an analogy,
reflection upon one kind of thing is transferred to something
different in kind. Symbols 'express concepts without employing a
direct intuition for the purpose, but only drawing upon an analogy
with one, i.e. transferring the reflection upon an object of intuition
to quite a new concept, and one with which perhaps no intuition
could ever directly correspond'.[30]

He then maintains that the beautiful is the symbol of the morally
good and spells out some of the points of the analogy upon which
the indirect presentation depends. One of the four points Kant
mentions as underpinning this analogy is that both judgements
concerning the beautiful and moral judgements are 'valid for
everyman'.

Now one cannot argue simultaneously that only if we see the
beautiful as a symbol of the morally good are we entitled to claim
that others ought to take pleasure as well, this is to claim that
judgements concerning the beautiful are universally valid; and that
part of the basis which underpins the analogy which justifies us in
speaking of the beautiful as the symbol of the moral is that they are
universally valid. If we take this remark of Kant's seriously we have
to see him as assuming in arguing that the beautiful is the symbol of
the moral what he claims to be able to show by regarding the
beautiful as the symbol of the moral, that is, that judgements
concerning the beautiful are, without any reference to their symbolising role, universally valid.

There is nothing inconsistent in Kant's contention that the
beautiful is the symbol of the moral, but if he is to maintain that view
upon his grounds, he cannot also use it to provide a *Deduction* for
the universality and necessity he finds in judgements concerning
the beautiful.

Using it so, would moreover be in conflict with many of his central contentions in the *Analytic of the Beautiful*. First, it would be in conflict with the criterion for a judgement concerning the beautiful which he laid down in the First Moment. Pleasure in the beautiful as symbol of morality although not 'interested' in the sense of resting upon an *antecedent* interest,[31] would be dependent upon interest drawn forth by morality and so would not satisfy the criterion of pleasure independent of all interest.

Secondly, one who takes pleasure in something beautiful seen as the symbol of the moral does not take pleasure in it in its own right. Although such pleasure is not exactly pleasure taken in something because it is a means to something else, it is very different from the immediate pleasure which Kant ascribes to both pleasure in the beautiful and the agreeable *in contrast* with pleasure in the good.[32] Moreover, acceding to another's claim to agreement because, and only because, one comes to see something which one did not previously see as a symbol of morality, does seem to be a case of treating the beautiful as being merely of derivative value.

Thirdly, pleasure in the beautiful will, on this account of the *Deduction* only be universal and necessary under the description 'symbol of the moral'. Although that is not exactly a concept, it does seem to make judgements concerning the beautiful much more like determinant judgements than they are made out to be in that part of their analysis which Kant conducts in the Second Moment.

Moreover, were the ground of the universality and necessity of pleasure in the beautiful provided by their symbolising relation to the moral, judgements concerning the beautiful would stand in no more need of a separate *Deduction* than do judgements concerning the sublime; and for the same reasons.[33]

Even if such an interpretation of how the claims to the agreement of others implicit in judgements concerning the beautiful is to be justified, were not in conflict with the rest of the book, it would still not provide a very convincing justification of such claims. There are no reasons for thinking that if something is a symbol of something in which we ought to take pleasure (e.g. the moral) we ought to take pleasure in it (the symbol) as well. If an evenly balanced beam-balanced is a symbol of impartial justice, and we ought to take pleasure in impartial justice, it does not follow that we ought to take pleasure in contemplating an evenly balanced beam-balance, or even that we ought to take pleasure in contemplating it as a symbol of impartial justice.

10

The Sublime

Kant's analysis of judgements concerning the sublime cannot but make the impression of an interruption in the development of the main theme of the *Critique of Aesthetic Judgement*. The analyses and justification of judgements concerning the beautiful carry over into his discussion of what is worthwhile in fine art; and are thus continuous with it. His discussion of the sublime breaks the train of this development. It does, however, advance the task of illuminating fine art a step. Although the sublime is not a necessary constituent of fine art, it may, so Kant believes, enter into it, on the condition that what is sublime is made to be, in addition, beautiful. Unfortunately we are not given many indications as to how that is to be done. However, we learn, at least, that 'beautiful' and 'sublime' are not thought by Kant to be incompatible terms.

Apart from the *Deduction of Pure Aesthetic Judgements* the major topics extensively discussed in the second part of the *Critique of Aesthetic Judgement* are the Sublime and Fine Art. Lest the discussion of the Sublime seem a total diversion from the main theme, it is as well to note that what ties these two discussions together, and provides the basis of a contrast between them and the analysis of the beautiful which precedes them, is that both introduce into the arena of aesthetic judgements the notion of 'ideas' as opposed to intuitions of sensibility, images of imagination and concepts or rules of understanding. In the case of the sublime the ideas are ideas of Reason (of the intellect and of morality) whereas in the case of fine art, the ideas are aesthetic ideas, which are ideas created (not reproduced) by the imagination. Both kinds of ideas are contrasted with concepts of the understanding but besides that they have little in common; as Kant describes them, they bear, instead, a kind of complementary relation to each other. The ideas of Reason are concepts to which no intuition can be adequate, whilst the aesthetic ideas are intuitions to which no concept can be adequate. Aesthetic ideas, however, can function as 'presentations' of the ideas of Reason, and presumably, as such, they are thought by Kant to be more 'adequate' to them than the ordinary intuitions of sense. We can think of Kant's point this way, in connection with an example. Eternity is an idea of Reason. No intuition of sense is adequate to it. We cannot perceive eternity. However, Vaughan's

> I saw Eternity the other night,
> Like a great Ring of pure and endless light,
> All calm as it was bright;[1]

presents something to sense in lieu of a sensory exemplification which does seem more 'adequate' to it than would, say, a dripping tap.

Besides the introduction of the notion of ideas into aesthetic matters, Kant's discussion of the sublime supplies a link in the development of Kant's conception of the importance of aesthetics. Throughout the *Critique of Aesthetic Judgement* he is not only concerned with the values which count within the sphere of aesthetics but also to develop theses to show why aesthetic activity is worthwhile.

His account of the importance of aesthetics is a complex one.[2] As he analyses aesthetic judgements, he develops a set of considerations which support a conception of aesthetic activity as worthwhile in its own right and as also worthwhile because it enhances culture and provides an intermediary step between the point of view of egocentric self-interest and the point of view of morality. The aesthetic judgements which are focal for Kant are judgements concerning the beautiful – be they free or dependently so. On these he bases his claims that aesthetics is autonomous and the principal aesthetic value intrinsic and non derivative. Judgements concerning the sublime according to Kant's analysis, involve values which although intrinsic because not merely instrumental are nonetheless derivative. The importance of contemplating the sublime derives from the importance of the ideas of the intellect and morality which supplement the mere perception of things we describe as 'sublime'. Rightly speaking, as Kant sees it, it is the state of mind in which we contemplate what we perceive which is 'sublime' rather than the starry heavens or the wild tiger which makes demands on our higher powers to be exercised with mastery, where imagination and understanding are felt with displeasure to be wanting.

Where the moral importance of contemplation of the sublime rates high, in contrast with the *moral* importance of contemplation of the beautiful, the importance of the sublime as a value within aesthetics rates low because it is not an autonomous but a derivative value. One cannot even judge which things are properly to be pronounced sublime without calling upon the ideas of the intellect and of morality to provide a basis for the communicability of pleasure in the sublime. For those wishing to cultivate their moral sensibilities, contemplation of the sublime, as Kant presents it, will seem more important than the contemplation of the beautiful.

Kant's treatment of the sublime is both provoking and suggestive. It is provoking because it seems to contain so many internal inconsistencies. It is suggestive because of its connections with both judgements concerning the beautiful and with judgements as to the worth of fine art. Kant elaborates the first of these connections in some detail but of the second he only hints in a way which exercises conjecture.

First, take the provoking aspects. *The Analytic of the Sublime* opens with an exercise in comparing and contrasting judgements concerning the beautiful with those concerning the sublime. The points of likeness are said to be, that both please on their own account, that both are judgements of reflection and not of sense or of understanding, that both express the accord of a given intuition of the faculty of imagination with the faculty of concepts or Reason, and that both are singular judgements which profess universal validity for every judging subject despite their non-cognitive nature.

The points of difference are said to be that, whereas the beautiful in nature is grounded on the perceptual form of the object, and hence applies to things which are limited, the things we judge to be sublime lack such a form and involve or invoke an impression of limitlessness alongside the thought of a totality. Kant says that whereas the beautiful seems as if it were the presentation of an indeterminate concept of understanding, the sublime seems as if it were an indeterminate concept of Reason.[3]

Secondly, Kant claims that whereas pleasure in the beautiful arises directly from the perception of the object, pleasure in the sublime arises indirectly because of the introduction of reference to the ideas of Reason. He therefore proposes to call pleasure in the beautiful 'positive' pleasure and pleasure in the sublime, thought of as admiration or respect, 'negative' pleasure.[4]

The most important difference between judgements concerning the sublime and those concerning the beautiful Kant pronounces to be that, whereas objects can quite properly be called 'beautiful' it is strictly incorrect to call them 'sublime', for what they do is to call up a 'presentation of a sublimity discoverable in the mind'[5] and it is that, rather than they, which is 'sublime'. He says that objects judged to be sublime do not exhibit finality in nature but only produce a final employment of a representation by the imagination.

This exercise, although it throws some light on the *Analytic of the Beautiful*, is far from satisfactory. If both the beautiful and the sublime are going to be said to 'please' on their own account then something more than Kant does say needs to be said about 'negative' pleasure. Off-hand, the phrase sounds like a contradiction and the explanation of it in terms of admiration, or respect, makes it involve cognitive judgement and therefore notions about the good, implications which Kant is concerned to deny. The judgements in 'Judgement of reflection' mentioned in the Introduction are explained as being those where a universal has to be found for a particular;[6] but here he takes the expression to mean judgements of neither sense nor understanding, that is judgements concerned with neither the agreeable nor the good.

It seems a travesty of his account of the sublime, which is that it is what affronts and outrages the imagination, to speak of judgements concerning the sublime as expressing 'accord' between imagination and the understanding, or with Reason. Adding 'or Reason' does not help out. The ideas of Reason are said to be felt to dominate the recalcitrant sensory material but not by 'accord'. The ideas of Reason seem to be better described as 'discordant' with those of imagination and understanding. Such a use of 'accord' weakens what was claimed for the chiming together of imagination and understanding in the case of the beautiful.

Since the universality and necessitation involved in judgements concerning the sublime are said to be based upon the ideas of Reason and on moral feeling,[7] and since the peculiarly aesthetic character of judgements concerning the beautiful were claimed to rest upon their independence of the determinate concepts of the understanding and hence their independence of 'the good', Kant really needs to say more about his reasons for thinking that reference to the ideas of Reason is a criterion for ruling a judgement to be an aesthetic judgement rather than a reason for ruling it not to be such.

Perceptual form, and formlessness too, are facilely contrasted by introducing the distinction between the limited and the limitless. Not all perceptually formless objects invoke the impression of limitlessness in the required sense,[8] although they are 'limitless' in the sense of not being limited in the way that objects having the Form of Finality are. This point is not covered by saying that in judgements concerning the beautiful, pleasure is connected with the representation of quality and in judgements concerning the sublime with judgements of quantity.[9]

Again, there is a puzzle with regard to why Kant is happy to say that beauty is, as it were, in or of, beautiful objects, whereas sublimity is something in our minds. We can just as well say that the 'sublime' objects are apt for outraging the imagination and thus for calling up the ideas of Reason, as we can say that beautiful objects are apt for setting the imagination and understanding into harmonious free play. Moreover, the pleasure taken in both must indisputably be placed 'in the mind'. However, Kant does think that the perceptual form of a thing is intrinsic to it, whereas 'greatness', be it numerical or dynamical, is relational and therefore extrinsic.[10] This does not, of course, show that 'greatness' is not a property of the thing since relational properties are just as much properties of a thing as intrinsic ones are. Kant owes us more than this, in explanation; but he does not give it. If he could show that whereas the object of pleasure (the Form of Finality) were internally related to pleasure in it, whereas the object of pleasure in sublimity were externally related to it, then he could make out a case for his conclusion. Suggestions to this effect are thrown out by Kant, but perhaps he did not formulate the notion of the object of pleasure clearly enough to fully distinguish such kinds?

Kant draws a distinction between what is 'mathematically' and what is 'dynamically' sublime. The first is that which is so great in size that it seems to be, or is, immeasurable, and the second is that which is so powerful or exerts such might, that it seems that it will, or that it can, overcome us.

In the case of the mathematically sublime, Kant thinks that imagination boggles, cannot get a grip and cannot make a whole of what is sensed. This helplessness in the face of recalcitrant sensory experience is only redeemed by the introduction of an idea of Reason, the thought, not the synthesis, of a totality.

In the case of the dynamically sublime, it is not that imagination cannot get a grip, but that we are fearful of destruction and what Kant thinks redeems the situation seems to be the thought of the power of righteousness, a power which no natural nor supernatural force can overcome.[11] Again it is an idea of Reason, this time of

practical Reason, which helps out in the face of something affront-
ing to sensibility, and this time it is a practical sensibility. Kant's
thought seems to be that in confronting the sublime the noumenal
self shows itself competent to the task to which the phenomenal self
profoundly feels itself to be inadequate.

Kant's account of the dynamically sublime is a radical departure
from everything which he hitherto included under the classification
of an aesthetic judgement, and this departure is only thinly
disguised by his customary equivocation on 'sensibility'.[12] Both
judgements concerning the beautiful and the mathematically sublime can plausibly be argued to please independently of all interest,
but judgements concerning the dynamically sublime cannot.

Kant says that the division of the moments of the *Analytic of the
Sublime* are, of quantity universally valid, of quality independent of
interest, of relation subjective finality and of modality, necessary.[13]
To bring home the extent to which Kant's account of the dynamically sublime parts company with those of the beautiful and of the
mathematically sublime, let us take 'in its quality, independent of
interest', seriously. What pleases independently of interest means
what pleases independently of the represented bond of connection
between subject and the real existence of the object. Thus what
pleases independently of interest, includes what pleases though it
be opposed to such interest. On that reading, judgements concerning the dynamically sublime would emerge as nothing more or less
than judgements concerning the beautiful.

Take the movement of a sting-ray. To judge it to be beautiful we
must judge it without reference to the represented bond between us
and the real object. We must not represent ourselves as either
catching and eating it or being caught and stung by it. If we do judge
it to be beautiful whilst being afraid of it, which we may do if we are
watching it not in an aquarium but being in the water with it, then
we judge it to be beautiful independent of that interest in it. Now we
can certainly do the same when,

> gazing upon the prospect of mountains ascending to heaven,
> deep ravines and torrents raging there, deep-shadowed solitudes
> that invite brooding melancholy . . .[14]

This description is of something taken by Kant to be dynamically
sublime. We can and do find such scenery beautiful, what more do
we have to do for it to count for Kant as a judgement not of the

beautiful, but of the sublime? We have to find it *fearful* but yet not be afraid of it. Kant says,

> The *sublime* is what pleases immediately by reason of its opposition to the interest of sense.[15]

that is, it pleases *because* it is fearful.

If this is so, and it must be or else a judgement concerning the dynamically sublime would not differ from a judgement concerning beauty, then the sublime and the beautiful cannot agree in their both being pleasing *independently of interest*. It is significant too, that Kant is silent upon whether judgements on the dynamically sublime are non-conceptual since it does seem that the application of determinant concepts such as 'mountains', 'ravines', 'torrents' are essential to the pleasure taken in viewing them, and to the claim to the assent of others made in judging them to be sublime. Neither imagination nor understanding boggle at those, nor does sensibility if we take it to be our capacity to register sense impressions. It is only what I dubbed 'practical' sensibility which boggles, that is we go wobbly at the knees. In fact, in the dynamically sublime we have a case where imagination and understanding must of necessity be working perfectly well together for us to find the scene 'fearful'. If imagination is still said in such cases to be outraged by sublime objects, it must be because 'imagination' means something different in this context. Imagination becomes how we picture or think it might be *for us* if the threat of the object seen as fearful were to be realised.[16]

With regard to the 'freedom' of the imagination claimed to be exhibited in both the estimation of beauty and sublimity alike, whereas in the case of beauty 'free' seems a reasonable description, in the case of the sublime what is described as taking place seems only ironically to be called 'free'. The description is,

> For though the imagination, no doubt, finds nothing beyond the sensible world to which it can lay hold, still this thrusting aside of the sensible barriers gives it a feeling of being unbounded; and that removal is thus a presentation of the infinite.[17]

In judging something to be mathematically sublime, Kant thinks that we have a feeling that the data of sensibility outstrip the powers of imagination and understanding. Presumably he thinks that imagination fails to synthesise that data and no concept seems applicable. Then we find, althouth no concept of the understanding is applicable, an idea of Reason does what imagination in collaboration with understanding has, and must have, failed to do.

Although he is reticent upon the matter, the case is not the same with judgements on the dynamically sublime. Here there is no question of imagination and understanding losing their grip. We have perfect *cognitive* control of raging torrents, storms and so on. We have no trouble in synthesising their manifolds and no trouble in bringing to bear concepts which apply to them. Kant has to fall back on a very different notion of 'sensibility' to be able to maintain that here also the data of sensibility outrages imagination and understanding. The notion of sensibility as susceptibility to wants and fears rather than to sensory data, is to the fore in Kant's ethical writings.[18] When 'sensibility' in this sense is outraged it is our wants and fears and not our powers of perception which are challenged.

To see something as an impending threat, imagination and understanding must needs be coping perfectly well. What Reason and the ideas of Reason are said to help out against is something seen as threatening. Man as noumena, as autonomous free agent, can stand up to all external power, that of the phenomenal world and that of the Almighty[19] by virtue of his own freedom. Stone walls do not a prison make.

The older commentators, such as Bosanquet and Lindsay,[20] used to ask whether the beautiful and the sublime were not, after all, two species of one another; and perhaps whether both were not in a deeper sense of the 'beautiful' 'beautiful'. Question-begging as that approach was, for they plainly believed that their question should be answered in the affirmative, it does, none the less, help to focus one's thoughts about Kant's treatment of the sublime. If we try to absorb Kant's dynamical sublime into his account of the beautiful what remains is that emotion which he emphatically excluded from non-barbarian aesthetic judgement.[21] The mathematical sublime cannot be absorbed at all, and Kant is inclined to treat the mathematical sublime as the paradigm of sublimity.[22] To invent a 'wider sense of beauty' which encompassed both would require both emotion and the ideas of Reason to be relevant and irrelevant to something's being, in the wider sense, 'beautiful'. There is no wider sense of 'beautiful' open to Kant; it involves him in contradiction.

We can now turn to what is suggestive in Kant's treatment of the sublime. Lindsay says perceptively of the *Critique of Judgement*:

The general plan of the work would suggest that the beautiful and the sublime are two species of what may in a wider sense be called beautiful. That is implied when Kant distinguishes the judgement of the beautiful from that of the agreeable on the one hand and that of the good on the other. But his distinction between the beautiful and the analytic of the sublime, and some of the things he says about the sublime, almost imply that the judgements of beauty and sublimity have no relation to one another.[23]

Lindsay is surprised because Kant is presupposing that there must be some one consideration or set of considerations which settle the issue as to whether any given thing is of aesthetic value. Hence he thinks that Kant ought to introduce 'beauty' in a wider sense. That is not Kant's point of view at all. He is comparatively liberal with the term 'aesthetic' and thinks of aesthetic merit in a variety of contexts.

Not only does Kant think both of judgements concerning the beautiful and judgements concerning the sublime as aesthetic and, as giving an estimate of aesthetic value, he is happy enough to speak in the same way *about* judgements of products of what he calls the arts of the agreeable (table-setting is one of his examples of an 'agreeable art'). In taking pleasure in a well-set table one is appreciating its aesthetic value; for he divides aesthetic *arts* into the agreeable and the fine arts.[24] Again, in taking pleasure in a worthwhile work of fine art, one is appreciating its aesthetic value, and that is a matter of taking note of different features again. None the less it is plain that he thinks that there is a strong family resemblance between them.

Kant really does think that in a way 'judgements of beauty and sublimity have no relation to one another'. They are both aesthetic judgements and what each separately relate importantly to, *is not each other*, but to judgements concerning the worth of works of fine art. However, whilst he is definite and explicit about the way in which judgements concerning the beautiful relate to judgements concerning the worth of works of fine art, he is offhand, and what he has to say is unsatisfactory, about the way in which judgements concerning the sublime relate to judgements as to the worth of works of fine art.

Works of fine art, to have aesthetic worth, must be beautiful. Being beautiful is a necessary but not a sufficient condition of a work of fine art having aesthetic worth.[25] Works of fine art may be sublime. He mentions when giving examples of the sublime St Peter's in Rome, the Pyramids, the inscription on the Temple of Isis, and tragedy and oratorio.[26] Although he thinks the beautiful and the sublime in nature are deeply different from each other, he thinks that they can and must, *if the sublime is to feature aesthetically at all in fine art*, be intentionally combined in the same work.

The trouble is that he does not say very much about how they are so to be combined; and what he does say is unsatisfactory. About the relationship in the *Critique of Judgement* he says,

> Even the presentation of the sublime, so far as it belongs to fine art, may be brought into union with beauty in a *tragedy in verse*, a *didactic poem* or an *oratorio*, and in this combination fine art is even more artistic. Whether it is also more beautiful (having regard to the multiplicity of different kinds of delight which cross one another) may in some of these instances be doubted.[27]

In the *Anthropology* he says,

> Beauty alone belongs before taste; the *sublime* does not, even though it belongs to the aesthetic judgement. The *representation* of the sublime, however, can and should be beautiful in itself; otherwise it is uncouth, barbarous, and repugnant to taste;[28]

and,

> The sublime, though the counterweight of the beautiful, is not its antagonist. For [on the one hand], the subject's endeavour and attempt to raise himself to the apprehension . . . of the object awakens in him a feeling of his own greatness and power; but, [on the other hand], the conception of the sublime in the *description* or presentation can and must always be beautiful; for if it is not, amazement becomes *abhorrence*, which is quite different from *admiration*, admiration being the kind of judgement or appraisal in which we never weary of being amazed . . .
>
> The sublime, then, is not an object of taste but for emotion. Yet its artistic presentation in describing and investing it (with accessories, *parerga*) can and must be beautiful, for otherwise it is wild, rough, and repulsive, and thus offensive to taste.[29]

Unfortunately, there is more than a hint that the sublime can only be incorporated into fine art by being represented. Kant does not discuss the kind of case which the Pyramids or St Peter's might, but did not, suggest to him, namely the case of the work of fine art which is, and does not represent, something sublime. Further, he implied that the sublime can, if it is to be successfully incorporated, only be represented as beautiful.[30] The proximity of this requirement with the requirement that the evil and the ugly as presented in fine art should be presented in beautiful form enforce this intepretation. He believes that the sublime, like diseases and the devastations of war,[31] must be represented as beautiful if it is to be satisfactorily incorporated into fine art.

In being something which must be mastered before being satisfactorily incorporated into a work of art, the sublime is analogous with the aesthetic ideas which men of genius express in them. Whereas the sublime is 'uncouth' if not properly integrated into a work, the aesthetic ideas are incomprehensible.[32] Kant thinks of them both as boundless and in need of having limitations set upon them. Embodiment in a beautiful form civilises the one and articulates the other and without such civilising and articulation they are, within the confines of a work of art, worse than worthless.

Although the *Analytic of the Sublime* is fraught with inconsistencies, and although its role in the *Critique of Judgement* is ill-defined, it is an extremely important section since it reveals how far Kant is from believing that there is one and only one feature or set of features by reference to which we can establish that a judgement is aesthetic, or that an object is of aesthetic value. His theory is much more like one suggested by the much vaunted Wittgensteinian figure of a rope or piece of string made up of many fibres.

Kant conceives of the sublime as being in one way like the beautiful, and in another like worthwhile works of art. Neither comparison turns upon a simple point of resemblance. Kant finds instead a string of similarities some of which are based upon analogy. The sublime is seen as being like the beautiful in being the object of communicable (i.e. universal and necessary) pleasure, despite the fact that communicability is backed by co-operation between imagination and Reason and not, as in the case of the beautiful, by harmonious free play of imagination and understanding. The sublime is seen as being like works of fine art in that, unlike the beautiful in nature, both involve reference to something more than mere perceptual form. In both, this additional factor involves ideas although the ideas related to the sublime are different from the ideas expressed by works of fine art, the one sort being ideas of Reason, the other, the aesthetic ideas which are ideas of the productive imagination and characteristic of genius.

11

Fine Art

Up to Section 43 Kant treats successful works of art and beautiful natural objects equally, as examples of beautiful things. Both, according to his analysis, are to be judged universally and necessarily pleasing in virtue of their being of a perceptual form which is suitable for setting the cognitive powers, imagination and understanding, into harmonious free play. Such universality and necessity is for both kinds of examples, underpinned by the finality of such forms for human perception. The pleasure taken in each, is the pleasure felt in realising the powers brought to bear in perception to the full. Critics as well as connoisseurs of nature must concentrate upon,

> the investigation of the faculties of cognition and their function in these judgements, and the illustration, by the analysis of examples, of their mutual subjective finality, the form of which in a given representation has been shown above to constitute the beauty of their object.[1]

From Section 43 onwards, Kant sets out to show how worthwhile works of art differ from beautiful natural objects. He finds the two main points of difference to be that first, worthwhile works of fine art are intended to be as they are; and second they are expressive of what he calls 'aesthethic ideas', ideas which are the distinctive contribution of men of genius.

WORKS OF FINE ART ARE ARTEFACTS

Kant is concerned both to show the relationship of fine art to natural objects and to place them within the field of artefacts. 'Fine art' means for him what 'art' means for us, as indicated earlier, where 'art' for him covers whatever men make, that is artefacts. He stresses that making is different from simply bringing something about,[2] and that artefacts exhibit skill and not just theoretical knowledge.[3] When men produce artefacts they therefore have an end in view.[4]

Some arts are mechanical, some free.[5] He has in mind a notion somewhat similar to Collingwood's conception of 'craft', yet it catches the spirit of the contrasts he wishes to make, to think of what we would describe as manufactured objects. He classes with fine art, and describes both as 'free', a group called 'the agreeable arts'. His examples are drawn from dinner parties:

Agreeable arts are those which have mere enjoyment for their object. Such are all the charms that can gratify a dinner party: entertaining narrative, the art of starting the whole table in unrestrained and sprightly conversation, or with jest and laughter inducing a certain air of gaiety. Here, as the saying goes, there may be much loose talk over the glasses, without a person wishing to be brought to book for all he utters, ... (Of the same sort is also the art of arranging the table for enjoyment, or, at large banquets, the music of the orchestra – a quaint idea intended to act on the mind merely as an agreeable noise fostering a genial spirit, which, without any one paying the smallest attention to the composition, promotes the free flow of conversation between guest and guest.)[6]

Both the 'agreeable arts' and fine art have, as their end in view, pleasure. The kind of pleasure, however, differs. In the case of the agreeable the pleasure is pleasure in sensation and the pleasure in fine art is pleasure in a 'representation which is intrinsically final' and is one of reflection. Thus,

Fine art ... is a mode of representation which is intrinsically final, and which, although devoid of an end, has the effect of advancing the culture of the mental powers in the interests of social communication.

The universal communicability of a pleasure involves in its very concept that the pleasure is not one of enjoyment arising out of mere sensation, but must be one of reflection.[7]

The apparent contradiction between saying that the end in view is pleasure and that 'the representation' is devoid of an end is, I believe, apparent only. He is contrasting as befits the case, proximate and ulterior 'ends'. Both an elegantly set table and a work of art are to be enjoyed in their own right.

Because all artefacts are deliberately produced, and the product of fine art is an artefact, to estimate its worth one must recognise it as 'art'.[8] One must recognise such objects as being deliberately and skilfully produced with a view to their being pleasing in the mere estimate of them. A major difference therefore between beautiful natural objects and beautiful works of fine art is that:

> To enable me to estimate a beauty of nature, as such, I do not need to be previously possessed of a concept of what sort of a thing the object is intended to be, i.e. I am not obliged to know its material finality (the end), but, rather, in forming an estimate of it apart from any knowledge of the end, the mere form pleases on its own account. If, however, the object is presented as a product of art, and is as such to be declared beautiful, then, seeing that art always presupposes an end in the cause (and its causality), a concept of what the thing is intended to be must first of all be laid at its basis. And, since the agreement of the manifold in a thing with an inner character belonging to it as its end constitutes the perfection of the thing, it follows that in estimating beauty of art the perfection of the thing must also be taken into account – a matter which in estimating a beauty of nature, as beautiful, is quite irrelevant.[9]

Beautiful natural objects have the Form of Finality by a kind of chance.[10] Worthwhile works of fine art have it by human contrivance. It is as if beautiful natural objects were designed to be as they are for our reflective pleasure,[11] but worthwhile works of art really are designed to be what they are for our reflective pleasure.[12]

As we have seen, in general ends and finality are treated by Kant as being quite independent of a necessary connection with human wills or human intentions. Once he begins his analyses of 'art in general' and 'fine art' those notions are related to what humans will and what they intend. He says that art is production through freedom, 'through an act of will that places reason at the basis of its action'[13] and that 'the thought of something as end must be present, or else its product would not be ascribed to an art at all, but would be a mere product of chance'.[14]

In not seeing a beautiful strawberry to be beautiful and in seeing it just as the fruit of the strawberry plant or as something to eat one does not violate any real end. However, in failing to appreciate the worth of a worthwhile work of art one does violate a real and not merely a 'formal' end. Its finality – the causation of the object by its concept and the perfection of the object in relation to that concept – is produced through a human act. Fine art is produced as art and must be recognised as art.[15]

This admission leaves Kant with a problem. His account of intention is that if something is as it is intentionally, 'its producing cause had an end in view to which the object owes its form', and 'its actuality must have been preceded by a representation of the thing in its cause',[16] then doing whatever is necessary to realise the object in a way which is adequate to the intention will constitute a mechanical art (not a fine art) and be made and appreciated by following rules.[17] Also, since judging the degree to which the intention in question is realised, amounts to judging the perfection of the thing after its kind according to rules of conceptual rather than perceptual form, whether the thing conforms with formulable rules for judgement, and is perfect of its kind, considerations which Kant has argued to be irrelevant or secondary when judging whether natural objects were beautiful, seem to be brought into the picture when judging works of art.

What Kant does in this quandary, is to say that although all this is so, it must not appear to be so. He expresses this point in a paradox,

> Nature proved beautiful when it wore the appearance of art; and art can only be termed beautiful, where we are conscious of its being art, while yet it has the appearance of nature;[18]

and goes on to say that,

> the finality in the product of fine art, intentional though it be, must not have the appearance of being intentional.[19]

If that were all he had to say he would not escape the charge of inconsistency. It is just disingenuous to say that we must pretend, whilst recognising something to be intentional, that it is not.

He meets the charge by claiming that this particular intention does not amount to the representation of the thing actualised in its cause being a definite one, and hence, if not a definite one, not realisable by mechanical rules.[20] Perfection after its kind he accepts[21] but this acceptance is harmless to his central thesis, since the kind is 'work of fine art' and perfection after that kind will be determined by reference to whether the thing in question is a product of genius, and genius, by definition, does not proceed upon formulable rules.

Before looking at the second major difference which Kant finds to hold between beautiful natural objects and beautiful works of fine art one should note one other remark which he makes. In Section 48 he says:

A beauty of nature is a *beautiful thing*; beauty of art is a *beautiful representation* of a thing.[22]

It has been thought that this commits Kant to the view that works of art must, of necessity, be depictive or representative of natural objects. He does, naturally enough, tend to think of them that way. He speaks of painting as the beautiful portrayal of nature. An interesting example is what he says in a footnote,

It seems strange that landscape gardening may be regarded as a kind of painting, notwithstanding that it presents its forms corporeally. But, as it takes its form bodily from nature (the trees, shrubs, grasses, and flowers taken, originally at least, from wood and field) it is to that extent not an art such as, let us say, plastic art. Further, the arrangement which it makes is not conditioned by any concept of the object or of its end (as is the case in sculpture), but by the mere free play of the imagination in the act of contemplation. Hence it bears a degree of resemblance to simple aesthetic painting that has no definite theme (but by means of light and shade makes a pleasing composition of atmosphere, land, and water).[23]

What is interesting here, is that in describing 'aesthetic painting' he comes near to thinking of a painter producing an abstract painting, but ends up interpreting it as depictive of 'atmosphere, land, and water'. He is not, however, unaware of non-depictive patterns: 'designs *à la grecque*, foliage for framework or on wallpapers, &c., have no intrinsic meaning; they represent nothing – no Object under a definite concept . . .'[24] and he certainly thinks of music and architecture as non-depictive. Interesting as this may be, it is of far less importance than the fact that there is nothing at all in his account of what art is and what constitutes excellence in it to rule out abstract art. Fidelity of depiction or representation, is never counted as a virtue of any work; and there is no reason at all why a non-depictive work could not be given a perceptual form suitable for setting imagination into harmonious free play and be used to

express aesthetic ideas. In fact 'a representation' is such a general-
ised notion in Kant's writing that it could be treated as marking, in
the passage under discussion, no more than the fact that the artist
makes, and does not find or is not 'given', the object in question.

WORKS OF FINE ART ARE WORKS OF GENIUS

The second major difference which Kant finds to hold between the
beauty of natural objects and worthwhile works of art is that,
whereas the aesthetic worth of natural objects is simply a matter of
their being beautiful, the aesthetic worth of works of fine art turns
upon their being beautiful and on their expressing aesthetic ideas.
Being expressive of aesthetic ideas shows a work of fine art to be a
work of 'genius'. In this connection Kant says,

> it is imperative at the outset accurately to determine the difference
> between beauty of nature, which it only requires taste to estimate,
> and beauty of art, which requires genius for its possibility (a
> possibility to which regard must also be paid in estimating such an
> object).[25]

Again, artefacts other than works of art may be beautiful and in
being so bear the 'form of fine art' but that is not sufficient for them
to be worthwhile works of fine art. To estimate a work as a work of
fine art one must take note of genius as well. Satisfying taste, which
is defined by Kant to be the faculty of judging beauty by means of
pleasure,[26] is not the only consideration which comes into account in
judging works of fine art. Thus we find Kant explaining that,

> Taste is, however, merely a critical, not a productive faculty; and
> what conforms to it is not, merely on that account, a work of fine
> art. It may belong to useful and mechanical art, or even to science,
> as a product following definite rules which are capable of being
> learned and which must be closely followed. But the pleasing
> form imparted to the work is only the vehicle of communication
> and a mode, as it were, of execution, in respect of which one
> remains to a certain extent free, notwithstanding being otherwise
> tied down to a definite end. So we demand that table appoint-
> ments, or even a moral dissertation, and, indeed, a sermon, must
> bear this form of fine art, yet without its appearing *studied*. But

one would not call them on this account works of fine art. A poem, a musical composition, a picture-gallery, and so forth, would, however, be placed under this head; and so in a would-be work of fine art we may frequently recognize genius without taste, and in another taste without genius.[27]

Worthwhile works of fine art must have more than the 'form of fine art'; they must have 'soul', an animating principle which brings the beautiful but dead creature alive.[28] It is Kant's belief that by expressing aesthetic ideas works have 'soul', or are animated.

A man of genius uses the work of art which he creates, to talk, as it were, to other men.[29] Not only is a work of fine art beautiful by design rather than apparent design, it is also used to express something. A work of fine art cannot be wholly worthwhile, rather than simply inoffensive to taste, unless it expresses and communicates these aesthetic ideas.

First, Kant is saying that a work will be no more than tasteful unless it expresses aesthetic ideas; he is not saying that given that it does express aesthetic ideas, it will have aesthetic merit. Secondly, it is the work of art which has the aesthetic merit not the aesthetic ideas.[30]

This second point is of the utmost importance. The contention that a work will not be worthwhile without 'soul' does not entail that the value of the work is dependent upon the value of that which gives 'soul' to the work. Moore's strictures are in order here. Even if it should be granted that a beautiful but soulless work were of no value at all and that it could come to have value by coming to have 'soul' it would not follow that the only thing of value was that which imparted 'soul' to it. Scrambled eggs may be tasteless without pepper – that does not mean one would do well to forego a dish of scrambled eggs in favour of a dish of pepper.[31]

One of the considerations to which regard must be paid when taking note of the contribution of 'genius' to a work is wealth of aesthetic ideas. A wealth of aesthetic ideas is, however, simply 'rich *material* for products of fine art'.[32] The other contribution of genius is the suitability of the work as an expression for the ideas. A man of genius must not only have ideas, he must be able 'to hit upon the expression for them'.[33]

Genius is evident in works of art when works are fit to function as original examples of works of art, when the work 'gives the rule to art'.[34] The fertility of aesthetic ideas may alone amount to originality

but as Kant says, there can be original nonsense.[35] Taste alone like
genius alone will not fit the work to function as an exemplar, each is
necessary but neither is sufficient. Taste is a critical and not a
productive faculty. An artist's correction of his work to satisfy 'taste'
is said to be a slow and even painful process of improvement
directed to making the form adequate to his thought[36] without
prejudice to the freedom in the play of these powers.

Thus we should interpret Kant as maintaining genius to be
productive on two counts, first as productive of aesthetic ideas and
secondly as productive of suitable expressions for those ideas. This
is how Kant himself speaks of it in the following:

> genius properly consists in the happy relation, which science
> cannot teach nor industry learn, enabling one to find out ideas for
> a given concept, and, besides, to hit upon the *expression* for them
> – the expression by means of which the subjective mental
> condition induced by the ideas as the concomitant of a concept
> may be communicated to others. This latter talent is properly that
> which is termed soul. For to get an expression for what is
> indefinable in the mental state accompanying a particular repre-
> sentation and to make it universally communicable – be the
> expression in language or painting or statuary – is a thing
> requiring a faculty for laying hold of the rapid and transient play
> of the imagination, and for unifying it in a concept (which for that
> very reason is original, and reveals a new rule which could not
> have been inferred from any preceding principles or examples)
> that admits of communication without any constraint of rules.[37]

Important as these contributions of genius are to the worth of a
work of fine art, just as taste is not sufficient, so too is the animating
presence of the aesthetic ideas not sufficient without beauty of form.

When Kant comes to consider which, of the two kinds of
considerations, those of genius or those of beauty, to favour in the
case of conflict, he comes down upon the side of beauty (because, in
being beautiful that which expresses the aesthetic ideas renders
them communicable). Thus he says,

> where the interests of both these qualities clash in a product, and
> there has to be a sacrifice of something, then it should rather be on
> the side of genius . . .[38]

Kant, in maintaining that in estimating the worth of works of art in contrast with estimating the beauty of natural objects one must pay regard to genius, introduces a rich variety of considerations which apply peculiarly to aesthetic judgements of works of art. How rich the variety is, is indicated by his account of what genius is, thus:

> *First*, that it is a talent for art – not one for science, in which clearly known rules must take the lead and determine the procedure. *Secondly*, being a talent in the line of art, it presupposes a definite concept of the product – as its end. Hence it presupposes understanding, but, in addition, a representation, indefinite though it be, of the material, i.e. of the intuition, required for the presentation of that concept, and so a relation of the imagination to the understanding. *Thirdly*, it displays itself, not so much in the working out of the projected end in the presentation of a definite *concept*, as rather in the portrayal, or expression of *aesthetic ideas* containing a wealth of material for effecting that intention. Consequently the imagination is represented by it in its freedom from all guidance of rules, but still as final for the presentation of the given concept. *Fourthly*, and lastly, the unsought and undesigned subjective finality in the free harmonizing of the imagination with the understanding's conformity to law presupposes a proportion and accord between these faculties such as cannot be brought about by any observance of rules, whether of science or mechanical imitation, but can only be produced by the nature of the individual.
>
> Genius, according to these presuppositions, is the exemplary originality of the natural endowment of an individual in the *free* employment of his cognitive faculties.[39]

The genius to which we must pay regard in estimating the worth of works of fine art is therefore not one thing (one constituent or aspect of a work) but several: intention, aesthetic ideas, the mode of their expression and the creation of original exemplars.

12
Exemplars of Fine Art and Genius

AN EXEMPLARY WORK IS ONE WHICH EXPRESSES AESTHETIC IDEAS

Although 'a product of fine art must be recognized to be art and not nature'[1] recognising it as art is recognising it as a work of genius.[2] Since genius is,

(1) a *talent* for producing that for which no definite rule can be given: and not an aptitude in the way of cleverness for what can be learned according to some rule; and that consequently *originality* must be its primary property.
(2) Since there may also be original nonsense, its products must at the same time be models, i.e. be *exemplary*; and, consequently, though not themselves derived from imitation, they must serve that purpose for others, i.e. as a standard or rule of estimating,[3]

genius is what 'gives the rule' to fine art.[4]

By contrast, what 'gives the rule' to 'mechanical art',[5] manufactured objects, is a concept. Such a concept articulates what the thing in question is to be, and its perfection. This is what Kant describes as 'the agreement of the manifold in a thing with an inner character belonging to it as its end . . .'[6] The production of such things is a matter of industry and learning.[7] It seems too, that it involves following a rule which can be set down in a formula which serves as a precept.[8]

In the case of fine art, genius and not the concept of 'fine art', articulates what the thing made is to be and its perfection. It is genius therefore which 'gives the rule of art', not by articulating a formula which functions as a rule, but by producing something which can function as a paradigm, an example of what a work of fine art is, which can be followed. Such examples serve the purpose of a standard or rule of judgement and models by reference to which others may 'put their talent to the test'.⁹ They supply both standards for judgement; and models for aspiring artists to follow and not merely to imitate.

What is it then for a work to be 'exemplary' in this way? Kant's answer to this question seems to contain three main considerations. First, the work must be an expression of aesthetic ideas. Secondly, it must be dependently beautiful. Thirdly, the work must render the ideas it expresses universally communicable. We must therefore look at each of these in turn.

For Kant, a worthwhile work of fine art is an intentionally produced beautiful thing which is expressive of aesthetic ideas, so we must ask: What is an aesthetic idea?

Kant's first step in explanation is given in terms of a comparison between aesthetic ideas and 'Rational ideas'. Both, as ideas, are contrasted with empirical concepts brought to bear upon experience in attaining perceptual knowledge. In perceptual knowledge a synthesis of intuitions is subsumed under an empirical concept and the synthesis is adequate to the concept and the concept is adequate to the synthesis. 'Rational ideas' (such as those of totality, God, free-will and virtue) are in contrast, concepts to which no syntheses of intuitions can be adequate. Rational ideas are 'indemonstrable concepts of Reason'. Aesthetic ideas are a kind of counterpart to Rational ideas in that they are syntheses of intuitions to which no concept can be adequate. In the case of Rational ideas concept outstrips experience, in the case of aesthetic ideas experience outstrips concept.

An aesthetic idea is a representation 'of the imagination which induces much thought, yet without the possibility of any definite thought whatever, that is *concept*, being adequate to it, and which language, consequently, can never get quite on level terms with or render completely intelligible'.¹⁰ Where Rational ideas are the indemonstrable concepts of Reason, aesthetic ideas are the inexponible representations of imagination.¹¹

Since in Kantian epistemology knowledge is possible only when concept coincides with synthesised intuition one cannot attain knowledge by applying either Rational or aesthetic ideas. Thus he maintains,

An *aesthetic idea* cannot become a cognition, because it is as an *intuition* (of the imagination) for which an adequate concept can never be found. A *rational idea* can never become a cognition, because it involves a *concept* (of the supersensible), for which a commensurate intuition can never be given.[12]

Kant's examples make it clear that he thinks that aesthetic ideas are typically expressed in symbolic uses of depictions (Jupiter's eagle with the lightning in its claws)[13] and in poetic figures of speech such as metaphor simile and personification. It would, however, be a mistake to think of these as the ideas, they rather express or 'furbish' the ideas. What Kant is concerned to stress is that such expressions invite and expand thought, 'animating the mind by opening out for it a prospect into a field of kindred representations stretching beyond its ken'.[14]

It is, I believe, no accident that Kant begins to speak in terms of sublimity here. There is, as I have indicated, a puzzle about the bearing of Kant's discussion of the sublime on his philosophy of art. This much is clear however, both experience of the Sublime and the entertaining of aesthetic ideas, by Kant's analysis, involve the experience of something which outstrips our conceptual powers.[15] It is to be borne in mind, however, that neither is thought by him to be paradigmatically aesthetic. Judgements upon the sublime are not 'pure'. They rest their inter-subjective validity upon communal moral feeling and the inter-subjectivity of Rational ideas;[16] and aesthetic ideas, whilst imparting 'soul' to fine art, simply entitle works to count as 'inspired' not 'fine' art;[17] only being also beautiful entitles them to count as 'fine'.

That aesthetic ideas are such that no concept can be adequate to them seems to be definitive of what Kant means by an aesthetic idea – he stresses 'cannot' rather than 'is not'. The importance he places upon that consideration is underlined by his emphasis upon the mind-expanding propensities of aesthetic ideas, and the affinity we have noted between what he says of them, and of our experience of the sublime in nature. Such considerations strongly suggest that he is theoretically committed to the view that the content of works of art and the meanings of figures of speech are of necessity non-paraphrasable in literal language. Is he so committed?

This question is far more difficult to answer than at first sight it would seem to be. Kant is, it is true, committed to the view that a paraphrase would not satisfy the role of an aesthetic idea in a work. The statement that 'Death is not final but a guarantee of the eternal return' will not satisfy the role of thoughts about the life cycle of the cicada in a funeral jade. The paraphrase by its very nature does not open up 'a field of kindred representations stretching beyond our ken'. However, that the function of the expression of an aesthetic idea is not satisfied by the paraphrase, does not decisively show that the paraphrase is incorrect; although it could be maintained that it does show that it is incomplete. What the cicada form suggests is a thought about death which the paraphrase asserts, and although that is not all the cicada form suggests, it is the focal part of what it suggests. There is nothing in Kant's theory which commits him to a denial of such paraphrases. In fact there are definite suggestions that he favours the view that there can be and are such paraphrases.[18]

However, there is something which is more important for understanding Kant's relation to the issue of a paraphrase, the fact that in his theory, aesthetic ideas cannot become knowledge.

Many contemporary writers, writing as they do after Croce had developed Kant's ideas in an entirely different way, of the non-paraphrasability of the cognitive content of works of art and poetic figures of speech, accept intuitive as well as conceptual forms of *knowledge*, and believe imagination can be an independent source of such knowledge. Kant's whole epistemology is a denial of the first of these beliefs and his handling of the imagination generally and specifically in relation to the arts implies rejection of the second. The major difference between the expression of the aesthetic ideas and the paraphrases for Kant, will therefore lie in the difference in propositional attitude. Such sentences as 'Death is not final but is a guarantee of the eternal return' are designed to *assert*. Unless we are told otherwise we take them to be in the assertive mode. The paraphrase therefore asserts the thought which the carving of the funeral jade invites us to entertain. It is, in Kantian theory, the thought and not its assertion which animates the mind and gives 'soul' to the sculpted cicada. The assertion of the thought constitutes a bit of transcendental metaphysics which is to be discouraged, since it is an attempt to apply concepts which are valid only within the bounds of our experience, outside these bounds.

Peirce, who was much influenced by Kant, said that iconic signs were in the problematic mode[19] and that does not seem to be a bad way of summing up the basic reason why Kant is committed to there being no paraphrase for the cognitive content of works of art or poetic figures of speech. This reason, however, is not in conflict with the tenet that no mysterious bit of non-discursive truth eludes us

when we try to capture it by discursive thought. Creative imagination for Kant, can be clarificatory, it can help to give expansion to a
concept; and being speculative, it can extend thought; but it cannot
give issue to self-validating truths.[20]

In relation to the contemporary dispute about paraphrasability as
with the contemporary dispute about 'the aesthetic attitude' Kant is
much more of a middle-of-the-road-man than he appears to be
when viewed through eyes accustomed to more recent theories
which import different presuppositions.

The way in which Kant treats of the relationship between Rational
ideas and aesthetic ideas tends to suggest that, in specifying that it is
aesthetic ideas that works of fine art are to express, Kant is
specifying a proper subject matter for works of art. He holds that,
although there are no syntheses of intuitions which instantiate
Rational ideas such as God, Hell, Eternity and so forth, imagination
can none the less 'body forth' such ideas to sense. It is said that Kant
was fond of Milton's poetry[21] so it does not take much by way of
interpretation to conjecture what he has in mind here. In *Paradise
Lost* we do, as it were, encounter just such creatures as these. When
an aesthetic idea bodies forth to sense a Rational idea, a synthesis of
intuitions to which no concept can be adequate is used to body forth
to sense a concept to which no intuition can be adequate. It is no
wonder that Kant describes this manoeuvre as 'straining after
something'.[22]

Although Kant is plainly fascinated by this function of aesthetic
ideas he does not, however, maintain that it is their only role. He
specifically mentions concepts other than Rational ideas which can
be 'bodied forth' to sense by aesthetic ideas. These are such notions
as death, envy, love and fame.[23] Unlike Rational ideas these
concepts are already instantiated in our experience but Kant
suggests such instantiations are in some way incomplete and that
their 'bodying forth' in poetry can be more complete than they are in
actual experience.[24] We can guess that what he means to contrast
here is the difference between experiences lived through, or
relationships and states of affairs observed, correctly categorised
and truly stated; and those which come fully home to us.

One can in our society illustrate the point forcefully in relation to
the first of his examples. Many of the institutionalised devices for
dealing with the disposal of dead bodies are designed to prevent the
bereaved from fully realising the full impact of the death of someone
close to them. It is part of the stock in trade of writers and film

makers to restore the full impact by interleaving aspects of the institutionalised devices with description of earthier facts. One can imagine that a bereaved person who had witnessed the death of someone, who had seen the laid-out body, the cremation and the funeral gathering, only fully grasping the finality of that death in reading a poem or short story, or witnessing a funeral scene in a play or film. Literary and dramatic exaggeration can, too, more clearly articulate mundane or inchoate experience – the look on the face of a depicted Judas or murderer, may enable one to recognise the look on the face of an erstwhile friend who has changed his allegiance; or the impression imparted to you as a pedestrian crossing a road by the postures and expressions of drivers behind the steering wheels of cars. There is no doubt that fine writing, painting and photography can and do body forth such things as these to sense 'with a completeness of which nature affords no parallel'.[25]

Noting this, however, does not completely dispel the belief that Kant is stipulating a special subject matter proper for aesthetic treatment, namely, imperfectly instantiated conceptions, endorsing the view for example, that whilst eternity and death are suitable for aesthetic presentation, plates[26] and ships[27] are not. Kant's development of his notion of an aesthetic idea as a correlate of a Rational idea draws him in that direction.

There is, however, another way in which he develops this notion, that in terms of a novel combination of intuitions, which leads to the conception of aesthetic ideas as providing not so much a special subject matter for fine art, but as a special mode of presentation of any subject matter whatever.[28] As well as being able to combine the data of perception in a way which processes it for the acquisition of perceptual knowledge, we are also able to combine it in novel ways which make the creation of aesthetic ideas possible.

In more technical language the job of combining or synthesising the data of sensation (intuitions) into an image or a representation, in Kant's epistemology, is done by the imagination, and imagination is involved both in acquiring perceptual knowledge and in the creation of the aesthetic ideas which 'give soul to', or inspire, works of art. In performing its role in perceptual knowledge, that is in 'the empirical employment of the imagination', it synthesises in a way which is governed by the laws of association and is hence called 'reproductive imagination'. Contrasted with this is imagination's activity in a synthesis which is not performed according to rules dependent upon the laws of association, one which gives the impression of being 'free' and which results in a new combination of intuitions. In this role it is called 'the productive imagination'. He describes it as 'a powerful agent for creating, as it were, a second nature out of the material supplied to it by actual nature'.[29]

The capacity to produce novel syntheses is, however, only a condition for the creation of aesthetic ideas. We can all, by virtue of possessing the cognitive faculty of the imagination[30] produce novel syntheses, for example we can think of a creature with the head of a fish and with human legs, we can think of a steam train as a kind of organ but that does not mean that these combinations are aesthetic ideas. It takes genius to create those. An 'aesthetic idea' as well as being a novel combination of intuitions must animate 'the mind by opening out for it a prospect into a field of kindred representations stretching beyond its ken'[31] and it must not be nonsense. Aesthetic ideas must be original, mind-stretching and followable.[32]

Kant thinks that when imagination is synthesising in the ordinary way it makes use of a thing's logical attributes, that is those of its attributes which satisfy what lies within the concept we apply to it, that is the attributes by reference to which it satisfies the concept ordinarily applied to it. These are, in the case of Jupiter's eagle with the lightning in its claws, those attributes in virtue of which we deem it to be an eagle, and in the case of Jupiter himself, those attributes in virtue of which we deem him to be majestic and powerful. These attributes Kant calls 'logical attributes'.[33] But there are also secondary representations of the imagination which he calls 'aesthetic attributes' and these can be used as a basis for synthesising not eagle with eagle, and god with god, but eagle with god, both of whom are majestic and powerful. The novel synthesis brings home the majesty and power of Jupiter not by reference to the logical attributes of Jupiter which make it true that he is majestic and powerful; but by reference to the 'aesthetic attributes' of eagles.

To take a case within the spirit of Kant's treatment, one could, if one believed the arguments to be conclusive, prove God's omniscience and avenging justice by *a priori* proofs or appeal to scripture. In speaking of God, one would then take oneself to be committed to his omniscience and avenging justice. In truly describing a state of affairs as a hawk surveying its territory from above and ready to strike, one is not necessarily committed to the belief that the hawk-eye watching is undetected, and that the hawk will strike unexpectedly. It is, however, these attributes, that of the unseen watcher from on high and the unpredictability of the strike, which permit the synthesising of hawk-eye and the eye-of-God which the Egyptian pattern of the eye of Horus expresses; and it is this which constitutes the aesthetic idea. The Egyptian pattern does not say God is omniscient and avenging; but it bodies forth to sense a prospect of representations connected with sharp sight and an unseen watcher from above, which might at any moment make itself felt, which can well be described as 'stretching beyond our ken'.

This example fits Kant's case of an aesthetic idea (the unseen watcher from the sky ready to strike) used to body forth a Rational idea (God's omniscience and vengeance) to sense, and it is that in Kant's theory, which suggests that he is implying a special subject matter proper to aesthetic presentation. I have been maintaining that the exposition of Kant's notion of an aesthetic idea in terms of a novel synthesis, points more towards a special manner of presentation than a special subject matter. How then can this be shown to hold in relation to the more humdrum concepts of the understanding contrasted as they must be with the ideas of Reason (Rational ideas)?

Because Kant's epistemology is as it is, and because in it there is no room for a radical distinction between intuitions had, and intuitions remembered,[34] Kant does not attend to the cases of ordinary conceptual knowledge of something not being currently experienced. To obtain knowledge, one must have intuition brought into accord with concept, but once one has had that, one can remember the knowledge obtained. In order to know that there are broad-leaved marigolds blooming in the garden of a certain house, in June, in the year 1979, one needs to have had certain intuitions synthesised by the imagination and brought under the concept 'broad-leaved marigold'. Once one has done that, however, one does not have to go on staring in order to maintain perceptual knowledge of the fact.

Knowing, in the absence of actually looking, smelling, etc. is however, being in the possession of concepts imperfectly 'bodied forth to sense'. This is of necessity so, because what Kant calls the 'logical attributes' of things (their defining characteristics, or those attributes in virtue of which deem them to fall under the concepts which we apply to them) are not the only attributes things have. It would not be an exaggeration to maintain that any given thing has an indefinitely large number of attributes which contrast forcibly with the more or less definite few made use of to assign it to a given class, or to apply a concept to it. Hence knowing, even on the basis of one's own experience, that there were broad-leaved marigolds blooming in a certain garden, in June in 1979, does very little towards bodying that knowledge forth to sense.

Now consider in this context Shakespeare's use of the 'aesthetic attributes' of both broad-leaved marigolds and eyes in his figure, 'The marigold which goes to bed with the Sun and with him rises weeping . . .'[35] What this novel synthesis does, amongst other things, is through the non-defining characteristics, of broad-leaved marigolds and eyes (both the flowers and the eyes tend to shut at night, and open in the morning; and both can accumulate moisture – drop of dew in the flower, tear in the eye) is to body forth the concept 'marigold' to sense; and that more completely than if Shakespeare had offered the simple bit of knowledge about broad-leaved marigolds, for example that the flowers close up at night and can accumulate dew in the mornings. Shakespeare's image opens up 'a prospect of a host of kindred representations stretching beyond our ken' and by doing so creates the impression of the fullness of the experience of currently looking at the marigolds, which is lost when the perceptual knowledge obtained in that experience is recorded and remembered. Shakespeare's synthesis creates the very freshness of the morning in which the flowers of broad-leaved marigolds open up.

Let me take one other case, a case used by Eisenstein to illustrate what it would be no misnomer to use Kant's expression 'bodying forth to sense' to describe in poetry and in film – a scene from Pushkin's *Poltava*. Eisenstein says,

> Here, for instance, is another scene from Pushkin's *Poltava*, in which the poet magically causes the image of a nocturnal flight to rise before the reader in all its picturesque and emotional possibilities:
>
> > But no one knew just how or when
> > She vanished. A lone fisherman
> > In that night heard the clack of horses' hoofs,
> > Cossack speech and a woman's whisper . . .
>
> Three shots:
>
> 1. Clack of horses' hoofs.
> 2. Cossack speech.
> 3. A woman's whisper.

Once more three objectively expressed representations (in sound!) come together in an emotionally expressed unifying image, distinct from the perception of the separate phenomena if encountered apart from their association with each other. The method is used solely for the purpose of evoking the necessary emotional experience in the reader. The emotional experience only, because the information that Marya has vanished has been given in a previous single line (*"She vanished. A lone fisherman"*). Having told the reader that she had vanished, the author wanted to give him the experience as well. To achieve this, he turns to montage. With three details selected from all the elements of flight, his image of nocturnal flight emerges into montage fashion, imparting the experience of the action to the senses.

To the three sound pictures he adds a fourth picture. It has the effect of a full stop. To attain this effect he chooses his fourth picture from another sense. This last 'close-up' is not in sound, but in sight.

> And eight horseshoes had left their traces
> Over the meadow morning dew . . .[36]

As the examples from Shakespeare and Pushkin show, Kant's notion of an 'aesthetic idea' developed as a certain kind of novel synthesis is compatible with the view that there is no special subject matter proper to aesthetics but makes it possible for any subject matter to be expressed as aesthetic ideas.

Whilst an aesthetic idea is for Kant a novel synthesis of intuitions which body forth concepts to sense, the role of aesthetic ideas in works of art is to extend the mind in thought. An aesthetic idea 'includes much thought, yet without the possibility of any definite thought whatever;'[37] it gives 'unbounded expansion to the concept itself . . . towards an extension of thought . . .',[38] it 'gives the imagination an incentive to spread its flight over a whole host of kindred representations that provoke more thought than admits of expression in a concept determined by words'.[39]

If we think of a work of art as comprised of a vehicle whose virtue is to be beautiful, and a tenor consisting of aesthetic ideas then, there is, I believe, an analogy in Kant's thinking between the way in which the beauty of the vehicle extends our perceptual powers by giving harmonious free play to our cognitive powers and the extension of thought induced by the tenor. In a thoroughly worthwhile work of art, a work fit to function as an exemplar of fine art, the vehicle makes demands upon our perceptual powers whilst the tenor makes comparable demands upon our intellectual powers.

The difference between a work of art which satisfies taste but is not worthwhile and one which is thoroughly worthwhile is that the first lacks what the second has, namely 'soul'.

> Soul (*Geist*) in an aesthetic sense, signifies the animating principle in the mind. But that whereby this principle animates the psychic substance (*Seele*) – the material which it employs for that purpose – is that which sets the mental powers into a swing that is final, i.e. into a play which is self-maintaining and which strengthens those powers for such activity.[40]

What the work of art expresses – the aesthetic ideas, and that it expresses them, makes all the difference between the vehicle being a dead and a living thing.

Neither at the level of subject matter – what the work expresses – nor at the level of the role of what is expressed in relation to the work as a whole, does Kant think of the aim of the exercise, that is creating a work of art, as being that of imparting knowledge. Knowledge is a matter of intuition being adequate to concept and concept adequate to intuition. The exercise of expressing aesthetic ideas is worthwhile in its own right, 'the mental powers are set into a swing that is final', but it also quickens the cognitive powers in such a way that if you are going to talk about an aim or an end or a proper function[41] it will be in terms of animating the mind and, indirectly, the culture of our mental powers. He says,

> Fine art . . . is a mode of representation which is intrinsically final, and which, although devoid of an end, has the effect of advancing the culture of the mental powers in the interests of social communication.[42]

On the other hand it ought to be transparently clear, that in so far as Kant puts forward a non-cognitive account of fine art it is non-cognitive only in his very special sense. What works of art express are ideas – not feelings or emotions. These ideas do not amount to knowledge in more familiar terminology, they are cognitive but not cognitions which are true.

Because the aesthetic ideas do not present us with truths Kant cannot plausibly be read as treating works of fine art as a substitute for a true transcendental metaphysic.

It is true that he puts forward a somewhat opaque account about the relation which sometimes holds between aesthetic ideas and Rational ideas that is that aesthetic ideas may body Rational ideas forth to sense, but he stresses that the function of this relationship is solely that of animating the mind not of advancing knowledge.[43] He does say too,

> Now, since the imagination, in its employment on behalf of cognition, is subjected to the constraint of the understanding and the restriction of having to be conformable to the concept belonging thereto, whereas aesthetically it is free to furnish of its own accord, over and above that agreement with the concept, a wealth of undeveloped material for the understanding, to which the latter paid no regard in its concept, but which it can make use of, not so much objectively for cognition, as subjectively for quickening the cognitive faculties, and hence also indirectly for cognitions . . .[44]

I think it is plain that Kant's emphasis is upon the proper use for the quickening of our cognitive powers with the indirect effect of their culture.[45]

There therefore seems to be to be little excuse for interpreting Kant to be saying that expressions of aesthetic ideas impart knowledge of any sort; and hence, little excuse for believing that he thought of works of art as providing any sort of a substitute for transcendental metaphysics. He is at much pains to distinguish 'inducing much thought' from imparting knowledge.

13

Exemplars of Fine Art and Taste

AN EXEMPLARY WORK IS ONE WHICH IS DEPENDENTLY BEAUTIFUL

The second condition of a work of fine art being an exemplar is that it should be beautiful. Kant does not explicitly say that this beauty is dependent and not free beauty; but that appears to be a direct consequence of what he does say. Something has 'dependent' rather than 'free' beauty, when what that thing is intended to be, and its perfection, enter into the judgement of its beauty. Since Kant explicitly states that they do so in the case of fine art, it seems to follow that the beauty of fine art is dependent beauty. Kant says,

> since the agreement of the manifold in a thing with an inner character belonging to it as its end constitutes the perfection of the thing, it follows that in estimating beauty of art the perfection of the thing must be also taken into account – a matter which in estimating a beauty of nature, as beautiful, is quite irrelevant.[1]

In the paragraph which follows this quotation he goes on to speak of 'dependent' beauty using substantially the same examples of dependent beauty in nature as he did when he introduced the distinction between 'free' and 'dependent' beauty.[2] It is natural to interpret this paragraph as unequivocally asserting that beauty of art counts as 'dependent' for Kant in just the same sense that the beauty of a horse or a handsome woman does. Such interpretation, I believe, conceals a contrast which may explain why Kant is so hesitant about pronouncing the beauty of art to be 'dependent' rather than 'free'.

The contrast is between the implications of taking note of perfection as well as beauty in the case of fine art, and in the case of nature. He seems to imply that taking note of perfection in the case of a natural object results in an aesthetic judgement which is not 'pure' but in the case of works of fine art it does not. What background assumptions can he bring to bear to underpin this implication?

The quick assimilation of the case of fine art and natural organisms in fact infringes one of the distinctions which Kant believes it to be essential to draw, that between 'objective' as opposed to 'subjective' finality. The opening discussions of the *Critique of Teleological Judgement* drive home this message. Whereas in the *Analytic of the Beautiful* the Form of Finality is analysed as, intrinsic, apparent, subjective finality, in the *Analytic of Teleological Judgement*, only organisms emerge as having intrinsic objective finality.[3] Utility and adaptability of the things of nature also count as being objectively final; but that finality is said to be both external and relative.

It is therefore possible, to read the paragraph in question as *contrasting* taking note of the perfection of fine art in relation to beauty, and taking note of perfection in relation to beauty in the case of natural objects because both the Form of Finality, which determines which objects have 'free' beauty, and the perfection of fine art are, in Kant's terminology, varieties of finalities which are 'subjective'.

The basic objection to this interpretation is that in the Third Moment of the *Analytic of the Beautiful*, the dependent beauty of churches, palaces and summer-houses are treated in exactly the same way as that of horses and humans. The account of what genius is, has, however, been developed between these two sections, and it could be argued that as Kant is now stressing the differences between the useful and the fine arts, that he is drawing distinctions between the cases he was treating as comparable in the Third Moment. There, he was stressing the difference between subjective, external finality and objective internal finality, the utility of man-made objects and the final ends of organisms. Here, in Section 48, he is stressing the likeness between apparent subjective internal finality, that is the Form of Finality in nature, and real subjective internal finality, that is what a creative artist makes intentionally, but without ulterior purpose.

However, we read this somewhat ambiguous paragraph, the upshot seems to be that Kant implies, and never retracts, the implication that the beauty of fine art is a kind of dependent beauty.

It is therefore necessary to work out what dependent beauty is in the case of fine art. In general, free beauty is universal and necessary pleasure in the perceptual form of a thing, irrespective of what that thing is taken to be. Natural beauty, when free, 'is only ascribed to the objects in respect of reflection upon the *external*[4] intuition of them and, therefore, only on account of their superficial form'.[5] Pleasure in the perfection of a thing is pleasure in its conceptual form, its inner structure rather than in its external appearance. Intrinsic natural perfection is possessed by things which are only possible because their parts are put together in the way they are.[6] When a thing is not a natural object but an artefact, such parts and such form are due to the conception that its maker had of it in the making of it,

> For the thing is itself an end, and is, therefore, comprehended under a conception or an idea that must determine *a priori* all that is to be contained in it. But so far as the possibility of a thing is only thought in this way, it is simply a work of art. It is the product, in other words, of an intelligent cause, distinct from the matter, or parts, of the thing, and of one whose causality, in bringing together and combining the parts, is determined by its idea of a whole made possible through that idea, and consequently, not by external nature.[7]

However, in both the case of a natural thing and an artefact,

> the delight in the manifold of a thing, in reference to the internal end that determines its possibility, is a delight based on a concept, whereas delight in the beautiful is such as does not presuppose any concept . . .[8]

Pleasure in the dependent beauty of a thing will therefore be universal and necessary pleasure in the answering of the form of a thing's external appearance to pleasure in its inner structure; of perceptual form answering to conceptual form. Hence the tattooed face,[9] whilst freely beautiful, does not answer to the perfection of a human face. Those looks do not answer to what a human face should be.

The case is even more complicated when it is a question of external appearance answering to inner character. Thus,

> The visible expression of moral ideas that govern men inwardly can, of course, only be drawn from experience; but their combina-

tion with all that our reason connects with the morally good in the idea of the highest finality – benevolence, purity, strength, or equanimity, &c. – may be made, as it were, visible in bodily manifestation (as effect of what is internal), and this embodiment involves a union of pure ideas of reason and great imaginative power, in one who would even form an estimate of it, not to speak of being the author of its presentation.[10]

Beauty of visage answering to inner moral perfection is what Bosanquet would call 'the difficult in beauty';[11] difficult as opposed to easy, 'formal', beauty.

In the case of an artefact, perceptual form has to answer to the inner structure of the thing which has been imparted to it by its maker according to his conception of it, that is of what it is, in Kant's language, 'to be'. When such an object is dependently beautiful its pleasing superficial form must answer to perfect inner structure.

In general:

> perfection neither gains by beauty, nor beauty by perfection. The truth is rather this, when we compare the representation through which an object is given to us with the Object (in respect of what it is meant to be) by means of a concept, we cannot help reviewing it also in respect of the sensation in the Subject. Hence there results a gain to the *entire faculty* of our representative power when harmony prevails between both states of mind.[12]

Pleasure in dependent beauty is therefore a combination of intellectual and aesthetic pleasure.[13] Because intellectual delight here is delight in the conceptual form of the thing, it is also delight in the good of a thing after its kind. Delight in the perfection of a thing is delight in 'the good, namely, of the manifold of the thing itself according to its end'.[14] Pleasure in dependent beauty therefore also combines aesthetic pleasure and pleasure in the good (of a kind).

Kant's examples of a church, of a tatooed face, and of a stern-faced soldier,[15] make his position clear.

It is to be noted that such a position implies that nothing can be dependently beautiful which is not, considered apart from the conception of perfection of such an object, freely beautiful. On the other hand, something which might otherwise be freely beautiful may not be dependently beautiful, given that its perceptual form does not answer to its conceptual form, its beauty to its perfection.

Many possible superficial perceptual forms which universally and necessarily please will not, when brought into relation with the inner structure of a thing, 'answer to it'. Think here, for example, of many of the early models of sewing machines. Their superficial forms did not 'answer to' their inner structure and yet they can, or at least parts of them can, turn up as 'art objects' or rudimentary sculptures.

Now, how are we to explicate dependent beauty in the special case of works of fine art? How are we to think of the perfection of a work to which its superficial form must answer if it is to be dependently beautiful?

We have seen that, in an artefact, the form is due to the conception which its maker had in the making of it. The possibility of an artefact depends upon a conception or idea which determines what it is to be. We have seen too, that in the case of fine art, that idea or conception is not a concept of what the particular thing to be made as a definite thing[16] is to be. 'Fine art' unlike 'industrial art' where the concept of its maker does give the rule to art, is the art of genius. Genius gives the rule to art by creating exemplars, creating that is, not only expressions of aesthetic ideas but expressions which are universally communicable. Hence works of art judged as perfect are works where that which expresses the aesthetic ideas, the vehicle, is a universally communicable expression of the ideas which constitute its tenor.

The vehicle, which is a conjoint of the matter and the form of sensation is beautiful in so far as the form is such that it sets the cognitive powers, imagination and understanding in harmonious free play. The aesthetic ideas are a free play of thought. Because the beauty of art is dependent beauty, the beauty of the work must answer to its perfection. The form which gives free play to the cognitive powers must 'answer to' the work as the universally communicable expression of aesthetic ideas.

Let us consider cicadas. Plato puts into the mouth of Socrates in the *Phaedrus* the following myth:

Once upon a time these creatures were men – men of an age before there were any Muses – and that when the latter came into the world, and music made its appearance, some of the people of those days were so thrilled with pleasure that they went on singing, and quite forgot to eat and drink until they actually died without noticing it. From them in due course sprang the race of cicadas, to which the Muses have granted the boon of needing no sustenance right from their birth, but of singing from the very first, without food or drink, until the day of their death, after which they go and report to the Muses how they severally are paid honor among mankind, and by whom.[17]

Now, contrast this set of ideas with those connected with the use of a cicada form, sculpted in jade, as an expression of the ideas connected with death and cyclic existence which can be thought of as 'the eternal return'. If one had to body forth to sense this myth, the perceptual form which would 'answer to' its expression would need to be of an entirely different kind from that of a funeral jade. The funeral jade is of a quiescent cicada-form, richly sombre. This myth requires instead a form quiveringly active and a material evocative of song, for example rock-crystal.

However, if this is the way in which to construe Kant's views, it contains a problem. To see perfection and beauty as 'answering to' each other, even if we concede the figurative nature of the expression, what 'answers to' something else must be distinct from it. One bird-cry, for example, answers to another. In the case of a work of art, the vehicle which is a conjoint of the matter and form of sensation, expresses and makes the aesthetic ideas universally communicable; and it is the very same vehicle which is beautiful. What 'answers' by way of perfection to beauty then, is the same object construed in different ways – as universally communicable of aesthetic ideas; and as beautiful. Using our example from Chapter 11, it is the same piece of carved jade which is a universally communicable expression of the play of thoughts about the eternal return, and which has been given a perceptual form which sets the cognitive powers into harmonious free play. Hence what answers to what, must be spelt out, not in terms of different entities such as one bird-cry answering to another, but one aspect of the same thing answering to another. The work as beautiful answering to the work as expressive of aesthetic ideas. Although not such a straightforward conception of 'answering to' as the conception of one bird song answering to another, one can still see how these two can answer to each other. The quiescent cicada-form in the richly sombre material of the jade can answer to the novel synthesis of human death with the life-cycle of the cicada expressed by it. Similarly, the sound patterns and verse form of 'The marigold which goes to bed with the sun, and with him rises weeping . . .' can answer to the novel synthesis of human eyes and marigolds which the poem expresses.

In the same way too the coal-like glow of lights and brights within the black-velvet texture of the darks and the crowding of the forms of the depicted people in the group constituting Goya's *Witches' Sabbath* answers to the novel synthesis of religious gathering and a gathering being addressed by the Great Goat. Toppling forms caught in the wider balance of the positions of the dance in *Disparate Alegre*[18] at once express 'merry folly', and as perceptual form set the imagination and understanding into harmonious free play: and the perceptual form answers to expression of aesthetic ideas.

In Chapter 2, we considered ways in which Kant might be able to answer Nelson Goodman's claims concerning the 'problem of the ugly'. We can now add a final consideration.

If the beauty of fine art, is for Kant, dependent beauty, then it is not at all surprising that the beauty of, for example, Monet's *Waterlilies*, can be contrasted with that of Goya's *Witches' Sabbath*. Since Kant grants that the tattooed pattern on a human face may be (freely) beautiful and yet dependently not beautiful, so he can argue that such patterns as those of Monet's *Waterlilies* are freely beautiful and dependently beautiful too in that they answer to Monet's aesthetic ideas, but yet they are entirely unsuited to the aesthetic ideas expressed by Goya's *Witches' Sabbath*, or his *Disparates*.

AN EXEMPLARY WORK IS ONE WHICH UNIVERSALLY COMMUNICATES AESTHETIC IDEAS BY BEING DEPENDENTLY BEAUTIFUL

Just as Kant believes that natural objects, in order to be beautiful, must not only give pleasure but must give pleasure which is universally communicable, so he also believes that, for a work to be an exemplar of fine art, it must not only express aesthetic ideas but must also render them universally communicable.

For Kant, a work which does not express aesthetic ideas is without 'soul'[19] Having 'soul' is, however, not enough,[20] it must also be dependently beautiful. These two conditions are still not sufficient for a work of fine art to be exemplary. In addition the work must render the aesthetic ideas which it expresses universally communicable.[21] As with the communicability of pleasure so with the communicability of aesthetic ideas, Kant does not maintain that *everyone will* grasp the aesthetic ideas, he asserts the expression of the aesthetic ideas must be such that *everyone can* grasp them by coming directly into contact with the work. So much is clear.

What is not so clear, however, is the way in which Kant believes rendering the expression of aesthetic ideas universally communicable is to be effected. For instance, there seems some doubt in Kant's mind as to whether it is the free productive faculty of genius or the orderly critical capacity of taste which he bills for the task of rendering the aesthetic ideas universally communicable.

In his most definitive statement about what genius is,[22] he not only takes 'soul' to include the universally communicable expression of the aesthetic ideas rather than the condition that the work must express aesthetic ideas, an inclusion which does not seem to be necessarily implied by his first account of what soul is,[23] he definitely attributes the work of rendering the aesthetic ideas universally communicable to genius.

However, in an earlier passage, he seems to attribute the same task to taste. In that passage he says:

So much for the beautiful representation of an object, which is properly only the form of the presentation of a concept, and the means by which the latter is universally communicated. To give this form, however, to the product of fine art, taste merely is required. By this the artist, having practised and corrected his taste by a variety of examples from nature or art, controls his work and, after many, and often laborious, attempts to satisfy taste, finds the form which commends itself to him. Hence this form is not, as it were, a matter of inspiration, or of a free swing of the mental powers, but rather of a slow and even painful process of improvement, directed to making the form adequate to his thought without prejudice to the freedom in the play of those powers.[24]

The opposition between the two passages can be partially accounted for by noting that throughout the whole discussion of fine art Kant has two uses of 'genius' in play. Sometimes he gives this term a wider use where it includes all that is necessary to make an exemplar of fine art 'possible'.[25] In this wider use 'genius' includes 'taste'. Sometimes he uses the term more narrowly to draw a contrast between one condition of a work's being an exemplar and another. In this narrower use 'genius' contrasts with 'taste'.

According to this use it is 'genius' which gives 'soul' to works and entitles us to call them 'original' and 'inspired';[26] whereas 'taste' prevents works in which aesthetic ideas are expressed from degenerating into nonsense[27] and entitles us to call them 'fine art'.

If then, Kant is thinking in terms of the wider meaning of 'genius' in the first of these passages above, and it does seem from the context that he is, there is a way of understanding the two passages which makes them compatible. We are thus able to solve the puzzle and come down upon the side of attributing the task of rendering the aesthetic ideas universally communicable to taste and not to 'genius' taken in the narrower sense.

Now, although this interpretation seems to be substantially correct, Kant's settled thought is that it is taste and not 'genius' in the narrow sense which is responsible for rendering the aesthetic ideas universally communicable; it is none the less too facile. In addition to the requirement that a work must be expressive of aesthetic ideas to function as an exemplar, there are two other requirements, not just one. A work must in addition to expressing aesthetic ideas render them universally communicable; and it must be dependently beautiful. A 'presentation'[28] (what I have been calling 'the vehicle' of a work) must have a perceptual form which sets the perceptual powers into a free play which is final and this form must 'answer to' the aesthetic ideas which constitute a play of thoughts which it expresses.

Moreover, there are unresolved puzzles about the two quotations. The description given in the first quotation of the process of finding a universally communicable expression for the aesthetic ideas as 'hitting upon an expression', hardly seems to be a description of the same process as the one which is described as the 'slow and even painful' process of the second quotation. The overall ambiguity of Kant's position remains. What are we to make of the matter?

It is possible to read him as saying that genius in the narrower sense, creates aesthetic ideas and 'hits upon an expression' for them, and that expression only renders the ideas universally communicable after it has been worked upon by taste. This is to allow that the two opposed descriptions from our two quotations describe different processes. Even so, we are still confronted with the fact that the 'slow and even painful process' seems to pick out something which is doing double duty in the theory. That process has to impart the Form of Finality to the presentation (i.e. the vehicle) and make it universally communicable of the aesthetic ideas. In his discussion of fine art Kant seems to stress the role of taste in making aesthetic ideas intelligible, but what we carry forward from the Introduction to the *Critique of Judgement* and the *Analytic of the Beautiful* is taste as that by which we discern the beautiful.

In the first of the above trains of thought we find him saying:

> Genius can do no more than furnish rich *material* for products of fine art; its elaboration and its *form* require a talent academically trained, so that it may be employed in such a way as to stand the test of judgement.[29]

He also says:

> Now, imagination rather entitles an art to be called an *inspired* (*geistreiche*) than a *fine* art. It is only in respect of judgement that the name of fine art is deserved. Hence it follows that judgement, being the indispensable condition (*conditio sine qua non*), is at least what one must look to as of capital importance in forming an estimate of art as fine art. So far as beauty is concerned, to be fertile and original in ideas is not such an imperative requirement as it is that the imagination in its freedom should be in accordance with the understanding's conformity to law. For in lawless freedom imagination, with all its wealth, produces nothing but nonsense; the power of judgement, on the other hand, is the faculty that makes it consonant with understanding.
>
> Taste, like judgement in general, is the discipline (or corrective) of genius. It severely clips its wings, and makes it orderly or polished; but at the same time it gives it guidance, directing and controlling its flight, so that it may preserve its character of finality. It introduces a clearness and order into the plenitude of thought, and in so doing gives stability to the ideas, and qualifies them at once for permanent and universal approval, for being followed by others, and for a continually progressive culture.[30]

When we compare such statements with his earlier definitions of taste the emphasis is very different. Consider:

> When the form of an object (as opposed to the matter of its representation, as sensation) is, in the mere act of reflecting upon

it, without regard to any concept to be obtained from it, estimated
as the ground of a pleasure in the representation of such an
Object, then this pleasure is also judged to be combined necessarily with the representation of it, and so not merely for the
Subject apprehending this form, but for all in general who pass
judgement. The object is then called beautiful; and the faculty of
judging by means of such a pleasure (and so also with universal
validity) is called taste.[31]

When we carry forward into the context of Kant's discussion of
fine art such accounts of what taste is; and bring them into relation
with the activity of taste as it is described in the second of the two
passages which are currently concerning us, and with which they
appear to agree; we are left wondering how the role of taste seen as
rendering the aesthetic ideas universally communicable, and its role
in ascertaining that the Form of Finality is imparted to 'the
presentation of the concept', connect with one another.

However, if we bring into the picture the fact that beauty of fine
art is a kind of dependent beauty and read our second quotation as
description of what it is for taste to impart dependent beauty to the
vehicle of art we can give some sort of reconstruction as to why it is
that Kant talks almost as if only the one operation, that of rendering
the aesthetic ideas universally communicable, were involved. We
can understand him to be saying that it is by rendering the vehicle
(or 'presentation') of the work of art *dependently* beautiful that taste
makes the aesthetic ideas universally communicable.

Kant's full story of what is involved in a work of fine art will
therefore be that an artist creates is 'a presentation' to sense which is
given not only a form which sets the perceptual powers into
harmonious free play; but which also 'answers to' its role as being
expressive of aesthetic ideas. The more a play of perceptual powers
'answers to' a play of thought, the more universally communicable
does the play of thought become. Or, to put it in the language of
synthesis: a synthesis of intuitions of sense is brought into relation
to the novel synthesis of the productive imagination whereby the
aesthetic ideas are created; and by the one 'answering to' the other,
it becomes the universally communicable expression for it. So
understood Kant's account of fine art is a true ancestor of Hegel's art
as the spiritual in sensuous form.

Any mystery which surrounds Kant's view about how the
aesthetic ideas are rendered universally communicable does not,

however, extend to the fact that he believes that in order to be an exemplar of fine art the vehicle of the work must be such that it renders the aesthetic ideas which it expresses universally communicable. An exemplar of fine art must express aesthetic ideas, and hence be original. It must also be dependently beautiful and hence manifest taste. It must also render the aesthetic ideas expressed by the work universally communicable. This too seems to constitute a manifestation of taste. I have been canvassing an interpretation of Kant's views which takes him to maintain that the last of these three conditions is satisfied by satisfying the second. If this interpretation be false it still is true that in order for a work to function as an exemplar or a model of fine art, to serve instead of a concept of what the product of fine art is to be, and instead of a formula according to which works of fine art can be constructed, Kant believes that the three conditions set out above must be satisfied. The articulation of what is contained in those three conditions completes the major tenets of Kant's philosophy of art.

14

The Strengths of Kant's Philosophy of Art

Whereas Kant's account of beauty in nature is to be compared with formalist theories of beauty such as those advanced by Plato in *Philebus* and Hogarth in the *Analysis of Beauty*, Kant's philosophy of art is best compared with expressionist theories of art such as the theories of Croce and Collingwood. It therefore enhances one's conception of the strengths of Kant's position to see how his theory fares when confronted with the difficulties and objections which affect their theories. Since Collingwood's is the more fully worked out theory of the two I address my discussion mainly to Collingwood.

For Collingwood exercising creative imagination is not merely a necessary condition for the creation of works of art, it is also sufficient. As creative imagination is roughly equivalent to 'genius' in Kant's narrower sense of 'genius'; we can say that, what Kant takes as merely necessary for something to be a work of art, that it shall bear the mark of genius, Collingwood takes to be sufficient. The creation of an imaginary experience of total activity which expresses our emotions is the creation of a work of art.[1] Thus his wholehearted emphasis on creative imagination leads Collingwood to contend that not only what is expressed by a work of art in the artist's head but so too is that which expresses it. The public object which is a mere externalisation of the real work is called a 'work of art' by courtesy title only. Techniques of artistic production pertain to the externalisations not to works of art properly so-called. The artist manifests creative imagination in creating the work in his own head.[2] There are no techniques for creative imagination.[3]

Kant's account of fine art makes creative imagination ('genius' in his narrow use of that term) necessary but not sufficient for the production of worthwhile works of art, which he thinks of as exemplars or models of fine art. Kant also assumes that the more intuitively obvious view of what a work of art is, and where it is, is correct. He locates the work of art in the public world. His account is not therefore vulnerable to the major objections which can be brought against Collingwood's theory.

As Wollheim points out, the two main objections to the Croce–Collingwood theory are that it severs the link between the artist and his audience and that it totally ignores the significance of the medium.[4] There is nothing in the Croce–Collingwood theory to show why, if administering a specific dosage of a certain drug should be found to induce the having of the required imaginative experience of total activity which expresses the feelings and emotions which the artist experienced when he created 'the work', we should not substitute that dosage of the drug for, for example, listening to Mozart's *Quintet for Clarinet and Strings*, or even, prefer taking the drug to listening to the 'noises'[5] that is to the *Quintet* which, on the Croce–Collingwood theory merely constitute the externalisation of the work. Similarly, there is no reason which we can draw from the Croce–Collingwood theory, which prevents literally the same 'imaginative experience of total activity' being 're-constructed' from externalisations in entirely different sensory modes, for example from a painting and a piece of music.

In accepting the more intuitively obvious account of what a work of art is, Kant is also in a position to justify his insistence upon the importance of 'form' in fine art. Collingwood voices direct opposition to Kant's insistence upon this, when he maintains that because, strictly speaking, works of art are imagined, not heard or seen, perceptual form is unimportant in the arts. Collingwood says:

> Music does not consist of heard noises, paintings do not consist of seen colours, and so forth. Of what, then, do these things consist? Not, clearly of a 'form', understood as a pattern or system of relations between the various noises we hear or the various colours we see. Such 'forms' are nothing but perceived structures of 'bodily works of art', that is to say, 'works of art' falsely so-called; and these formalistic theories of art, popular though they have been and are, have no relevance to art proper and will not be further considered in this book. The distinction between form and matter, on which they are based, is a distinction belonging to the philosophy of craft, and not applicable to the philosophy of art.[6]

Since Kant holds that the 'bodily work of art' is the work of art, and that it is that and not something in the artist's head which expresses the aesthetic ideas, he is perfectly entitled to lay stresses upon the importance of perceptual form. Nor is he open to the criticisms which Collingwood launches against those who distinguish between form and matter; or what, in Collingwood's opinion is worse, between form and content. Collingwood maintains:

> When people have spoken of matter and form in connexion with art, or that strange hybrid distinction, form and content, they have in fact been doing one of two things, or both confusedly at once. Either they have been assimilating art to an artifact, and the artist's work to a craftsman's; or else they have been using terms in a vaguely metaphorical way as a means of referring to distinctions which really do exist in art, but are of a different kind. There is always in art a distinction between what is expressed and that which expresses it; there is a distinction between the initial impulse to write or paint or compose and the finished poem or picture or music; there is a distinction between an emotional element in the artist's experience and what may be called an intellectual element. All these deserve investigation but none of them is a case of the distinction between form and matter.[7]

Kant does not assimilate the artist's work to that of a craftsman.[8] Even if he sometimes fails to make full use of it, he has at his disposal what Collingwood lacks, the distinction between an external end, or use, of something; and its internal end or perfection.[9] He also draws the distinction between subjective and objective ends.[10] He therefore has the theoretical equipment to speak of human makers making things for subjective ends which are either intrinsic or external. Fine art is for Kant, 'a mode of representation which is intrinsically final'.[11] It must be that, since the notions in terms of which he unpacks 'fine art', 'genius', and 'taste', involve reference to a play of thoughts (the aesthetic ideas) which is intrinsically final; and to the Form of Finality which is defined as subjective internal finality. Within the terms of his own account of art he is in a position to argue just as forcibly as Collingwood does, and more cogently, against the pseudo-arts which Collingwood describes as 'magical' and 'amusement' arts. These, for Kant, would not constitute 'fine' art since they are not intrinsically, but only extrinsically, final; and they would have to be made according to a formulable rule which would determine in advance what they were to be.

Kant too has at his disposal another distinction which permits him to draw a contrast which Collingwood's theory is ill-equipped to handle, the contrast between man-made objects which are genuinely crafted and manufactured items which are the result of rule-following activities according to an articulated formula. This distinction is the distinction between 'science' and 'art' (that is what Kant calls 'art in general' – not 'fine art'). His test for determining where 'art' as distinct from 'science' is involved, is whether the most complete knowledge of what the thing is to be yields there and then the skill to do something, and where it does not. He says:

> To art that alone belongs for which the possession of the most complete knowledge does not involve one's having then and there the skill to do it.[12]

And again:

> what one *can* do the moment one only *knows* what is to be done, hence without anything more than sufficient knowledge of the desired result, is not called art.[13]

The example of 'art' which Kant mentions in this context is shoe-making. To this he adds the following footnote:

> Where I come from if you set a common man a problem such as Columbus and his egg – he is wont to reply: 'This is not a matter of art, only of knowledge', i.e. If you know the answer you can do it; he would say the same of all the so-called arts of the card-trickster. But he had no resistance at all towards calling tightrope-dancing an art.[14]

It is important to see that, as well as opposing doing and knowing, Kant rightly spells out the difference between doing which involves skill, and doing which does not. He does not make the mistake of thinking that those arts which he describes as 'mechanical', and whose products he dubs 'handicraft', in contrast with free fine art, are unskilled. Production line activities involved in manufacturing machine-made shoes would not, within his theory, count as 'arts' at all.

Collingwood, to the impoverishment of both his philosophy of art, and his philosophy of craft, maintains that artefacts, or 'bodily works of art' if these are thought of as works of art proper, can only be designed as means to external ends, for example to amuse an audience or to achieve a propagandist end. That, together with his almost total reduction of the notion of skill to a form of *knowing that*, that is knowing that doing this is the means to some desired end, makes his theory quite unfitted to draw the distinction between a genuinely crafted object, for example a hand-made shoe and a machine-made one. Technique for Collingwood, is always just a matter of knowing the means to some external end.[15]

Collingwood's cobblers, carpenters, weavers and smiths are no 'craftsmen'; and how odd their ends are! He says:

> The cobbler or carpenter or weaver is not simply trying to produce shoes or carts or cloth. He produces them because there is a demand for them; that is they are not ends for him, but means to the end of satisfying a specific demand. What he is really aiming at is the production of a certain state of mind in his customers, the state of having these demands satisfied.[16]

In the same vein he says:

> a horseshoe is a means to a certain state of mind in the man whose horse is shod.[17]

This failure to grasp the importance of skill and not mere knowledge of means to external ends to the crafts, is of course all of one piece with Collingwood's general contempt for technique. The artist needs no technique because *all* the artistic work is done 'in his head'.[18]

Kant is therefore clearly in better control of the distinction between the artist's work and that of a craftsman than Collingwood is. In distinguishing between form and matter and form and content in fine art, he is not therefore failing to make one of the distinctions which Collingwood holds to be at the basis of such a mistaken point of view.

It is also absolutely clear that Kant does not use 'form' and 'matter' in a vaguely metaphorical way, to refer to the difference between what is expressed, and that which expresses or is expressive of it, in a work of art. 'Form' and 'matter' are for Kant, the form and matter of sensation.[19] He uses the distinction to oppose perceptual form to the perceptual items which are configured in that form. *Both* pertain to what Collingwood calls, 'works of art falsely so-called'. Form for Kant is indeed the 'perceived structure of the bodily work of art'.[20] That which expresses and that which is expressed is, in Kant's theory, the whole complex of 'the presentation' or vehicle, which is both the matter and the form of sensation on the one hand; and the aesthetic ideas on the other.[21] There is a perfectly sensible use to which the 'content' of a work of art can be spoken of in relation to Kantian theory; but even if he did speak of the 'aesthetic ideas' as 'the content' of works of fine art, he could not be accused of making use of that 'hybrid distinction' to which Collingwood refers. 'Form' for Kant is the form and not the matter of sensation, not the form of the 'aesthetic ideas' which constitute 'the content' of works of fine art.

In the Introduction of this work I used the terminology which I. A. Richards invented to talk about two constituents of metaphors, the 'vehicle' and the 'tenor' to clarify Kant's analysis of two different constituents of works of fine art. I have continued to apply this terminology to Kant's account of fine art throughout this book. It ought to be evident from the above discussion of his views in relation to the contentions under attack by Collingwood, why such terminology is necessary. It is important not only for the distinctions it permits one to draw, but also because I. A. Richards uses his terminology as applied to metaphors, to argue that the meaning of a metaphor is due to the interaction of the vehicle with the tenor; and that too seems to me to be true of anything which could be thought of as 'the meaning' of a work of fine art as Kant construes it.

Kant's philosophy of art considered as an expressionist theory can withstand the criticisms to which Collingwood's theory falls; and it does not do so by infringing the distinctions which Collingwood maintains must be infringed by theories such as his. Kant's theory, unlike that of Collingwood, does not sever the link between the artist and his audience; nor does it totally ignore the importance of the medium. Although Kant shows very little interest in the medium his theory leaves a great deal of scope for both the importance of the medium, and of technique in manipulating it, to be incorporated.

On my interpretation of Kant, the successful artist has to impart to the vehicle of a work of art a perceptual form which sets the perceptual powers, imagination and understanding, into harmonious free play. He has to impart to the vehicle the Form of Finality. By doing this, and by making this perceptual form 'answer to' the work as expressive of the aesthetic ideas he renders these aesthetic ideas universally communicable. Working the matter of sensation into the Form of Finality and making that form 'answer to' the aesthetic ideas, leaves a great deal of room for the importance of the medium and of artistic technique. It is true that Kant does not labour the point. It is true too, however, that in carefully placing fine art as a species of art in general in radical opposition to 'science', and by stressing that there is something mechanical in all the fine arts,[22] he provides the general structure into which more specific investigation into the varied techniques and media of the different art forms need to be slotted. His theory provides a place in the general philosophy of art for these investigations.

The superiority of Kant's philosophy of art as an expressionist theory over that of Collingwood, can be seen also in that it can withstand a further important criticism which emerges from something Wittgenstein says in *Lectures and Conversations* and which is fatal to a theory such as that of Collingwood. Wittgenstein, in the context of discussing the role of associations in connection with poems, pictures and music makes the point that:

> You can't say: 'That's just as good as the other: it gives me the same associations.'[23]

Then he immediately generalises his remark to a word 'doing just as well' as another *tout court*; not just with regard to the associations it has for someone. Thus he says:

> You could select either of two poems to remind you of death, say. But supposing you had read a poem and admired it, could you say: 'Oh, read the other, it will do the same.'
>
> How do we use poetry? Does it play this role that we say such a thing as 'Here is something just as good . . .'?[24]

Since the answer to Wittgenstein's question is, 'Certainly not',[25] if a theory implies that such a recommendation is possible that constitutes a criticism of it.

Suppose we advance this Wittgensteinian criticism against Collingwood's theory. In that theory the only thing we could proffer someone whilst saying, 'Here is something just as good . . .' is what Collingwood refers to as a mere externalisation, the real and true work being in the artist's head. Of any one of two externalisations, that is two different poems improperly called 'works of art'

Collingwood's theory renders it perfectly intelligible to say, 'Here is something just as good . . .'. Since the auditor has to reconstruct the real and true work of art from the public item, he might as well reconstruct it from one rather than another; and indeed, he might find one not only as good as, but better than another on that count. This could be true even if the public externalisations were in different sensory modes. One of the differences between the externalisations and the real work of art in Collingwood's account of the matter is that whilst the externalisation can be in one sensory mode, that is appeal to sight, or to hearing alone, the work of art proper is an experience of *total activity*, that is is in no particular sensory mode or is imagined in all.

Now at times Kant hints that it might be possible to maintain that two different works and even two works in different sensory modes, express the same aesthetic ideas. Within his theory such a remark would make sense. What the work expresses is not the work. We could be of the opinion that, for example, the large bronze of Athena in the National Museum in Athens expresses the same aesthetic ideas as Shakespeare's sonnet XCIV which commences with the words, 'Those which have power to hurt and will do none . . .'. That is not a too outlandish suggestion. However, even on the basis of this view, it would be no consolation at all to tell someone who could not go to Athens to see the Athena, to read Shakespeare's sonnet instead, saying, 'That will do just as well'.

On Kantian theory the person who regrets that he cannot go to see the statue not only regrets not having the aesthetic ideas communicated to him, he also regrets not being able to directly feel its beauty. He regrets not being able to feel the pleasure involved in reflecting upon its perceptual form as engaging his perceptual faculties in harmonious free play.

On a deeper level, within Collingwood's theory it is not possible to say of one of two real works of art, because they are both imaginative experiences of total activity which express the same feelings and emotions of the artist, 'That one will do just as well as the other'. The imaginative experience of total activity and the feelings and emotions expressed are for Collingwood both constitutive of the work, in the way in which for Kant both the beautiful sensory object and the aesthetic ideas it expresses are constitutive of the work. One might, on this count, therefore, think that Collingwood's expressionist theory fares as well against the Wittgensteinian objection as does Kant's. Such a view assumes, for

Collingwood's theory, what Kant attempts to explain within his own, how it is that two different people are able to have what the work of art expresses communicated to them. We have already noted that securing identity of reference in, 'That one will do just as well as the other' as applied to real works rather than externalisations within Collingwood's theory is a major problem.

Kant's account fares only as well and not better than Collingwood's in the face of the Wittengensteinian criticism if we treat the beauty of a work of art as fortuitously connected with what it expresses. If, however, my interpretation of Kant's beliefs on that matter is correct, Kant does not believe the connection between a work and its expressive power is merely fortuitous. He believes that the beauty of art is a species of dependent beauty and that the aesthetic ideas which are expressed by a work are rendered universally communicable by the dependent beauty of the vehicle of the work which expresses them.

As we have seen even on the supposition that the bronze Athena and Shakespeare's sonnet XCIV express the same aesthetic ideas, it does not follow that one will do just as well as the other, since contemplating the beauty of the one will be very different from contemplating the beauty of the other. Taking into account that such beauty is dependent beauty implies noting that not merely does contemplating the beauty of one differ from contemplating the beauty of the other, but also the way in which the sculptural form 'answers to' the aesthetic ideas, differs from the way in which the poetical form 'answers to' the aesthetic ideas. Taking into account that Kant believes that the aesthetic ideas are rendered universally communicable by the dependent beauty of the bronze and the poem, implies taking note of the fact that someone who cottons on to the aesthetic ideas, without appreciating the dependent beauty of the vehicle of the work, has not fully come to grips with the work of art. If he should think that the one work would do as well or better than the other, it is because he has fortuitously hit upon the conception of the work as expressive of the aesthetic ideas it is expressive of, but not because he has had those ideas communicated to him by the work. Such a person would be in the same position as one who jumps to the meaning of a linguistic expression in a foreign language which he does not understand.

Kant's theory of fine art requires that one personally experience the dependent beauty of the vehicle of the work as a condition of having the aesthetic ideas which are expressed by it communicated to one. He seems to think that the dependent beauty of the work renders the aesthetic ideas universally communicable in the way in which the rules of the foreign language in our example render the meaning of the expression communicable. Appreciating the dependent beauty of the vehicle of the work is a necessary condition of having those particular aesthetic ideas communicated to one, and that is quite a different matter than fortuitously cottoning on to them.

Given these two considerations, that the beauty of art is a kind of dependent beauty, and that it is the dependent beauty of a work which renders the aesthetic ideas expressed in it universally communicable, Kant's theory rules out the possibility of telling the person who cannot see the bronze Athena in the museum in Athens that reading Shakespeare's sonnet XCIV will 'do just as well'. The one will not do just as well as the other, since personally experiencing beauty and fit are conditions of having the appropriate aesthetic ideas communicated to one; and such personal experience of the Athena is of neccessity different from such personal experience of Shakespeare's sonnet XCIV. There is more than a contingent connection between the vehicle and the tenor of a work. In addition, as we have seen, it is the vehicle 'ensouled' by the tenor which constitutes the work of art.

Once again it is worth noting a contrast between the ways in which Collingwood thinks of the public item called the work of art. For Collingwood this vehicle is a poor externalisation of a richer and more subtle reality. Kant thinks of the vehicle and the tenor as analogous with body and soul. To appreciate the full force of this analogy for Kant, one needs to realise that despite the distinction he draws between the noumenal and phenomenal self, it is not right to think of him as holding a view of body and soul which is a kind of Descartean dualism. He is, after all, particularly scathing about such a philosophical position in the Paralogisms of the *Critique of Pure Reason*. Kant thinks that the aesthetic ideas give 'soul' to art because he thinks of them as animating that which expresses them; and he thinks of what expresses them in an exemplar of fine art as being beautiful in the ways in which natural objects may be. He also speaks of aesthetic ideas which are not expressed in a universally communicable form as 'bodiless and evanescent'.[26] What greater contrast could this conception of the relation between the vehicle and tenor of a work and Collingwood's, where mere bodily works of art are not real works of art at all. For Kant that which gives 'soul' to fine art is not that alone which can be properly called the work of fine art and 'soul' is more than contingently connected to 'body'.

15

The Importance of Aesthetics

One of the main tasks of aesthetics is to provide a rationale for judging that one thing is aesthetically better than another. The scope of such judgements may be thought of narrowly, as simply covering the field of the arts; or it may be thought of more generally, in the way that Kant thinks of it, as extending across the whole extent of our experience of things, and so including natural objects, humble artefacts and works of fine art. This first task concerns questions of value within aesthetics. Assuming that aesthetic appraisals are made, one proceeds to ask what is it that makes it fit to prize one thing rather than another, to consider one thing aesthetically better than another.

There is, however, another way in which questions of value emerge in connection with aesthetics. There are those who, standing outside aesthetic appraisals and theoretical attempts to give a rationale for them, wonder whether and why such activities are worthwhile. Such a person may feel, when confronted with aesthetic matters of this kind, just as perplexed as a person quite unaffected by the pursuits and joys of trout-fishermen would be when confronted with appraisals of different kinds of flies, and the arguments which fishermen produce to back up their claims that one kind is better than another. Such a person might well ask, as he might also ask of these activities of fishermen, 'What is all this to me?' His question would concern not merely the appraisals and the proposed theoretical justifications of them; but the whole cluster of aesthetic activities in which they are embedded. Such perplexity might include puzzlement as to why some people prefer to spend their time in absorbing what they consider to be aesthetically good rather than in doing other things. The overall value of aesthetic matters deserves attention in a thorough-going aesthetics. One who asks how one should rate aesthetic values in relation to other values deserves an answer.

It is a measure of Kant's stature that, in the *Critique of Aesthetic Judgement*, he not only produces an account of appraisals within aesthetics; he also presents a whole series of considerations which bear upon why aesthetic activities are of value for human beings. Together with an unusually detailed comprehensive and sustained attempt to give an account of what it is to appraise and appreciate things aesthetically, he offers reasons for thinking that appraising and appreciating things aesthetically is important, and consequently, why understanding what is involved in them is important.

As we have seen, Kant believes that the central value within aesthetics, the beautiful, is not dependent for its value on values of other sorts, such as the value of knowledge, the values of things perfect of their kind or of the morally good. Things which are beautiful just because they are beautiful have a distinctive kind of value. He thinks of this as a value, of and for imagination (in all its roles), rather than of sense on the one hand, or of understanding and reason on the other. The value of that which is sublime, according to Kant's analysis, in contrast with the value of that which is beautiful, is not a distinctive kind of value. It derives from the values of the intellect and morality. This is one of the reasons which make it seem that Kant's discussion of the sublime is something of a diversion from the central thesis of his book.

There are three major ways in which Kant analyses what it is for one thing to be aesthetically better than another. These concern aesthetic appraisals in terms of the beautiful, the sublime and the worthwhile in fine art. Since worthwhile fine art must be dependently beautiful, Kant's account of what it is for something to be beautiful forms part of what it is for something to be a worthwhile work of art. His analysis of the sublime breaks into the continuity of this connection. Judgements about what is sublime count as aesthetic because they involve universal and necessary pleasure; but their universality and necessity are, so Kant believes, grounded upon entirely different considerations from the universal and necessary pleasure which is a constituent of judgement upon the beautiful. The value of contemplating the sublime is derivative but it still counts as aesthetic because the non-aesthetic values from which it is derived enter into the judgement not as cognitions but as feeling.

As has been stressed Kant's analysis of appraisal of something as beautiful is designed to cover such things as flowers, the plumage of birds, crystals, animals human and non-human, artefacts of various kinds ranging from table-appointments and sermons, as well as summer-houses, churches, and poems, to pictures and musical compositions. Some of each of these kinds of thing we judge to be beautiful and others not. In appraising some as beautiful, we judge them to be, in one way, aesthetically better than those we judge not to be beautiful. Saying what it is about them in virtue of which we so judge them is therefore an attempt to give a rationale of a value within aesthetics.

According to Kant, judgements concerning the beautiful can be distinguished as being of two different kinds, the one being 'free', the other being 'dependent' beauty. That in virtue of which, for example, some crystalline formation is judged to be beautiful whilst another lump of stone is not, is that the perceptual form of the one and not of the other sets the perceptual powers, imagination and understanding, in pleasurable, harmonious, free play. Kant describes this as the one having the Form of Finality, the other not. Which perceptual forms set the perceptual powers into such a play, is not a matter for intellectual discrimination, but of personal experience. Kant says we have to try things as it were on our own palates as if to ascertain a sensation.

In the case of dependent beauty, the perceptual form of a thing is judged must not only set the perceptual powers into pleasurable harmonious free play but it must also 'answer to' the kind of thing it is. 'Answering to' seems to amount to there being a kind of fit between a thing's superficial perceptual form, and its deeper structure.

In both cases of 'free' and of 'dependent' beauty, one thing's being aesthetically better than another turns upon its having the Form of Finality when the other does not. For free beauty the crystalline formation has what the other lacks, a form which sets the imagination and understanding into pleasurable harmonious free play where the other does not.

In the case of dependent beauty, for example that of a carving dish, one carving dish will be aesthetically better than another either because one has a perceptual form which sets imagination and understanding in harmonious free play and another does not; or, where each is of such a form one answers to what the thing is intended to be, namely a carving dish, and the other does not. Appraisals of both free and dependent beauty are internal to aesthetics, although the judgement on dependent beauty is qualified by reference to non-aesthetic considerations.

Aesthetic judgements concerning the sublime are also appraisals internal to aesthetics, although their universality and necessity are grounded in non-aesthetic values. Strictly speaking, Kant believes that making judgements about which things are sublime is to be described as making such judgements about a state of mind, rather than about an object of nature. He means that it is as much what we bring to the perception of, for example, the starry heavens or a wild tiger, as the perception of it, which is under assessment. One prospect of the starry heavens or one tiger may, whilst another may not, allow us to bring to bear ideas of reason which enable us to overcome with a feeling of pleasure in the mastery, the initial check to our senses brought about by the impact on our perceptions of the night sky or the wild beast. Such ideas of reason will be those of an intellectual kind such as those of totality and infinity, in the case of the mathematically sublime; and of a moral kind, such as that of a free moral agent, in the case of the dynamically sublime. The feeling of pleasure in intellect overcoming sense, is, according to Kant's theory, pleasure in the *feeling* of the power of our intellectual and moral nature. He thinks that when we are confronting the sublime we are confronting something which brings home to us the subjective side of the conception of rational creatures as having more than mere relative value, their having 'dignity', and being priceless.

In appraising works of fine art as worthwhile or not, or to bring it closer to Kant's own language, in estimating which works are models or exemplars of fine art, Kant, as we have seen, uses three criteria. These criteria are: being expressive of aesthetic ideas, being dependently beautiful, and, being universally communicable of the aesthetic ideas expressed. According to Kant's analysis then, one work of art is aesthetically better than another if it satisfies all, where another satisfies none or only some, of these. Exemplars of fine art must be works of genius, that is they must express aesthetic ideas; and must satisfy taste, that is they must, by being dependently beautiful render the aesthetic ideas which give the work 'soul' universally communicable. Presumably then, a work which satisfies taste but lacks genius, and a work which, although it was produced by a genius, is unintelligible, are to be estimated as aesthetically inferior to an exemplar. Both presumably are to be appraised aesthetically better than works which are neither works of genius nor satisfy taste.

So much can be said in summary of Kant's answers to what is to be counted as better within aesthetics. How this summary is spelt out in detail we have already seen. But what of the other issue which I claimed to be part of a project for a thorough-going aesthetic? What can we draw from Kant from which to compose an answer to the person who asks of these aesthetic appraisals, and of the activities in which they are embedded, whether they are worthwhile? Why does Kant think that one should engage oneself in making aesthetic appraisals, try to understand what is involved in them, and to spend one's time in contemplation of what is aesthetically better rather than what is essentially worse?

We must draw Kant's answers to these questions from various discussions in the *Critique*; from the *Deduction of Pure Judgements of Taste*, from the *Analytic of the Sublime*, from his discussion of fine art and of beauty as the symbol of the moral.

Of these, that of the *Deduction* is the most important, since Kant's claims for the autonomy of aesthetics depend on it. However, because the *Deduction* underpins values within aesthetics in the way it does, there is only a short step needed to be made from what is of value within aesthetics, to what is more generally so. If contemplation of things beautiful is, as Kant claims it is, worthwhile in its own right, and if this is universally and necessarily so, that is if everybody should and any dissenter ought, to take pleasure in things which have the Form of Finality; then contemplation of the beautiful is *a* good. Such a conclusion marks off the activities connected with appreciating the beautiful generally, and in connection with fine art, from such activities as those connected with trout-fishing etc. Although the activity of trout-fishing is enjoyable in its own right, and many fishermen enjoy it even though they seldom catch any fish, trout-fishing in general is *worthwhile* because of the eminent desirability of having fresh trout to eat, and so is not worthwhile in its own right. There are no grounds upon which we can argue that everyone should and anyone ought to seek to go trout-fishing, that those who do go shall enjoy it, and that anyone who does not ought to do so. If Kant's argument of the *Deduction* is correct, then we can argue in just that way, about the activity of appreciating things which are beautiful. Those who do not engage in such activity do not simply lack a special interest which others have; they are less, as human beings, than those who do.

Because Kant's conception of the rationality of humans is somewhat complicated, including as it does, not only the powers of the intellect or Reason, but also the active powers of the mind involved in perception as opposed to the passive capacity to sense, it is not often noted that Kant sees this failure as a failure of human rationality. To make the point in a way which is more faithful to the way in which Kant thinks of what is involved in aesthetic appreciation, it is a failure of a person as rational animal.[1] Because things which have the Form of Finality can engage the active powers involved in perception in pleasurable harmonious free play, it is part of being rational to seek such things out and to enjoy them.[2]

Although this is what is implicit in Kant's position, it is also important not to overstate its implications. If it is sound, the *Deduction* establishes that aesthetic appreciation is worthwhile in its own right, that it is *a* good. It does not, however, establish anything concerning its value in comparison with other things and activities which are worthwhile in their own right. To say that this activity is worthwhile in its own right, is not to say it is the only activity which is worthwhile in its own right, nor is it to say that in competition with other activities worthwhile in their own right, that it is the one which must always prevail. Throughout the *Critique of Judgement* and his other works, Kant consistently presents morality as another activity worthwhile in its own right, and as the most important amongst such activities. In the case of aesthetic appreciation, he simply argues that it is a good, not the good.

His position in this is to be compared with that of G. E. Moore. In the last chapter of *Principia Ethica* Moore defines beauty as that of which the admiring contemplation is good in itself.[3] Thus Moore maintains aesthetic appreciation is a good, one variety of thing which is intrinsically good. It is central to Moore's ethical standpoint to maintain that there is no one thing which alone is intrinsically good but many; one of the deficiencies of Moore's theory is that he gives no well-developed account of how his plurality of things which are intrinsically good stand relative to each other. What is important here in consulting a comparison with Moore, is to note that this comparison underpins the difference between whether something is or not worthwhile in its own right and the issue as to how things worthwhile in their own right stand to each other as a matter of comparative value.

Unfortunately, Kant always takes intellectual values for granted. It is none the less clear that he thinks that the contention that human beings have unconditional worth is to be supported, at least in part, by references to the fact that they are able to understand and think. What he feels called upon to *argue* for, as distinct from what he takes for granted, is the intrinsic value of morality; and its preeminent status in relation to values which are relative to individual, private and personal aims, and goals. We do know, however, that he believes that people have a moral obligation to realise their capacities. We might therefore dally with the idea that he thinks that, since we have the capacity for aesthetic appreciation, we *morally* ought to realise that capacity. He does not, however, say so. What is more, I doubt very much whether he is thinking of that sort of capacity at all when he takes, as his third example when applying the categorical imperative in *The Groundwork*, the man who fancies living after the style of the South Sea Islanders in neglect of the cultivation of his talents in pursuit of pleasure of the senses.[4] There, I believe, he is talking of personal endowments rather than human capacities common to us all.

Secondly, he only thinks that we have a *moral* obligation to appreciate beautiful things in the special case of the beautiful things *of nature*, which we not only properly judge to be beautiful and also which please us by existing. He shows no more sign of thinking that we have a general *moral* obligation to appreciate beautiful things than he does of thinking that we have a general *moral* obligation to exercise our higher intellectual capacities. Yet it seems obvious that he does take for granted that we ought to exercise them; and that our worth as human beings depends upon our capacity to realise them.

The contemplation of the sublime is not for Kant, as the contemplation of the beautiful is, something both worthwhile in its own right and also non-derivatively good. Contemplation of the sublime is only contemplation of the sublime rather than experience of something horrifying if we bring to bear upon what we perceive ideas of Reason which are part of our intellectual and moral endowment. The value of such contemplation derives from these ideas, and not solely from the perception of the object as a natural occurrent.

The lines of connection between contemplation of the sublime and of the beautiful are, for Kant, basically that both universally and necessarily please. The bases of this universality and necessity, subjective in both cases, differ. The beautiful has an independent basis of its own, whilst the basis of the sublime is the universality and necessity of the ideas of Reason. Contemplation of things sublime brings home the power of our intellectual and moral nature; and it is of value because they are. We are entitled to demand that everyone shall and anyone ought to take pleasure as we do in things judged to be sublime, because we are entitled to demand that everyone shall and anyone ought to believe that human beings as rational, are of unconditional worth, that is have 'dignity'. However, contemplation of the sublime does not involve the cognition that human beings have unconditional worth or dignity, but rather the *feeling* of that unconditional worth or dignity in our own person.

Once again, we could interpret Kant to be implying that we *morally* ought to take pleasure in contemplating the sublime because we *morally* ought to treat all rational creatures, including humanity in our own person, as having dignity; and this is a way of doing so. Such an interpretation would, I believe, fail to take account of Kant's emphasis of the difference between knowing that humans have dignity; and feeling oneself to have it. What Kant represents contemplation of the sublime as doing, is not the job of imparting the truth of the proposition, 'Rational creatures have dignity'; but of bringing home that truth to us as a truth about our own person, through feeling.

It is to be noted too, that although Kant believes that the value of contemplating the sublime is, in this way a derivative value, he does not present it as merely an instrumental value.[5] He does not argue that contemplation of the sublime makes us morally better persons, that is persons more likely to act in accordance with the moral law out of respect for it, than we would be without it. He implies that it could have such a consequence and perhaps he even believes that it is likely that such a consequence should accrue; but he does not argue that the contemplation of things which are sublime is worthwhile because it might have, or is likely to have, such a consequence.

It is perhaps because Kant believes that the value of contemplation of things sublime is derivative in this way, that he contends that the sublime can only enter into fine art, that is only feature in it, if it is made by the artist to be beautiful as well.

In his discussion of fine art Kant is concerned to distinguish the various aspects of works which fit them to function as models or exemplars of fine art. In the first place then, he is concerned with values within aesthetics or the philosophy of art. However, because all the other topics discussed come together in his discussion of fine art, because an exemplar of fine art must be dependently beautiful, because the subject can be sublime and can be a presentation of Rational ideas, what he has to say of the value of dependent beauty, sublimity and the presentation of Rational ideas is carried forward into the context of fine art.

Kant's account of fine art is therefore concerned both with what is worthwhile within the field of art and also from without that standpoint. He believes, as we have seen, that a work of fine art must be expressive of aesthetic ideas and dependently beautiful. The importance of the second of these has already been accounted for. The contemplation of beautiful objects extends our perceptual powers to the full, and this in a way which is pleasurable; and such pleasure is communicable to others.

The importance of a work of art's being expressive of aesthetic ideas is taken to be both intrinsic and extrinsic. The contemplation of that which is expressive of aesthetic ideas extends our powers of thought in much the same way as contemplation of beautiful objects extends our perceptual powers. The coupling of that which extends thought with that which extends our perceptual powers, echoes the coupling of imagination and understanding in the contemplation of beauty. Kant seems to envisage a synchronised free play of thought with imagination and understanding. He thinks of this, in the same way as he thinks of the free play of understanding and imagination involved in contemplation of the beautiful generally, as pleasurable in a way which is communicable to others. The harmony between the faculties in the case of an exemplar of fine art is guaranteed by the fit between the beautiful vehicle of the work, and the aesthetic ideas of the creative imagination which constitutes its tenor, a fit imparted by the activity of the artist. The beauty of a work of fine art is dependent beauty. It is in terms of this free engagement of the faculties that Kant construes the intrinsic value of contemplation of exemplars of fine art.

In addition to such value, Kant also maintains that such works, and the contemplation of them, have extrinsic value. He maintains, without developing the theme very far, that they advance culture.

Kant offers one further reason why contemplation of the beautiful, be it of nature or of art, is worthwhile. It is the consideration that the aesthetic point of view, because it is akin to the moral point of view, provides us with a transitional step away from an egocentric outlook towards a fully moral one.[6] Kant expresses the relationship which he finds to hold between beauty and morality or the morally good, by saying that beauty is 'the symbol' of morality. His discussion of *Beauty as the Symbol of Morality*, is, I believe, intended to trace a different connection between aesthetic and moral matters from the one he has already traced in the section called *The Intellectual Interest in the Beautiful*.[7] In that discussion he maintains that a feeling for beauty in nature, in contrast with preoccupation with fine art, presupposes and is indicative of capacity for moral feeling. He says, 'One . . . who takes such interest in the beautiful in nature can only do so in so far as he has previously set his interest deep in the foundations of the morally good.'[8] In his discussion of beauty as the symbol of morality he is not, to my mind, speaking of a likeness between aesthetic feeling and interest and moral feeling and interest, but the similarities between the states of mind required for taking pleasure in the beautiful be it of nature or of art, and taking pleasure in the moral; hence I have described Kant's contention as being that the aesthetic point of view is akin to the moral.

Kant says, then, that beauty is the symbol of the morally good.[9] By 'symbol' he explains that he means more than a conventional mark of something. He says that symbols are 'indirect presentations of concepts' and he says that they work by analogy and that such analogies are based on points of resemblance which are themselves analogous, similarities rather than strict identities.[10] The points of resemblance picked out by Kant to back up his claim that beauty is the symbol of the moral show what he has in mind. Each, he says, involves a kind (but a different kind) of autonomy, gives a kind (but a different kind) of immediate and disinterested pleasure, each exhibits a kind of freedom in accordance with law (but each a different kind) and each is concerned with universality (although the kind of universality is different).

In more detail: Kant propounds the comparison by explaining that both in judging the beautiful and ascertaining the morally good, one of our higher cognitive faculties 'gives the law' rather than finds itself subject to a heteronomy of empirical laws. Taste gives the law to itself in judging of beauty, whilst Reason gives the law to itself whilst judging of the moral. Judgements of the beautiful and of the moral each involve taking immediate pleasure in what is judged but the immediate pleasure involved in the beautiful is pleasure apart from a concept, and the pleasure involved in the moral is pleasure in a concept. Both involve disinterested pleasure, since both presuppose no interest antecedent to that judgement; but the moral judgement 'calls forth' a consequent interest, whereas the judgement concerning beauty does not. Both involve freedom in accordance with law; but the freedom involved in the judgement of beauty is freedom of the imagination in accordance with the law of understanding, whereas the freedom of morality is freedom of the will in conformity to the law of Reason, that is the moral law. Both too, concern what is universal, albeit that the universality of the beautiful is subjective, whilst that of morality is objective.

If we see beauty as the symbol of the moral, then we see it as a step taken away from the strictly egocentric point of view preoccupied with the private pleasures of sense[11] and the relative personal and subjective ends and goals of individuals.[12] Because an aesthetic judgement is what it is a person who takes pleasure in something which has the Form of Finality has already parted company with an outlook centred entirely upon self-interest, and is on the way to the adoption of the point of view required for morality, which is a matter of conforming with universal laws which would make a Kingdom of Ends[13] possible and requires one to take pleasure in what is for the good of all alike. Looking at things with a view to estimating what subjectively, universally, and necessarily pleases (i.e. what is beautiful) seen as the symbol of what objectively, universally and necessarily pleases (i.e. what is moral) is to see the pleasures of the beautiful as transitionary between the pleasures of sense and of morality. Kant says:

> Taste makes, as it were, the transition from the charm of sense to habitual moral interest possible without too violent a leap . . .[14]

To sum up the main points in what Kant has to say about values within aesthetics, and what is worthwhile about aesthetics:

Within aesthetics conceived generally, and not simply as the special case of excellence within the arts, judgements concerning what is beautiful function as focal for him. He asks what it is for one thing to be beautiful and another not. To this question he gives the answer that it is for the thing in question to have (whilst the other has not) a perceptual form which is the object of a communicable, that is a universal and necessary, pleasure; to have the Form of Finality.

To the conjectured questioner who asks, 'What is that to me?' 'What is so good about a thing's having the Form of Finality?' Kant would be able to reply that, the perception of things having such forms enables us as humans to realise our perceptual powers with pleasure. To fail to contemplate such things would be to fail to come alive[15] to our surroundings and a failure in ourselves as Rational animals.[16]

Within aesthetics, as philosophy of art, to the question of what it is that accounts for one work being an exemplar or model of fine art when another is not, Kant replies that is its being dependently beautiful, expressive of aesthetic ideas and expressive of them in a way which renders them universally communicable.

To those who raise the questions, 'What is that to me?' 'What is so good about doing that?' Kant can reply, first, as beautiful, contemplating such a thing will realise our perceptual powers as human beings. Secondly, because such a work will be expressive of aesthetic ideas, it will also realise our cognitive powers. A perceptual form which extends our perceptual powers, in being expressive of aesthetic ideas, also extends our powers of thought. In addition, if my interpretation of Kant's view of the role of taste in fine art is correct, Kant is able to reply that the contemplation of such work is of value because it extends our cognitive powers, extends thought, by extending our perceptual powers. Last of all, he can reply that it is internal to his account of aesthetic judgement that it does all these with pleasure.

Notes and References

All references to the works of Immanuel Kant are given to the relevant translation into English, and to the German text of the edition of the Royal Prussian Academy, now the German Academy of Sciences, in Berlin, and published from 1902 onwards.

1 Introduction

1. Richard Wollheim, *Art and Its Objects; an Introduction to Aesthetics* (New York and Evanston, 1968), sections 42–3.
2. Nelson Goodman, *Languages of Art – an Approach to the Theory of Symbols* (Indianapolis, New York, 1969) ch. VI, 6.
3. R. G. Collingwood, *The Principles of Art* (Oxford, 1938) ch. V.
4. James Creed Meredith, Kant's *The Critique of Judgement*, translated with Analytical Indexes (Oxford, 1952, originally published 1911) p. 62; Kant's *gesammelte Schriften*, vol. 5, §11, p. 221, lines 1–27.
5. Marshall Cohen, 'Aesthetic Essence', in *Philosophy in America* ed. Max Black (London, 1964) pp. 115–33; 'Appearance and the Aesthetic Attitude, *Journal of Philosophy*, vol. 56 (1959) pp. 915–26.
6. George Dickie, The Myth of the Aesthetic Attitude, *American Philosophical Quarterly*, vol. 1 (1964) pp. 56–65.
7. Meredith, *Critique of Judgement, Part I, Critique of Aesthetic Judgement*, pp. 146–7; Kant's *gesammelte Schriften*, vol. 5, §38, p. 289, line 30–p. 290, line 14.
8. Meredith, *Aesthetic Judgement*, pp. 175–6; Kant's *gesammelte Schriften*, vol. 5, §49, p. 313, line 35–p. 314, line 8.
9. Meredith, *Aesthetic Judgement*, pp. 168–9, 181; Kant's *gesammelte Schriften*, vol. 5, §46, p. 308, lines 1–5; §49, p. 318, lines 6–8.
10. Meredith, *Aesthetic Judgement*, p. 168; Kant's *gesammelte Schriften*, vol. 5, §46, p. 307, lines 11–15.
11. Meredith, *Aesthetic Judgement*, p. 31; Kant's *gesammelte Schriften*, vol. 5, Einleitung VII, p. 190, lines 20–1.

2 Kant's Methodology and Presuppositions

1. Meredith, *Aesthetic Judgement*, pp. 55, 72, 80 (footnote); Kant's *gesammelte Schriften*, vol. 5, §8, p. 215, lines 15–22; §16, p. 229, lines 18–21; §17, p. 236 (footnote).
2. Meredith, *Aesthetic Judgement*, pp. 72, 217; Kant's *gesammelte Schriften*, vol. 5, §16, p. 229, lines 24–8; §58, p. 347, line 28–p. 348, line 2.
3. Meredith, *Aesthetic Judgement*, p. 219; Kant's *gesammelte Schriften*, vol. 5, §58, p. 349, lines 15–19.
4. Meredith, *Aesthetic Judgement*, p. 73; Kant's *gesammelte Schriften*, vol. 5, §16, p. 230, line 6.

5.   Meredith, *Aesthetic Judgement*, p. 187; Kant's *gesammelte Schriften*, vol. 5, §51, p. 323, lines 8–14.
6.   Meredith, *Aesthetic Judgement*, p. 187; Kant's *gesammelte Schriften*, vol. 5, §51, p. 322, line 37–p. 324, line 12.
7.   Meredith, *Aesthetic Judgement*, pp. 52, 139; Kant's *gesammelte Schriften*, vol. 5, §7, p. 212, lines 24–9; §33, p. 284, lines 5–7.
8.   Meredith, *Aesthetic Judgement*, p. 188; Kant's *gesammelte Schriften*, vol. 5, §51, p. 324, line 13–p. 325, line 21.
9.   Meredith, *Aesthetic Judgement*, pp. 121–2; Kant's *gesammelte Schriften*, vol. 5, §29, p. 270, lines 7–15.
10. Meredith, *Aesthetic Judgement*, p. 105; Kant's *gesammelte Schriften*, vol. 5, §26, p. 256, line 28–p. 257, line 5.
11. Meredith, *Aesthetic Judgement*, p. 121; Kant's *gesammelte Schriften*, vol. 5, §29, p. 269, lines 12–22.
12. Meredith, *Aesthetic Judgement*, p. 99; Kant's *gesammelte Schriften*, vol. 5, §26, p. 252, lines 10–13.
13. Meredith, *Aesthetic Judgement*, p. 100; Kant's *gesammelte Schriften*, vol. 5, §26, p. 252, lines 20–2.
14. Meredith, *Aesthetic Judgement*, p. 179 (footnote); Kant's *gesammelte Schriften*, vol. 5, §49, p. 316, lines 31–7.
15. Wollheim, *Art and Its Objects*, section 42, p. 83.
16. Ibid., section 43, p. 86.
17. Ibid., section 42, p. 84.
18. Ibid.
19. Ibid., p. 83.
20. Ibid., p. 85.
21. Ibid., section 43, p. 85.
22. Ibid., p. 86.
23. Ibid., p. 88.
24. Meredith, *Aesthetic Judgement*, p. 167; Kant's *gesammelte Schriften*, vol. 5, §45, p. 306, line 27.
25. Meredith, *Aesthetic Judgement*, pp. 175–82; Kant's *gesammelte Schriften*, vol. 5, §49, p. 313, line 2–p. 319, line 10.
26. Meredith, *Aesthetic Judgement*, p. 172; Kant's *gesammelte Schriften*, vol. 5, §48, p. 311. lines 9–13.
27. William Morris, *The Haystack in the Flood*.
28. Goodman, *Languages of Art*, p. 255.
29. Goodman does not use the Gruenewald example but it is a stock in trade example used by philosophers who mount arguments concerned with 'the problem of the ugly'.
30. Meredith, *Aesthetic Judgement*, pp. 174–5; Kant's *gesammelte Schriften*, vol. 5, §48. p. 312, line 28–p. 313, line 5.
31. I. A. Richards, *The Philosophy of Rhetoric* (New York, 1965, originally published 1936) p. 96.
32. Meredith, *Aesthetic Judgement*, p. 49; Kant's *gesammelte Schriften*, vol. 5, §5, p. 210, lines 6–9.
33. See Chapter 4.
34. Goodman, *Languages of Art*, p. 243.
35. R. G. Collingwood, *The Principles of Art*, ch. V.

36. Monroe Beardsley, *Aesthetics: Problems in the Philosophy of Criticism* (New York, 1958) pp. 524–43.
37. Goodman, *Languages of Art*, pp. 242–3.
38. Gilbert Ryle: *The Concept of Mind* (London, 1949), ch. IV (6); *Dilemmas* (London, 1954), IV; *Collected Essays* (London, 1971) vol. 2, 25. Terence Penelhum, 'The Logic of Pleasure', *Essays in Philosophical Psychology*, ed. Donald F. Gustafson (London, Melbourne, 1967) pp. 227–47. Mary A. McCloskey, 'Pleasure', *Mind*, vol. LXXX, No. 320 (1971) pp. 542–51.
39. Meredith, *Aesthetic Judgement*, pp. 215–6; Kant's *gesammelte Schriften*, vol. 5, §58, p. 346, lines 32–5.
40. See, for example, R. W. Beardsome, *Art and Morality* (London, 1971) pp. 46–50.
41. Meredith, *Aesthetic Judgement*, pp. 172, 175, 179–80; Kant's *gesammelte Schriften*, vol. 5, §48, p. 311, lines 6–13; §49. p. 313, line 21–p. 314, line 1; p. 316, line 19–p. 319, line 10.
42. Clive Bell, *Art* (London, 1914) pp. 49–50.
43. Roger Fry, *Transformations* (London, 1926) ch. 1.
44. William Hogarth, *The Analysis of Beauty*, Plates 1 and 2.
45. Meredith, *Aesthetic Judgement*, pp. 33–9; Kant's *gesammelte Schriften*, vol. 5, Einleitung VIII, p. 192, line 13–p. 198. See also Immanuel Kant, translated by Walter Cerf, *Analytic of the Beautiful from the Critique of Judgement with excerpts from Anthropology from a Pragmatic Point of View* (Indianapolis, New York, 1963) p. 65; Kant's *gesammelte Schriften*, vol. 7, §67, p. 240, line 26–p. 241, line 5.
46. H. J. Paton, *The Moral Law, or Kant's Groundwork of the Metaphysic of Morals* (London, 1948) p. 95; Kant's *gesammelte Schriften*, vol. 4, p. 428, lines 7–11.

3 Pleasure

1. John T. Goldthwait (translator), *Kant's Observations on the Feeling of the Beautiful and the Sublime* (Berkeley, Los Angeles, London, 1960) p. 46; Kant's *gesammelte Schriften*, vol. 2, p. 208, lines 10–24.
2. Goldthwait, *Observations*, p. 47; Kant's *gesammelte Schriften*, vol. 2, p. 209, line 7.
3. Meredith, *Aesthetic Judgement*, pp. 44–5; Kant's *gesammelte Schriften*, vol. 5, §3, p. 205, line 25–p. 207, line 12.
4. Meredith, *Aesthetic Judgement*, p. 44; Kant's *gesammelte Schriften*, vol. 5, §3, p. 206, lines 4–13.
5. Meredith, *Aesthetic Judgement*, p. 45; Kant's *gesammelte Schriften*, vol. 5, §3, p. 206. lines 31–6.
6. James Ellington (translator), Kant's *The Metaphysical Principles of Virtue* (Indianapolis, New York, 1964) pp. 9–10; Kant's *gesammelte Schriften*, vol. 6, p. 211, line 19–p. 212, line 1.
7. Meredith, *Aesthetic Judgement*, p. 41; Kant's *gesammelte Schriften*, vol. 5, §1, p. 203, lines 9–12.
8. A. D. Lindsay, *Kant* (London, 1934) p. 234.
9. Meredith, *Aesthetic Judgement*, p. 49; Kant's *gesammelte Schriften*, vol. 5, §5, p. 209, line 29–p. 210, line 2.

4 The Analytic of the Beautiful – Preliminaries

1. Meredith, *Aesthetic Judgement*, p.52; Kant's *gesammelte Schriften*, vol. 5, §7, p. 212, line 24–p. 213, line 7.
2. Meredith, *Aesthetic Judgement*, p. 53; Kant's *gesammelte Schriften*, vol. 5, §8, p. 213, line 35–p. 214, line 10.
3. Meredith, *Aesthetic Judgement*, p. 50; Kant's *gesammelte Schriften*, vol. 5, §6, p. 211, lines 12–29.
4. Ludwig Wittgenstein, *Lectures and Conversations on Aesthetics, Psychology and Religious Belief* (Oxford, 1966) p. 2.
5. Meredith, *Aesthetic Judgement*, p. 50; Kant's *gesammelte Schriften*, vol. 5, §5, p. 211, lines 2–4.
6. Meredith, *Aesthetic Judgement*, p. 60; Kant's *gesammelte Schriften*, vol. 5, §9, p. 219, line 25.
7. Meredith, *Aesthetic Judgement*, p. 80; Kant's *gesammelte Schriften*, vol. 5, §17, p. 236, lines 9–11.
8. Meredith, *Aesthetic Judgement*, p. 85; Kant's *gesammelte Schriften*, vol. 5, §22, p. 240, lines 18–19.
9. Meredith, *Aesthetic Judgement*, pp. 50–1; Kant's *gesammelte Schriften*, vol. 5, §6, p. 211, line 7–p. 212, line 5.
10. Meredith, *Aesthetic Judgement*, pp. 29–31, 62–3, 81; Kant's *gesammelte Schriften*, vol. 5, Einleitung VII, p. 188, line 33–p. 190, line 32; §11, p. 221, lines 1–27; §18, p. 236, line 15–p. 237, line 18.
11. Meredith, *Aesthetic Judgement*, p. 31; Kant's *gesammelte Schriften*, vol. 5, Einleitung VII, p. 190, lines 13–19.
12. Meredith, *Aesthetic Judgement*, p. 66; Kant's *gesammelte Schriften*, vol. 5, §14, p. 224, lines 8–21.

5 The First Moment – Disinterested Pleasure

1. Meredith, *Aesthetic Judgement*, p. 42; Kant's *gesammelte Schriften*, vol. 5, §2, p. 204, lines 22–4.
2. Meredith, *Aesthetic Judgement*, p. 49; Kant's *gesammelte Schriften*, vol. 5, §5, p. 210, lines 20–1.
3. Meredith, *Aesthetic Judgement*, p. 43; Kant's *gesammelte Schriften*, vol. 5, §2, p. 204, line 30–p. 205, line 8.
4. Meredith, *Aesthetic Judgement*, p. 48; Kant's *gesammelte Schriften*, vol. 5, §4, p. 209, lines 10–12.
5. Bernadetto Croce, *Aesthetic*, translated Douglas Ainslie (London, 1909) ch. III, pp. 36–7.
6. Meredith, *Aesthetic Judgement*, p.55; Kant's *gesammelte Schriften*, vol. 5, §8, p. 215, lines 14–5.
7. Meredith, *Aesthetic Judgement*, p. 48; Kant's *gesammelte Schriften*, vol. 5, §4, p. 209, lines 9–10.
8. Meredith, *Aesthetic Judgement*, p. 224; Kant's *gesammelte Schriften*, vol. 5, §59, p. 353, line 37–p. 354, line 4.
9. Meredith, *Aesthetic Judgement*, pp. 43–4; Kant's *gesammelte Schriften*, vol. 5, §2, p. 205, lines 31–6.
10. Paul Guyer, *Kant and the Claims of Taste* (Cambridge, Massachusetts and London, England, 1979) pp. 361–73.

11. Meredith, *Aesthetic Judgement*, pp. 154–6; Kant's *gesammelte Schriften*, vol. 5, §41. p. 296, line 14–p. 298, line 12.

12. Meredith, *Aesthetic Judgement*, pp. 157–62; Kant's *gesammelte Schriften*, vol. 5, §42, p. 298, line 13–p. 303, line 4.

13. Meredith, *Aesthetic Judgement*, p. 48; Kant's *gesammelte Schriften*, vol. 5, §5, p. 209, lines 19–21.

14. Marshall Cohen, 'Appearance and the Aesthetic Attitude', *Journal of Philosophy*, vol. LVI (1959) p. 920.

15. Arthur Schopenhauer, *The World as Will and Representation*, translated E. F. J. Payne (New York, 1958) vol. 1, p. 198.

16. See Chapter 4 (p. 27).

17. Meredith, *Aesthetic Judgement*, p. 44; Kant's *gesammelte Schriften*, vol. 5, §3, p. 205, lines 26–7.

18. Meredith, *Aesthetic Judgement*, p. 45; Kant's *gesammelte Schriften*, vol. 5, §3, p. 207, lines 9–10.

19. See Chapter 4 (p. 27).

20. Meredith, *Aesthetic Judgement*, pp. 49–51; Kant's *gesammelte Schriften*, vol. 5, §5, p. 210, lines 26–7.

21. Meredith, *Aesthetic Judgement*, pp. 51–2; Kant's *gesammelte Schriften*, vol. 5, §7, p. 212, lines 12–19.

22. Meredith, *Aesthetic Judgement*, p. 45; Kant's *gesammelte Schriften*, vol. 5, §3, p. 207, lines 2–3.

23. Meredith, *Aesthetic Judgement*, p. 54 (my emphasis); Kant's *gesammelte Schriften*, vol. 5, §8, p. 214, lines 10–15.

6 The Aesthetic Attitude?

1. George Dickie, *Art and the Aesthetic* (Ithaca, New York and London, 1974) p. 12.

2. Marshall Cohen, Aesthetic Essence, in *Philosophy in America*, ed. Max Black (London, 1965) p. 117.

3. Meredith, *Aesthetic Judgement*, pp. 172, 212; Kant's *gesammelte Schriften*, vol. 5, §48, p. 311, lines 9–13; §57, p. 344, lines 4–7.

4. Meredith, *Aesthetic Judgement*, pp. 70–1; Kant's *gesammelte Schriften*, vol. 5, §15, p. 228, line 6–p. 229, line 5.

5. George Dickie, 'The Myth of the Aesthetic Attitude, *American Philosophical Quarterly*, vol. 1, 1964, p. 57.

6. M. Rader and B. Jessop, *Art and Human Values* (Englewood Cliffs, N.J., 1976) p. 61.

7. Consider Lawrence Durrell's description in the *Alexandrian Quartet*.

8. Consider Epstein's *Bust of a Sick Child*.

7 The Second and Fourth Moments – Communicable Pleasures

1. Meredith, *Aesthetic Judgement*, p. 60; Kant's *gesammelte Schriften*, vol. 5, §9, p. 219, line 25.

2. Meredith, *Aesthetic Judgement*, p. 85; Kant's *gesammelte Schriften*, vol. 5, §22, p. 240, lines 18–19.

3. C. L. Stevenson. *Ethics and Language* (New Haven, 1944) p. 21.

4. Meredith, *Aesthetic Judgement*, p. 52; Kant's *gesammelte Schriften*, vol. 5, §7, p. 212, line 24–p. 213, line 7.

5. Meredith, *Aesthetic Judgement*, p. 131–2; Kant's *gesammelte Schriften*, vol. 5, §29, p. 278, lines 7–14.

6. Meredith, *Aesthetic Judgement*, pp. 131–2; Kant's *gesammelte Schriften*, vol. 5, §29, p. 278, lines 18–26.

7. Meredith, *Aesthetic Judgement*, p. 54; Kant's *gesammelte Schriften*, vol. 5, §8, p. 214, lines 26–9.

8. Meredith, *Aesthetic Judgement*, p. 147; Kant's *gesammelte Schriften*, vol. 5, §38, p. 290, line 16–p. 291, line 3.

9. Meredith, *Aesthetic Judgement*, p. 32; Kant's *gesammelte Schriften*, vol. 5, Einleitung VII, p. 191, lines 12–16.

10. Meredith, *Aesthetic Judgement*, p. 53; Kant's *gesammelte Schriften*, vol. 5, §7, p. 213, lines 20–3.

11. Meredith, *Aesthetic Judgement*, pp. 53, 81; Kant's *gesammelte Schriften*, vol. 5, §7, p. 213, lines 20–4; §18, p. 237, lines 2–6.

12. Meredith, *Aesthetic Judgement*, p. 48; Kant's *gesammelte Schriften*, vol. 5, §4, p. 209, lines 7–8.

13. Meredith, *Aesthetic Judgement*, p. 46; 73; Kant's *gesammelte Schriften*, vol. 5, §4, p. 207, lines 15–24; §16, p. 230, lines 4–13.

14. Meredith, *Aesthetic Judgement*, p. 49; 149; Kant's *gesammelte Schriften*, vol. 5, §5, p. 210, lines 14–20; §39, p. 292, lines 3–9.

15. Meredith, *Aesthetic Judgement*, pp. 31–2; Kant's *gesammelte Schriften*, vol. 5, Einleitung VII, p. 190, line 37–p. 191, line 11.

16. Stephen Korner, *Kant* (Harmondsworth, 1955), p. 48.

17. Meredith, *Aesthetic Judgement*, p. 55; Kant's *gesammelte Schriften*, vol. 5, §8, p. 215, lines 14–15.

18. Lewis Beck White (translator), Kant's *Prolegomena to Any Future Metaphysics* (Indianapolis, New York, 1950) p. 46; Kant's *gesammelte Schriften*, vol. 4, §18, p. 298, lines 9–12.

19. Meredith, *Aesthetic Judgement*, p. 56; Kant's *gesammelte Schriften*, vol. 5, §8, p. 215, lines 36–7.

20. Meredith, *Aesthetic Judgement*, p. 81; Kant's *gesammelte Schriften*, vol. 5, §18, p. 237, lines 6–10.

21. Meredith, *Aesthetic Judgement*, p. 53; Kant's *gesammelte Schriften*, vol. 5, §7, p. 213, lines 20–24.

22. Meredith, *Aesthetic Judgement*, p. 81; Kant's *gesammelte Schriften*, vol. 5, §18, p. 237, lines 2–6.

23. Meredith, *Aesthetic Judgement*, p. 53; Kant's *gesammelte Schriften*, vol. 5, §8, p. 213, line 35; p. 214, line 10.

24. Meredith, *Aesthetic Judgement*, p. 82; Kant's *gesammelte Schriften*, vol. 5, §20, p. 238, lines 4–6.

8 The Third Moment – the Form of Finality

1. Meredith, *Aesthetic Judgement*, p. 45; Kant's *gesammelte Schriften*, vol. 5, §3, p. 206, lines 26–36.

2. Meredith, *Aesthetic Judgement*, p. 148; Kant's *gesammelte Schriften*, vol. 5, §39, p. 291, lines 23–8.

3. Meredith, *Aesthetic Judgement*, pp. 51–2; Kant's *gesammelte Schriften*, vol. 5, §7, p. 212, lines 16–17, p. 207, line 12.

4. Meredith, *Aesthetic Judgement*, p. 70; Kant's *gesammelte Schriften*, vol. 5, §15, p. 228, lines 1–11.

5. See Chapter 4, p. 27.

6. Meredith, *Aesthetic Judgement*, pp. 66–7; Kant's *gesammelte Schriften*, vol. 5, §14, p. 224, lines 8–37.

7. Jack D. Flamm, *Matisse on Art* (London, 1973), p. 37 (from *Notes of a Painter* 1908).

8. Paton, *The Moral Law*, p. 95; Kant's *gesammelte Schriften*, vol. 4, p. 428, lines 7–11.

9. Meredith, *Teleological Judgement*, p. 13; Kant's *gesammelte Schriften*, vol. 5, §63, p. 367, lines 11–23.

10. Meredith, *Teleological Judgement*, p. 7; Kant's *gesammelte Schriften*, vol. 5, §62, p. 362, lines 6–15.

11. Meredith, *Teleological Judgement*, p. 18; Kant's *gesammelte Schriften*, vol. 5, §64, p. 370, line 35–p. 371, line 6.

12. Meredith, *Teleological Judgement*, p. 13; Kant's *gesammelte Schriften*, vol. 5, §63, p. 367, lines 3–10.

13. Paton, *The Moral Law*, pp. 95–6; Kant's *gesammelte Schriften*, vol. 4, p. 427, line 19–p. 429, line 13.

14. For a discussion of the possible meaning of this expression see Mary A. McCloskey, 'Kant's Kingdom of Ends', *Philosophy*, vol. 51 (1976) pp. 391–9.

15. Meredith, *Aesthetic Judgement*, p. 80 (footnote); Kant's *gesammelte Schriften*, vol. 5, §17, p. 236 (footnote).

16. Meredith, *Aesthetic Judgement*, p. 49; Kant's *gesammelte Schriften*, vol. 5, §5, p. 210, lines 6–11.

17. Paton, *The Moral Law*, p. 95; Kant's *gesammelte Schriften*, vol. 4, p. 428, lines 7–11.

18. Paton, *The Moral Law*, pp. 95–6; Kant's *gesammelte Schriften*, vol. 4, p. 428, lines 14–17.

19. Meredith, *Aesthetic Judgement*, p. 119; Kant's *gesammelte Schriften*, vol. 5, §29, p. 267, lines 30–7.

20. Meredith, *Aesthetic Judgement*, p. 56; Kant's *gesammelte Schriften*, vol. 5, §8, p. 215, line 35–p. 216, line 4.

21. Meredith, *Aesthetic Judgement*, p. 71; Kant's *gesammelte Schriften*, vol. 5, §15, p. 228, lines 27–31.

22. Meredith, *Aesthetic Judgement*, pp. 83–4; Kant's *gesammelte Schriften*, vol. 5, §21, p. 238, line 19–p. 239, line 2.

23. Meredith, *Aesthetic Judgement*, p. 88; Kant's *gesammelte Schriften*, vol. 5, §22, p. 242, lines 18–20.

24. Meredith, *Aesthetic Judgement*, p. 88; Kant's *gesammelte Schriften*, vol. 5, §22, p. 242, lines 16–18.

25. Meredith, *Aesthetic Judgement*, pp. 88–9; Kant's *gesammelte Schriften*, vol. 5, §22, p. 243, lines 4–19.

26. Meredith, *Aesthetic Judgement*, pp. 85–9; Kant's *gesammelte Schriften*, vol. 5, §22, p. 240, line 20–p. 244, line 2.

27. Meredith, *Aesthetic Judgement*, p. 88; Kant's *gesammelte Schriften*, vol. 5, §22, p. 242, line 34–p. 243, line 2.

28. Meredith, *Aesthetic Judgement*, pp. 86–7; Kant's *gesammelte Schriften*, vol. 5, §22, p. 241, lines 18–24.

29. Meredith, *Aesthetic Judgement*, pp. 72, 89; Kant's *gesammelte Schriften*, vol. 5, §16, p. 229, line 18; §22, p. 243, lines 12–24.

30. Meredith, *Aesthetic Judgement*, pp. 139–40; Kant's *gesammelte Schriften*, vol. 5, §33, p. 284, line 5–p. 285, line 2.

31. Meredith, *Aesthetic Judgement*, p. 140; Kant's *gesammelte Schriften*, vol. 5, §33, p. 284, lines 32–3.

32. Meredith, *Aesthetic Judgement*, p. 139; Kant's *gesammelte Schriften*, vol. 5, §33, p. 284, lines 9–11.

33. Meredith, *Aesthetic Judgement*, p. 137; Kant's *gesammelte Schriften*, vol. 5, §32, p. 282, lines 21–3.

34. Meredith, *Aesthetic Judgement*, p. 137; Kant's *gesammelte Schriften*, vol. 5, §32, p. 282, lines 27–30.

35. Meredith, *Aesthetic Judgement*, p. 139; Kant's *gesammelte Schriften*, vol. 5, §32, p. 283, lines 28–32.

36. Meredith, *Aesthetic Judgement*, p. 141 (my emphasis); Kant's *gesammelte Schriften*, vol. 5, §34, p. 286, lines 3–11.

37. Meredith, *Aesthetic Judgement*, p. 174 (my emphasis); Kant's *gesammelte Schriften*, vol. 5, §48, p. 312, lines 31–5.

38. Meredith, *Aesthetic Judgement*, p. 72. Kant's *gesammelte Schriften*, vol. 5, §16, p. 229, lines 10–17.

39. Thomas Aquinas, St, *Summa Theologica*, literally translated by Fathers of the English Dominican Province, 1st American edn (3 vols, New York, 1947), Part I, Qn 5, Article 4, vol. I, p. 26.
Or

> A good thing is also in fact a beautiful thing, for both epithets have the same basis in reality, namely, the possession of form; and this is why *the good is esteemed beautiful*. Good and beautiful are not however synonymous. For good (being *what all things desire*) has to do properly with desire and so involves the idea of end (since desire is a kind of movement towards something). Beauty, on the other hand, has to do with knowledge, and we call a thing beautiful when it pleases the eye of the beholder. This is why beauty is a matter of right proportion, for the senses delight in rightly proportioned things as similar to themselves, the sense-faculty being a sort of proportion itself like all other knowing faculties. Now since knowing proceeds by imaging, and images have to do with form, beauty properly involves the notion of form. (Thomas Aquinas, Saint, *Summa Theologiae*, Latin and English (60 vols, London, 1969 onwards), vol. II, 1a. 5, 4, p. 73.)

40. Aquinas, *Summa Theologica*, 1st American edn, Part II (first part), Qn 27, Article 1, vol. I, p. 707.
Or

> 'Good' and 'beautiful' have the same reference but differ in meaning. For the good, being 'What all things want', is that in which the orexis comes to rest, whereas the beautiful is that in

which the orexis comes to rest through contemplation or knowledge. (Aquinas, *Summa Theologiae*, Latin and English, vol. XIX, 1a,
2ae, 27, 2, p. 77.)

41. Thomas Aquinas, St, *Commentary on the Metaphysics of Aristotle*
translated by John P. Rowan (2 vols, Chicago, 1961) vol. I, Commentary §764, pp. 305–6.
42. Ibid., Commentary §771, p. 307.
43. Ibid., Commentary §781, p. 311.
44. My emphasis. W. D. Ross, *Aristotle*, 5th edn (London, 1953) p. 74.
45. Ludwig Wittgenstein, *The 1914–16 Notebooks*, p. 77e, entry dated
24.7.16.
46. Meredith, *Aesthetic Judgement*, p. 73; Kant's *gesammelte Schriften*, vol.
5, §16, p. 230, lines 14–20.

9 The Deduction

1. Meredith, *Aesthetic Judgement*, p. 18; Kant's *gesammelte Schriften*, vol.
5, Einleitung IV, p. 179, lines 19–26.
2. Meredith, *Teleological Judgement*, pp. 23–4; Kant's *gesammelte Schriften*, vol. 5, §65, p. 375, line 7–p. 376, line 2.
3. Meredith, *Teleological Judgement*, pp. 98–139; Kant's *gesammelte
Schriften*, vol. 5, §§84–90, p. 434, line 5–p. 466, line 37.
4. Meredith, *Teleological Judgement*, p. 111; Kant's *gesammelte Schriften*,
vol. 5, §86, p. 444, lines 15–17.
5. Paton, *The Moral Law*, p. 63; Kant's *gesammelte Schriften*, vol. 4,
p. 395, lines 4–12.
6. Meredith, *Aesthetic Judgement*, pp. 87–8, 219–21; Kant's *gesammelte Schriften*, vol. 5, §22, p. 242, lines 10–20; §58, p. 350, line
3–p. 351, line 12.
7. *Ethica Nicomachea*, BK X, 4, 1174C15, as translated by W. D. Ross,
The Works of Aristotle, translated into English under the editorship of
W. D. Ross (12 vols, Oxford, 1928) vol. IX.
8. Meredith, *Aesthetic Judgement*, pp. 69–70, 220; Kant's *gesammelte
Schriften*, vol. 5, §15, p. 227, line 10–p. 228, line 5; §58, p. 350, lines
13–20.
9. Meredith, *Aesthetic Judgement*, p. 135; Kant's *gesammelte Schriften*,
vol. 5, §31, p. 281, lines 5–8.
10. Meredith, *Aesthetic Judgement*, §§33, 34, see particularly p. 141;
Kant's *gesammelte Schriften*, vol. 5, §§33, 34, p. 286, lines 3–6.
11. Meredith, *Aesthetic Judgement*, p. 91; Kant's *gesammelte Schriften*, vol.
5, §23, p. 244, line 31–p. 245, line 1.
12. Meredith, *Aesthetic Judgement*, p. 52; Kant's *gesammelte Schriften*, vol.
5, §7, p. 213, lines 2–7.
13. Meredith, *Aesthetic Judgement*, p. 146; Kant's *gesammelte Schriften*,
vol. 5, §38, p. 289, line 30–p. 290, line 14.
14. Meredith, *Aesthetic Judgement*, pp. 148–50; Kant's *gesammelte Schriften*, vol. 5, §39, p. 291, line 22–p. 293, line 8.

15. Meredith, *Aesthetic Judgement*, p. 150; Kant's *gesammelte Schriften*, vol. 5, §39, p. 293, lines 2–7.

16. Meredith, *Aesthetic Judgement*, pp. 88–9; Kant's *gesammelte Schriften*, vol. 5, §22, p. 243, lines 4–19.

17. Donald W. Crawford, *Kant's Aesthetic Theory* (Madison, Wisconsin, 1974).

18. Meredith, *Aesthetic Judgement*, pp. 221–5; Kant's *gesammelte Schriften*, vol. 5, §59, p. 351, line 15–p. 354, line 30.

19. Meredith, *Aesthetic Judgement*, pp. 118–19; Kant's *gesammelte Schriften*, vol. 5, §29, p. 267, lines 25–37.

20. Meredith, *Aesthetic Judgement*, pp. 83–4; Kant's *gesammelte Schriften*, vol. 5, §21, p. 238, line 19–p. 239, line 10.

21. Meredith, *Aesthetic Judgement*, p. 83; Kant's *gesammelte Schriften*, vol. 5, §21, p. 238, lines 23–9.

22. I. Kant, *Prolegomena to Any Future Metaphysics*, translated by Lewis White Beck, p. 59; Kant's *gesammelte Schriften*, vol. 4, §29, p. 312, lines 1–29.

23. Meredith, *Aesthetic Judgement*, p. 140; Kant's *gesammelte Schriften*, vol. 5, §33, p. 284, line 24–p. 285, line 10.

24. Crawford, *Kant's Aesthetic Theory*, pp. 152–9.

25. Meredith, *Aesthetic Judgement*, pp. 157–62; Kant's *gesammelte Schriften*, vol. 5, §42, p. 298, line 13–p. 303, line 4.

26. Meredith, *Aesthetic Judgement*, pp. 221–5; Kant's *gesammelte Schriften*, vol. 5, §59, p. 351, line 14–p. 354, line 30.

27. Meredith, *Aesthetic Judgement*, p. 154; Kant's *gesammelte Schriften*, vol. 5, §40, p. 296, lines 11–13.

28. Meredith, *Aesthetic Judgement*, p. 158; Kant's *gesammelte Schriften*, vol. 5, §42, p. 299, lines 14–15.

29. Meredith, *Aesthetic Judgement*, pp. 223–4; Kant's *gesammelte Schriften*, vol. 5, §59, p. 353, lines 13–16.

30. Meredith, *Aesthetic Judgement*, p. 223; Kant's *gesammelte Schriften*, vol. 5, §59, p. 352, line 31–p. 353, line 2.

31. Meredith, *Aesthetic Judgement*, p. 224; Kant's *gesammelte Schriften*, vol. 5, §59, p. 353, line 37–p. 354, line 4.

32. Meredith, *Aesthetic Judgement*, pp. 46–7; Kant's *gesammelte Schriften*, vol. 5, §4, p. 207, line 22–p. 208, line 11.

33. Meredith, *Aesthetic Judgement*, pp. 116, 134; Kant's *gesammelte Schriften*, vol. 5, §29, p. 265, line 31–p. 266, line 8; §30, p. 280, lines 8–15.

10 The Sublime

1. Henry Vaughan, *The World*.

2. See Chapter 15.

3. Meredith, *Aesthetic Judgement*, p. 91; Kant's *gesammelte Schriften*, vol. 5, §23, p. 244, lines 26–9.

4. Meredith, *Aesthetic Judgement*, p. 91; Kant's *gesammelte Schriften*, vol. 5, §23, p. 245, lines 6–11.

5. Meredith, *Aesthetic Judgement*, p. 92; Kant's *gesammelte Schriften*, vol. 5, §23, p. 245, lines 29–31.

6. Meredith, *Aesthetic Judgement*, p. 18; Kant's *gesammelte Schriften*, vol. 5, Einleitung IV, p. 179, lines 24–6.

7. Meredith, *Aesthetic Judgement*, p. 116; Kant's *gesammelte Schriften*, vol. 5, §29, p. 265, lines 33–6.

8. Meredith, *Aesthetic Judgement*, pp. 121–2; Kant's *gesammelte Schriften*, vol. 5, §29, p. 270, lines 7–26.

9. Meredith, *Aesthetic Judgement*, p. 91; Kant's *gesammelte Schriften*, vol. 5, §23, p. 244, lines 29–31.

10. Meredith, *Aesthetic Judgement*, p. 97; Kant's *gesammelte Schriften*, vol. 5, §25, p. 250, lines 12–13.

11. Meredith, *Aesthetic Judgement*, pp. 111–12; Kant's *gesammelte Schriften*, vol. 5, §28, p. 261, line 25–p. 262, line 13.

12. Paton, *The Moral Law*, pp. 119–20; Kant's *gesammelte Schriften*, vol. 4, p. 450, line 35–p. 452, line 22.

13. Meredith, *Aesthetic Judgement*, p. 93; Kant's *gesammelte Schriften*, vol. 5, §24, p. 247, lines 7–12.

14. Meredith, *Aesthetic Judgement*, p. 121; Kant's *gesammelte Schriften*, vol. 5, §29, p. 269, lines 14–16.

15. Meredith, *Aesthetic Judgement*, p. 118; Kant's *gesammelte Schriften*, vol. 5, §29, p. 267, lines 28–9.

16. Meredith, *Aesthetic Judgement*, pp. 120–1; Kant's *gesammelte Schriften*, vol. 5, §29, p. 269, lines 12–22.

17. Meredith, *Aesthetic Judgement*, p. 127; Kant's *gesammelte Schriften*, vol. 5, §29, p. 274, lines 15–19.

18. Paton, *The Moral Law*, pp. 114–31; Kant's *gesammelte Schriften*, vol. 4, p. 446, line 1; p. 463, line 33.

19. Meredith, *Aesthetic Judgement*, pp. 113–4; Kant's *gesammelte Schriften*, vol. 5, §28, p. 263, line 10–p. 264, line 12.

20. Bernard Bosanquet, *History of Aesthetics*, 2nd edn (London, 1934) pp. 275–6; A. D. Lindsay, *Kant* (London, 1934) p. 238.

21. Meredith, *Aesthetic Judgement*, p. 65; Kant's *gesammelte Schriften*, vol. 5, §13, p. 223, lines 12–14.

22. Meredith, *Aesthetic Judgement*, p. 90; Kant's *gesammelte Schriften*, vol. 5, §23, p. 244, lines 23–9.

23. Lindsay, *Kant*, p. 238.

24. Meredith, *Aesthetic Judgement*, p. 165; Kant's *gesammelte Schriften*, vol. 5, §44, p. 305, lines 20–1.

25. Meredith, *Aesthetic Judgement*, p. 172; Kant's *gesammelte Schriften*, vol. 5, §48, p. 311, lines 6–13.

26. Meredith, *Aesthetic Judgement*, p. 190; Kant's *gesammelte Schriften*, vol. 5, §52, p. 325, lines 29–35.

27. Meredith, *Aesthetic Judgement*, p. 190; Kant's *gesammelte Schriften*, vol. 5, §52, p. 325, lines 29–35.

28. Walter Cerf (translator), *Analytic of the Beautiful* from Kant's *Critique of Judgement*, with excerpts from *Anthropology from a Pragmatic Viewpoint – Second Book* (Indianapolis, New York, 1963) p. 65; Kant's *gesammelte Schriften*, vol. 7, §67, p. 241, lines 26–9.

29. Cerf, *Analytic of the Beautiful*, p. 68; Kant's *gesammelte Schriften*, vol. 7, §68, p. 243, lines 13–32.

30. Cerf, *Analytic of the Beautiful*, p. 66; *Kant's gesammelte Schriften*, vol. 7, §67, p. 241, lines 24–9.
31. Meredith, *Aesthetic Judgement*, p. 173; *Kant's gesammelte Schriften*, vol. 5, §48, p. 312, lines 10–12.
32. Meredith, *Aesthetic Judgement*, p. 168; 183; *Kant's gesammelte Schriften*, vol. 5, §46, p. 308, lines 1–5; §50, p. 319, lines 25–27.

11 Fine Art

1. Meredith, *Aesthetic Judgement*, p. 141; *Kant's gesammelte Schriften*, vol. 5, §34, p. 286, lines 7–11.
2. Meredith, *Aesthetic Judgement*, p. 162; *Kant's gesammelte Schriften*, vol. 5, §43, p. 303, lines 7–10.
3. Meredith, *Aesthetic Judgement*, p. 163; *Kant's gesammelte Schriften*, vol. 5, §43, p. 303, line 29–p. 304, line 3.
4. Meredith, *Aesthetic Judgement*, p. 163; *Kant's gesammelte Schriften*, vol. 5, §43, p. 303, lines 21–3.
5. Meredith, *Aesthetic Judgement*, pp. 164, 165; *Kant's gesammelte Schriften*, vol. 5, §43, p. 304, lines 4–5; §44, p. 305, lines 17–20.
6. Meredith, *Aesthetic Judgement*, pp. 165–6; *Kant's gesammelte Schriften*, vol. 5, §44, p. 305, line 24–p. 306, line 1.
7. Meredith, *Aesthetic Judgement*, p. 166; *Kant's gesammelte Schriften*, vol. 5, §44, p. 306, lines 3–8.
8. Meredith, *Aesthetic Judgement*, p. 166; *Kant's gesammelte Schriften*, vol. 5, §45, p. 306, lines 14–15.
9. Meredith, *Aesthetic Judgement*, pp. 172–3; *Kant's gesammelte Schriften*, vol. 5, §48, p. 311, lines 16–29.
10. Meredith, *Aesthetic Judgement*, p. 171, 219–20; *Kant's gesammelte Schriften*, vol. 5, §47, p. 310, lines 11–13; §58, p. 350, lines 3–28.
11. Meredith, *Aesthetic Judgement*, p. 217; *Kant's gesammelte Schriften*, vol. 5, §45, p. 347, line 28–p. 348, line 2.
12. Meredith, *Aesthetic Judgement*, p. 167; *Kant's gesammelte Schriften*, vol. 5, §45, p. 306, lines 24–34.
13. Meredith, *Aesthetic Judgement*, p. 163; *Kant's gesammelte Schriften*, vol. 5, §43, p. 303, lines 11–13.
14. Meredith, *Aesthetic Judgement*, p. 171; *Kant's gesammelte Schriften*, vol. 5, §47, p. 310, lines 11–13.
15. Meredith, *Aesthetic Judgement*, p. 173. See also p. 166. *Kant's gesammelte Schriften*, vol. 5, §47, p. 311, lines 20–9; §45, p, 306, lines 14–15.
16. Meredith, *Aesthetic Judgement*, p. 163; *Kant's gesammelte Schriften*, vol. 5, §43, p. 303, lines 23–6.
17. Meredith, *Aesthetic Judgement*, p. 165; *Kant's gesammelte Schriften*, vol. 5, §44, p. 305, lines 17–20.
18. Meredith, *Aesthetic Judgement*, p. 167; *Kant's gesammelte Schriften*, vol. 5, §45, p. 306, lines 20–3.
19. Meredith, *Aesthetic Judgement*, p. 167; *Kant's gesammelte Schriften*, vol. 5, §45, p. 306, line 35–p. 307, line 2.

20.   Meredith, *Aesthetic Judgement*, p. 171; Kant's *gesammelte Schriften*, vol. 5, §47, p. 309, lines 28–35.
21.   Meredith, *Aesthetic Judgement*, p. 173; Kant's *gesammelte Schriften*, vol. 5, §48, p. 311, lines 20–9.
22.   Meredith, *Aesthetic Judgement*, p. 172; Kant's *gesammelte Schriften*, vol. 5, §48, p. 311, lines 14–15.
23.   Meredith, *Aesthetic Judgement*, p. 187 (footnote); Kant's *gesammelte Schriften*, vol. 5, §51, p. 323, lines 26–34.
24.   Meredith, *Aesthetic Judgement*, p. 72; Kant's *gesammelte Schriften*, vol. 5, §16, p. 229, lines 28–30.
25.   Meredith, *Aesthetic Judgement*, p. 172; Kant's *gesammelte Schriften*, vol. 5, §48, p. 311, lines 9–13.
26.   Meredith, *Aesthetic Judgement*, pp. 50, 174–5; Kant's *gesammelte Schriften*, vol. 5, §5, p. 211, lines 2–4; §48, p. 313, lines 3–11.
27.   Meredith, *Aesthetic Judgement*, pp. 174–5; Kant's *gesammelte Schriften*, vol. 5, §48, p. 313, lines 3–17.
28.   Meredith, *Aesthetic Judgement*, p. 175; Kant's *gesammelte Schriften*, vol. 5, §49, p. 313, lines 21–34.
29.   Meredith, *Aesthetic Judgement*, p. 184; Kant's *gesammelte Schriften*, vol. 5, §51, p. 320, lines 17–22.
30.   Meredith, *Aesthetic Judgement*, pp. 175, 182; Kant's *gesammelte Schriften*, vol. 5, §49, p. 313, lines 21–34; §50, p. 319, lines 17–27.
31.   G. E. Moore, *Principia Ethica* (Cambridge, 1903) pp. 27–8, 95–6, 202.
32.   Meredith, *Aesthetic Judgement*, p. 171; Kant's *gesammelte Schriften*, vol. 5, §47, p. 310, lines 20–1.
33.   Meredith, *Aesthetic Judgement*, pp. 179–80; Kant's *gesammelte Schriften*, vol. 5, §49, p. 317, lines 6–11.
34.   Meredith, *Aesthetic Judgement*, p. 168; Kant's *gesammelte Schriften*, vol. 5, §46, p. 307, lines 11–15.
35.   Meredith, *Aesthetic Judgement*, p. 168; Kant's *gesammelte Schriften*, vol. 5, §46, p. 307, line 33–p. 308, line 5.
36.   Meredith, *Aesthetic Judgement*, p. 174; Kant's *gesammelte Schriften*, vol. 5, §48, p. 312, line 30–p. 313, line 2.
37.   Meredith, *Aesthetic Judgement*, pp. 179–80; Kant's *gesammelte Schriften*, vol. 5, §49, p. 317, lines 6–19.
38.   Meredith, *Aesthetic Judgement*, p. 183; Kant's *gesammelte Schriften*, vol. 5, §50, p. 319, line 35–p. 320, line 2.
39.   Meredith, *Aesthetic Judgement*, pp. 180–1; Kant's *gesammelte Schriften*, vol. 5, §49, p. 317, line 21–p. 318, line 8.

12   Exemplars of Fine Art and Genius

1.   Meredith, *Aesthetic Judgement*, p. 166; Kant's *gesammelte Schriften*, vol. 5, §45, p. 306, lines 14–15.
2.   Meredith, *Aesthetic Judgement*, p. 168, cf. p. 141; Kant's *gesammelte Schriften*, vol. 5, §46, p. 307, lines 11–21; cf. §34, p. 286, lines 7–11.
3.   Meredith, *Aesthetic Judgement*, pp. 168–9; Kant's *gesammelte Schriften*, vol. 5, §46, p. 307, line 33–p. 308, line 5.

4. Meredith, *Aesthetic Judgement*, pp. 167, 168, 171; Kant's *gesammelte Schriften*, vol. 5, §45, p. 307, lines 3–8; §46, p. 307, lines 11–12; §47, p. 309, line 28–p. 310, line 5.

5. Meredith, *Aesthetic Judgement*, pp. 165, 171; Kant's *gesammelte Schriften*, vol. 5, §44, p. 305, lines 17–19; §47, p. 310, lines 6–11.

6. Meredith, *Aesthetic Judgement*, p. 173; Kant's *gesammelte Schriften*, vol. 5, §48, p. 311, lines 24–6.

7. Meredith, *Aesthetic Judgement*, p. 169; Kant's *gesammelte Schriften*, vol. 5, §47, p. 308, lines 23–32.

8. Meredith, *Aesthetic Judgement*, p. 171; Kant's *gesammelte Schriften*, vol. 5, §47, p. 309, lines 29–31.

9. Meredith, *Aesthetic Judgement*, p. 171; Kant's *gesammelte Schriften*, vol. 5, §47, p. 309, lines 31–3.

10. Meredith, *Aesthetic Judgement*, pp. 175–6; Kant's *gesammelte Schriften*, vol. 5, §49, p. 314, lines 1–5.

11. Meredith, *Aesthetic Judgement*, pp. 210; Kant's *gesammelte Schriften*, vol. 5, §57, p. 342, lines 20–6.

12. Meredith, *Aesthetic Judgement*, p. 210; Kant's *gesammelte Schriften*, vol. 5, §57, p. 342, lines 15–19.

13. Meredith, *Aesthetic Judgement*, p. 177; Kant's *gesammelte Schriften*, vol. 5, §49, p. 315, lines 14–15.

14. Meredith, *Aesthetic Judgement*, pp. 177–8; Kant's *gesammelte Schriften*, vol. 5, §49, p. 315, line 26–p. 316, line 29.

15. Meredith, *Aesthetic Judgement*, pp. 177–8; Kant's *gesammelte Schriften*, vol. 5, §49, p. 315, lines 22–4.

16. Meredith, *Aesthetic Judgement*, pp. 92, 93, 116, 120, 134; Kant's *gesammelte Schriften*, vol. 5, §23, p. 245, line 35–p. 246, line 4; §23, p. 246, lines 25–8; §29, p. 265, lines 27–30; §29, p. 268, lines 21–30; §30, p. 280, lines 8–15.

17. Meredith, *Aesthetic Judgement*, p. 182; Kant's *gesammelte Schriften*, vol. 5, §50, p. 319, lines 17–19.

18. Meredith, *Aesthetic Judgement*, p. 178; Kant's *gesammelte Schriften*, vol. 5, §49, p. 316, lines 2–7.

19. *The Elements of Logic: Collected Papers of Charles Sanders Peirce: Book II*, edited by Charles Hartshorne and Paul Weiss (6 vols, Harvard, 1931–60), vol. II, §291, p. 165.

20. Meredith, *Aesthetic Judgement*, pp. 209–13; Kant's *gesammelte Schriften*, vol. 5, §57, p. 341, line 35–p. 344, line 21.

21. Lindsay, *Kant*, p. 237; and also Cerf, *The Analytic of the Beautiful*, pp. 65–6; Kant's *gesammelte Schriften*, vol. 4, §67, p. 241, lines 30–1.

22. Meredith, *Aesthetic Judgement*, p. 176; Kant's *gesammelte Schriften*, vol. 5, §49, p. 314, lines 21–2.

23. Meredith, *Aesthetic Judgement*, pp. 176–7; Kant's *gesammelte Schriften*, vol. 5, §49, p. 314, lines 28–33.

24. Meredith, *Aesthetic Judgement*, pp. 176–7; Kant's *gesammelte Schriften*, vol. 5, §49, p. 314, lines 26–33.

25. Meredith, *Aesthetic Judgement*, p. 177; Kant's *gesammelte Schriften*, vol. 5, §49, p. 314, lines 32–3.

26. Norman Kemp Smith (translator), *Immanuel Kant's Critique of Pure*

Reason (London, 1933, first published 1929) p. 180; Kant's *gesammelte Schriften*, vol. 3, p. 134, lines 3–6.

27.　Kemp Smith, *Critique of Pure Reason*, pp. 219–21; Kant's *gesammelte Schriften*, vol. 3, p. 169, line 31; p. 170, line 10.

28.　Meredith, *Aesthetic Judgement*, p. 177; Kant's *gesammelte Schriften*, vol. 5, §49, p. 315, lines 16–21.

29.　Meredith, *Aesthetic Judgement*, p. 176; Kant's *gesammelte Schriften*, vol. 5, §49, p. 314, lines 9–11.

30.　Meredith, *Aesthetic Judgement*, p. 177; Kant's *gesammelte Schriften*, vol. 5, §49, p. 314, lines 35–6.

31.　Meredith, *Aesthetic Judgement*, pp. 177–8; Kant's *gesammelte Schriften*, vol. 5, §49, p. 315, lines 21–4.

32.　Meredith, *Aesthetic Judgement*, pp. 182–3; Kant's *gesammelte Schriften*, vol. 5, §50, p. 319, lines 23–6.

33.　Meredith, *Aesthetic Judgement*, p. 177; Kant's *gesammelte Schriften*, vol. 5, §49, p. 315, lines 9–21.

34.　Kemp Smith, *Critique of Pure Reason*, pp. 131–8; Kant's *gesammelte Schriften*, vol. 3, p. 119, line 1; p. 121, line 22.

35.　William Shakespeare, *A Winter's Tale*.

36.　Sergei Eisenstein, *The Film Sense* (London, 1943) p. 46.

37.　Meredith, *Aesthetic Judgement*, pp. 175–6; Kant's *gesammelte Schriften*, vol. 5, §49, p. 314, lines 2–3.

38.　Meredith, *Aesthetic Judgement*, p. 177; Kant's *gesammelte Schriften*, vol. 5, §49, p. 315, lines 3–8.

39.　Meredith, *Aesthetic Judgement*, pp. 177–8; Kant's *gesammelte Schriften*, vol. 5, §49, p. 315, lines 28–31.

40.　Meredith, *Aesthetic Judgement*, p. 175; Kant's *gesammelte Schriften*, vol. 5, §49, p. 313, lines 30–4.

41.　Meredith, *Aesthetic Judgement*, p. 179; Kant's *gesammelte Schriften*, vol. 5, §49, p. 316, line 27–p. 317, line 6.

42.　Meredith, *Aesthetic Judgement*, p. 166; Kant's *gesammelte Schriften*, vol. 5, §44, p. 306, lines 3–5.

43.　Meredith, *Aesthetic Judgement*, p. 177; Kant's *gesammelte Schriften*, vol. 5, §49, p. 315, lines 21–4.

44.　Meredith, *Aesthetic Judgement*, p. 179; Kant's *gesammelte Schriften*, vol. 5, §49, p. 316, line 27–p. 317, line 11.

45.　Meredith, *Aesthetic Judgement*, pp. 166, 226; Kant's *gesammelte Schriften*, vol. 5, §44, p. 306, lines 3–5; §60, p. 355, lines 24–32.

13　Exemplars of Fine Art and Taste

1.　Meredith, *Aesthetic Judgement*, p. 173; Kant's *gesammelte Schriften*, vol. 5, §48, p. 311, lines 24–9.

2.　Meredith, *Aesthetic Judgement*, p. 72; Kant's *gesammelte Schriften*, vol. 5, §16, p. 229, line 10–p. 230, line 20.

3.　Meredith, *Teleological Judgement*, p. 24; Kant's *gesammelte Schriften*, vol. 5, §65, p. 375, line 26–p. 376, line 2.

4.　Kant's emphasis.

5. Meredith, *Teleological Judgement*, p. 23; Kant's *gesammelte Schriften*, vol. 5, §65, p. 375, lines 7–10.
6. Meredith, *Teleological Judgement*, p. 23; Kant's *gesammelte Schriften*, vol. 5, §65, p. 375, lines 10–14.
7. Meredith, *Teleological Judgement*, pp. 20–1; Kant's *gesammelte Schriften*, vol. 5, §65, p. 373, lines 6–13.
8. Meredith, *Aesthetic Judgement*, p. 73; Kant's *gesammelte Schriften*, vol. 5, §16, p. 230, lines 21–4.
9. Meredith, *Aesthetic Judgement*, p. 73; Kant's *gesammelte Schriften*, vol. 5, §16, p. 230, lines 16–18.
10. Meredith, *Aesthetic Judgement*, p. 80; Kant's *gesammelte Schriften*, vol. 5, §17, p. 235, lines 17–25.
11. Bosanquet, *History of Aesthetics*, p. 406.
12. Meredith, *Aesthetic Judgement*, p. 74; Kant's *gesammelte Schriften*, vol. 5, §16, p. 231, lines 3–10.
13. Meredith, *Aesthetic Judgement*, p. 73; Kant's *gesammelte Schriften*, vol. 5, §16, p. 230, lines 21–31.
14. Meredith, *Aesthetic Judgement*, p. 73; Kant's *gesammelte Schriften*, vol. 5, §16, p. 230, lines 14–20.
15. Meredith, *Aesthetic Judgement*, p. 73; Kant's *gesammelte Schriften*, vol. 5, §16, p. 230, lines 14–20.
16. Meredith, *Aesthetic Judgement*, p. 167; Kant's *gesammelte Schriften*, vol. 5, §45, p. 306, lines 27–34.
17. Plato, *Phaedrus*, 259b–c.
18. Goya, *The Disparates* or *Proverbios*.
19. Meredith, *Aesthetic Judgement*, p. 175; Kant's *gesammelte Schriften*, vol. 5, §49, p. 313, lines 30–4.
20. Meredith, *Aesthetic Judgement*, p. 183; Kant's *gesammelte Schriften*, vol. 5, §50, p. 319, lines 24–7.
21. Meredith, *Aesthetic Judgement*, p. 174; Kant's *gesammelte Schriften*, vol. 5, §48, p. 312, line 28–p. 313, line 2.
22. Meredith, *Aesthetic Judgement*, pp. 179–80; Kant's *gesammelte Schriften*, vol. 5, §49, p. 317, lines 6–19.
23. Meredith, *Aesthetic Judgement*, p. 175; Kant's *gesammelte Schriften*, vol. 5, §49, p. 313, lines 30–4.
24. Meredith, *Aesthetic Judgement*, p. 174; Kant's *gesammelte Schriften*, vol. 5, §48, p. 312, line 28–p. 313, line 2.
25. Meredith, *Aesthetic Judgement*, pp. 171–2; Kant's *gesammelte Schriften*, vol. 5, §47, p. 310, lines 20–3.
26. Meredith, *Aesthetic Judgement*, p. 182; Kant's *gesammelte Schriften*, vol. 5, §50, p. 319, lines 15–17.
27. Meredith, *Aesthetic Judgement*, p. 183; Kant's *gesammelte Schriften*, vol. 5, §50, p. 319, lines 24–7.
28. Meredith, *Aesthetic Judgement*, pp. 186–7; Kant's *gesammelte Schriften*, vol. 5, §51, p. 321, line 36–p. 323, line 3.
29. Meredith, *Aesthetic Judgement*, pp. 171–2; Kant's *gesammelte Schriften*, vol. 5, §47, p. 310, lines 20–3.
30. Meredith, *Aesthetic Judgement*, pp. 182–3; Kant's *gesammelte Schriften*, vol. 5, §50, p. 319, lines 17–34.

31. Meredith, *Aesthetic Judgement*, p. 31; Kant's *gesammelte Schriften*, vol. 5, Einleitung VII, p. 190, lines 13–21.

14 The Strengths of Kant's Philosophy of Art

1. Collingwood, *Principles of Art*, p. 151.
2. Ibid., p. 139.
3. Ibid., p. 151; see also p. 111.
4. Wollheim, *Arts and Its Objects*, pp. 34–5.
5. Collingwood, *Principles of Art*, p. 142.
6. Ibid., pp. 141–2.
7. Ibid., p. 24.
8. Meredith, *Aesthetic Judgement*, pp. 162–6; Kant's *gesammelte Schriften*, vol. 5, §§43, 44, p. 303, line 5–p. 306, line 10.
9. Meredith, *Aesthetic Judgement*, p. 69; Kant's *gesammelte Schriften*, vol. 5, §15, p. 226, lines 31–2.
10. Meredith, *Aesthetic Judgement*, pp. 33, 69; Kant's *gesammelte Schriften*, vol. 5, Einleitung VIII, p. 192, lines 16–23; §15, p. 226, lines 24–30.
11. Meredith, *Aesthetic Judgement*, p. 166; Kant's *gesammelte Schriften*, vol. 5, §44, p. 306, lines 3–5.
12. Meredith, *Aesthetic Judgement*, p. 163; Kant's *gesammelte Schriften*, vol. 5, §43, p. 303, line 34–p. 304, line 1.
13. Meredith, *Aesthetic Judgement*, p. 163; Kant's *gesammelte Schriften*, vol. 5, §43, p. 303, lines 32–4.
14. Kant's *gesammelte Schriften*, vol. 5, §43, footnote to p. 304 (Reading *Tachenspieler* as card-trickster. Translated by J. T. J. Srzednicki.)
15. Collingwood, *Principles of Art*, p. 18.
16. Ibid., p. 18.
17. Ibid., p. 20.
18. Ibid., p. 139.
19. Meredith, *Aesthetic Judgement*, pp. 31, 65, 66, 151; Kant's *gesammelte Schriften*, vol. 5, Einleitung VII, p. 190, lines 13–19; §13, p. 223, lines 15–25; pp. 223–6; §40, p. 293, line 30–p. 294, line 8.
20. Collingwood, *Principles of Art*, p. 142.
21. Meredith, *Aesthetic Judgement*, pp. 183–90; Kant's *gesammelte Schriften*, vol. 5, §51, p. 320, line 10–p. 325, line 21.
22. Meredith, *Aesthetic Judgement*, pp. 164, 171; Kant's *gesammelte Schriften*, vol. 5, §43, p. 304, lines 17–25; §47, p. 310, lines 6–11.
23. Ludwig Wittgenstein, *Lectures and Conversations on Aesthetics and Psycho-Analysis* (New York, 1968) p. 34.
24. Ibid., p. 34.
25. Ibid., p. 34.
26. Meredith, *Aesthetic Judgement*, p. 164; Kant's *gesammelte Schriften*, vol. 5, §43, p. 304, line 19–21.

15 The Importance of Aesthetics

1. Meredith, *Aesthetic Judgement*, p. 49; Kant's *gesammelte Schriften*, vol. 5, §5, p. 210, lines 12–14.

2. Meredith, *Aesthetic Judgement*, pp. 5, 147; Kant's *gesammelte Schriften*, vol. 5, Borrede, p. 169, lines 15–26; §38, p. 290, lines 11–14.
3. Moore, *Principia Ethica*, p. 201.
4. Paton, *The Moral Law*, p. 90; Kant's *gesammelte Schriften*, vol. 4, p. 422, line 28–p. 423, line 16.
5. Meredith, *Aesthetic Judgement*, pp. 111–2; Kant's *gesammelte Schriften*, vol. 5, §28, p. 261, line 25–p. 262, line 13.
6. Meredith, *Aesthetic Judgement*, pp. 221–5; Kant's *gesammelte Schriften*, vol. 5, §59, p. 351, line 15–p. 354, line 30.
7. Meredith, *Aesthetic Judgement*, pp. 157–62; Kant's *gesammelte Schriften*, vol. 5, §42, p. 298, line 15–p. 303, line 4.
8. Meredith, *Aesthetic Judgement*, p. 160; Kant's *gesammelte Schriften*, vol. 5, §42, p. 300, lines 33–6.
9. Meredith, *Aesthetic Judgement*, p. 223; Kant's *gesammelte Schriften*, vol. 5, §59, p. 353, line 13.
10. Meredith, *Aesthetic Judgement*, p. 223; Kant's *gesammelte Schriften*, vol. 5, §59, p. 352, line 22–p. 353, line 2.
11. Meredith, *Aesthetic Judgement*, pp. 150–4; Kant's *gesammelte Schriften*, vol. 5, §40, p. 293, line 11–p. 296, line 13.
12. Paton, *The Moral Law*, pp. 95–6; Kant's *gesammelte Schriften*, vol. 4, p. 427, line 32–p. 428, line 2.
13. Paton, *The Moral Law*, pp. 100–2; Kant's *gesammelte Schriften*, vol. 4, p. 433, line 12–p. 434, line 30.
14. Meredith, *Aesthetic Judgement*, p. 225; Kant's *gesammelte Schriften*, vol. 5, §59, p. 354, lines 25–7.
15. Meredith, *Aesthetic Judgement*, p. 91; Kant's *gesammelte Schriften*, vol. 5, §23, p. 244, line 32–p. 245, line 1.
16. Meredith, *Aesthetic Judgement*, p. 116; Kant's *gesammelte Schriften*, vol. 5, §29, p. 265, line 31–p. 266, line 8.

Bibliography

ANSCOMBE, G. E. M., *Intention* (Oxford, Blackwell, 1957) reprinted 1976.

——, 'The Intentionality of Sensation: a Grammatical Feature', in *Analytical Philosophy* (second series) ed. J. Butler (Oxford, Blackwell, 1965) reprinted 1976.

AQUINAS, St T., *Summa Theologiae* (London, Blackfriars in conjunction with Eyre & Spottiswoode; New York, McGraw-Hill Book Co., 1969 onwards).

ARISTOTLE, *Ethica Nicomachea. The Works of Aristotle*, vol. IX, translated into English, ed. W. D. Ross (Oxford, Oxford University Press, 1908–52).

BEARDSLEY, M., *Aesthetics: Problems in the Philosophy of Criticism* (New York, Harcourt Brace & Co., 1958).

——, *Aesthetics from Classical Greece to the Present: A Short History* (Alabama, University of Alabama Press, 1966).

BEARDSMORE, R. W., *Art and Morality* (London and Basingstoke, Macmillan, 1971).

BECK, L. W., *Essays on Kant and Hume* (Yale, Yale University Press, 1978).

BELL, C., *Art* (London, Chatto & Windus, 1914).

BENTHAM, J., *An Introduction to the Principles of Morals and Legislation* (London, 1789) new edition 1823.

BERNARD, J. H. (trans.), *Immanuel Kant: Critique of Judgement*, Hafner Library of Classics (New York, Hafner, 1951).

BOSANQUET, B., *A History of Aesthetics* (London, George Allen & Unwin, 1892) reprinted 1966.

BULLOUGH, E., *Aesthetics; Lectures and Essays*, ed. Elizabeth M. Wilkinson (Stanford University Press, 1957).

BURKE, E., *Philosophical Enquiry into the Origin of Our Ideas on the Sublime and the Beautiful*, ed. J. T. Boulton (London, Routledge & Kegan Paul, 1958).

CARY, J., *Art and Reality* (London, Cambridge University Press, 1958).

CASSIRER, E., *Rousseau, Kant and Goethe* (New York and London, Evanston, 1945).

CASSIRER, H. W., *Commentary on Kant's Critique of Judgement* (London, Methuen, 1938).

CERF,W. (trans.), *Kant. Analytic of the Beautiful*, The Library of Liberal Arts (Indianapolis, New York, Bobbs-Merrill, 1963).

CHISHOLM, R., *Perceiving: A Philosophical Study*. (Ithaca, New York, Cornell University Press, 1957).

COHEN, M., 'Aesthetic Essence' in *Philosophy in America* ed. Max Black (London, Allen & Unwin, 1965).

COHEN, T. and GUYER, P. (eds), *Essays in Kant's Aesthetics* (Chicago, University of Chicago Press, 1982).

COLEMAN, F. X. J., *The Harmony of Reason; A study in Kant's Aesthetics* (Pittsburgh, University of Pittsburgh Press, 1974).

——, *The Aesthetic Thought of the French Enlightenment* (Pittsburgh, University of Pittsburgh Press, 1971).

COLLINGWOOD, R. G., *The Principles of Art* (Oxford, Oxford University Press, 1938) reprinted 1962, 1970.

CRAWFORD, D. W., *Kant's Aesthetic Theory* (Madison, Wisconsin, University of Wisconsin Press, 1974).

CROCE, B. *Aesthetic: as Science of Expression and General Linguistic*, trans. Douglas Ainslie (London, Vision, 1922).

DICKIE, G., *Aesthetics: An Introduction*, Pegasus Traditions in Philosophy (Indianapolis, 1971).

——, *Art and the Aesthetic* (Ithaca, New York and London, 1974).

EISENSTEIN, S., *The Film Sense* (London, Faber, 1943).

ELLIOTT, R. K., 'The Unity of Kant's "Critique of Aesthetic Judgement"', *British Journal of Aesthetics*, 8 (1968).

FRY, R., *Transformations* (London, Chatto & Windus, 1926).

——, *Vision and Design* (London, Chatto & Windus, 1920).

——, *Last Lectures* (London, Cambridge University Press, 1939).

GIBSON, A. B., *Muse and Thinker* (London, Watts & Co. Ltd, 1969).

GOODMAN, N., *Languages of Art; An Approach to a Theory of Symbols* (Indianapolis, New York, Bobbs-Merrill 1968).

GOTSHALK, D. W., *Art and the Social Order* (Chicago, University of Chicago Press, 1947).

——, 'Form and Expression in Kant's Aesthetics', *British Journal of Aesthetics*, 7 (1967).

GUYER, P., *Kant and the Claims of Taste* (Cambridge, Mass., Harvard University Press, 1979).

HEYL, B. C., *New Bearings in Esthetics and Art Criticism* (New Haven, Yale University Press, 1943).

HOGARTH, W., *The Analysis of Beauty*, ed. with an introduction by J. Burke (Oxford, Clarendon Press, 1955).

HUME, D., *Treatise on Human Nature*, ed. L. Selby-Bigge (Oxford, Clarendon Press) 1st edn 1888, reprinted 1967.

——, *An Enquiry Concerning Human Understanding* ed. L. Selby-Bigge, 2nd ed. (Oxford, Clarendon Press, 1902, 1965).

——, 'The Standard of Taste', in *Essays Political and Literary*, vol. I (London, Longman Green & Co., 1975).

JOYCE, J., *The Portrait of the Artist as a Young Man* (London, 1914–15); *Stephen Hero* (London, 1944).

KANT, I., *gesammelte Schriften* – the edition of the Royal Prussian Academy, now the German Academy of Sciences (Berlin, 1902 onwards).

KNOX, I., *The Aesthetic Theories of Kant, Hegel and Schopenhauer* (New York, Columbia University Press, 1936).

KORNER, S., *Kant* (Harmondsworth, Penguin, reprinted 1955).

LINDSAY, A. D., *Kant* (Oxford, Oxford University Press, 1934).

McCLOSKEY, Mary A., 'Pleasure', in *Mind*, LXXX, 1971.

MARITAIN, J., *Art and Scholasticism: With Other Essays*, trans. J. F. Scanlan (London, Sheed & Ward, 1930), reprinted 1946.

MEREDITH, J. C., *Introductory Essays to Kant's 'Critique of Aesthetic Judgement'* (Oxford, Oxford University Press, 1911).

——, *Critique of Judgement* (Oxford, Clarendon Press, reprinted 1957).

MILL, J. S., *Utilitarianism*, Collected Works (Toronto and London, 1963).

MOORE, G. E., *Principia Ethica* (Cambridge, Cambridge University Press, 1954).

MORRIS, W., *The Haystack in the Flood*, poem.

MURDOCH, I., *The Fire and the Sun: Why Plato Banished the Artists* (Oxford, Clarendon Press, 1977).

NAGEL, T., *The Possibility of Altruism* (Oxford, Oxford University Press, 1970) reprinted 1975.

OSBORNE, H. *Aesthetics and Art Criticism* (London and Harlow, Longman Green & Co., 1968).

——, *The Art of Appreciation* (London, Oxford University Press, 1970).

——, *Aesthetics*, ed. and introduction, pp. 1–24. (Oxford, Oxford University Press, 1972).

PENELHUM, T., 'The Logic of Pleasure' in *Essays in Philosophical Psychology*, ed. D. F. Gustafson (London, Macmillan, 1967) reprinted London and Basingstoke, 1973.

PLATO, *Hippias Major, Protagoras, Republic, Philebus*.

PLOTINUS, *The Enneads* (London, Faber & Faber, 1917–30).

PODRO, M. I., *The Manifold in Perception: Theories of Art From Kant to Hildebrand*, Oxford-Warbury Studies (Oxford, Clarendon Press, 1972).

RADER, M. M. and JESSOP, B. E., *Art and Human Values* (Englewood Cliffs, Prentice-Hall, 1976).

RICHARDS, I. A., *The Philosophy of Rhetoric; the Mary Flexner Lectures on the Humanities III* (New York, Oxford University Press, 1965).

RYLE, Gilbert, *The Concept of Mind* (London, Hutchinson, 1949) reprinted 1966, 1969.

——, *Dilemmas. Tanner Lectures, 1953* (Cambridge, Cambridge University Press, 1966, 1975).

——, 'Pleasure' in *Collected Works*, vol. II (London, Hutchinson, 1971).

SARTRE, J.-P., *The Psychology of Imagination*, first published in France with the title *L'Imaginaire*, 1940; first published in Great Britain, 1972.

SCHAPER, E., *Studies in Kant's Aesthetics* (Edinburgh, Edinburgh University Press, 1979).

SCHOPENHAUER, A., *The World as Will and Representation*, translated by E. F. J. Payne (New York, 1958).

SCRUTON, R., *Art and Imagination, A Study in the Philosophy of Mind* (London, Methuen, 1974).

STEVENSON, C. L., *Ethics and Language* (New Haven, Yale University Press, 1944).

STRAWSON, P. F., *The Bounds of Sense; An Essay on Kant's Critique of Pure Reason* (London, Methuen, 1966) reprinted 1968.

——, *Freedom and Resentment and Other Essays* (London, Methuen, 1974).

UELING, T. E., *The Notion of Form in Kant's 'Critique of Aesthetic Judgement'* (The Hague, Mouton, 1971).

VAN DE PITTE, F. P., *Kant as Philosophical Anthropologist* (The Hague, Martinus Nijhoff, 1971).

WEITZ, Morris, *Philosophy of the Arts* (New York, Russell & Russell, 1950).

——, 'The Place of Theory in Aesthetics', *Journal of Aesthetics and Art Criticism*, XV, 1956.

WITTGENSTEIN, L., *Lectures and Conversations on Aesthetics and Psycho-Analysis*, ed. C. Barrett (New York, 1966).

WOLLHEIM, Richard, *Art and Its Objects: An Introduction to Aesthetics* (New York and Evanston, Harper & Row, 1968, 1971).

——, *Art and Its Objects*, 2nd edn with six supplementary essays (Cambridge, Cambridge University Press, 1980).

——, *On Art and the Mind* (London, Allen Lane, 1973).

Index